アメリカESL教育の第一人者が厳選!

TOEFL®テスト対策必須語彙力トレーニング

400 MUST-HAVE WORDS FOR THE TOEFL® TEST

ローレンス・J・ツヴァイヤー + リン・スタッフォード-ユルマズ[著]

島崎由里子 + 野津麻紗子[訳]

かんき出版

本書を、聡明で、無私の人であった亡き父、
リチャード・J・ツヴァイヤーに捧げる。
そして、我が親愛なる友人であり、
英語の語彙とイディオムの優れた使い手であるセピデ・ファルサイに捧げる。

本書の出版社（マグロウヒル・エデュケーション）は、
この第２版を故リン・スタッフォード-ユルマズに捧げる。

400 MUST-HAVE WORDS FOR THE TOEFL® TEST
by
Lawrence J. Zwier and Lynn Stafford-Yilmaz

はじめに

本書はマグロウヒル社のベストセラー*400 Must-Have Words for the TOEFL®*の増補・改訂新版です。読解文が更新され、新しいLESSONも追加されました。初版同様、TOEFL® iBT（インターネット方式によるTOEFL®テスト）のスコアアップに役立つ１冊です。iBTで好成績を取得するには語彙力が大変重要なため、本書はとても有効な学習教材です。

自習用として使いやすいように構成されており、各LESSON、約25分間でひと通り終わらせることができます。今回の増補・改訂新版は、TOEFL®対策の授業でも大変役立ちます。

各LESSONは10個の必須単語のリストで始まります。まずこれら必須単語の定義と簡単な例文を学習します。多くの単語には使い方のヒントも示されています。またその単語に、よく使われる別の品詞の関連語がある場合は、それらもリストアップされています。

その後、これらの必須単語を３つの練習問題で学習します。「TOEFLプレップ１」と「TOEFLプレップ２」は、さまざまな形式のシンプルな練習問題です。最後の「TOEFLサクセス」は、実際のTOEFL®形式の読解文と問題が１問または２問ついている練習問題です。ほとんどの「TOEFLサクセス」の読解文には10個の必須単語がすべて含まれており、多くの場合、「読解のポイント」も示されています。各LESSONの最後には学習成果を確認できる解答がついています。

さらに本書では、巻頭に「TOEFL®成功のための６つのヒント」を掲載しています。このような基本的なテスト攻略法をおさえておくことは、TOEFL®で良い成績を修めるために必要不可欠です。

*400 Must-Have Words for the TOEFL®*の初版が出版された後、本書の共著者の１人であるリン・スタッフォード・ユルマズが亡くなり、私たちは悲嘆にくれていました。リンは優れた書き手であると同時に、献身的な教師でもありました。生徒たちが勉強や試験準備に邁進できるよう、いつも熱心に指導していました。私たちはこの新版を通してリンを懐かしく思い出しています。本書が提供するアドバイスや練習問題が１人でも多くの方のお役に立てれば、彼女もとても誇らしく思えることでしょう。

皆さんのTOEFL®テストに向けた語彙学習の成果が発揮されることをお祈りしています。

TOEFL®成功のための6つのヒント

1 読解もリスニングも、まずは全体として理解しよう

従来とは異なり新バージョンのTOEFLでは、より長い読解文の中でさまざまな論点の関わり合い方を理解できるかどうかが問われます。

2 メモを取ろう

特にリスニングセクションでは、聞いたことを忘れないようにメモを取る必要があります。メモを取ることで、集中力を鍛えることもできます。ニュースやドキュメンタリー、講義を聞きながらメモを取り、練習しましょう。

3 文法は、それ自体にとらわれるのではなく、つねに文脈の中で学ぼう

従来のバージョンのTOEFLとは異なり、新バージョンには文法セクションがありません。文法の知識は、読解やリスニングを理解するのに役立つものであって、文法に特化した問題に答えるためのものではありません。

4 あるテーマについて、自分の意見を述べるエッセイを書く練習をしよう

新バージョンのTOEFLのライティングセクションには、日常のさまざまなトピックについて意見を問われる問題があり、制限期間があります。自分の考えを整理し、充実したエッセイに仕上げる練習をしましょう。

5 学術的な語彙を増やそう

文章の理解力は、学術的な語彙力にかかっています。できるだけ英文を読み、単語帳の作成や、新しい単語を文脈の中で使って文章を書くなどして、語彙を増やしましょう。豊富な語彙は、読解力だけでなく、リスニング、ライティング、スピーキングの力を高めるのにも役立ちます。

6 テストに集中しよう

テストで扱われるトピックの中には、興味のないものもあるかもしれません。それでも、集中すればテストのスコアは向上するでしょう。テスト中は他のことを考えず、テスト問題に集中しましょう。

目次

Society
(社会)

Money
(お金)

Government and Justice
(政府と正義)

翻訳協力／株式会社リベル
校正／小林　祥子
本文デザイン・ＤＴＰ／石澤　義裕

Food Crops

Target Words

1. abandon
2. adversely
3. aggregate
4. cultivation
5. fertilize
6. intensify
7. irrigation
8. obtain
9. photosynthesis
10. precipitation

Definitions and Samples

1. abandon *v.* To leave; to give up
To save their lives, the sailors had to **abandon** the sinking ship.
Parts of speech abandonment *n*

2. adversely *adv.* In a harmful way; negatively
Excessive rainfall early in the spring can **adversely** affect the planting of crops.
Usage tips *Adversely* is often followed by *affect*.
Parts of speech adversity *n*, adverse *adj*

3. aggregate *adj.* Gathered into or amounting to a whole
It is impossible to judge last year's performance without knowing the **aggregate** sales numbers.
Usage tips *Aggregate* is often followed by a term like *sum*, *total*, or *numbers*.
Parts of speech aggregate *v*, aggregate *n*

4. cultivation *n.* Preparing the land to grow crops; improvement for agricultural purposes
With the development of land **cultivation**, hunters and gatherers were able to settle in one place.
Parts of speech cultivate *v*

5. fertilize *v.* To supply with nourishment for plants by adding helpful substances to the soil

Tomatoes grow well here because the farmers **fertilize** their soil with nitrogen.

Parts of speech fertilizer *n*, fertilization *n*

6. **intensify** *v.* To increase in power; to act with increased strength

Jacob's long absence from Rose **intensified** his certainty that he should marry her.

Parts of speech intensification *n*, intense *adj*, intensity *n*

7. **irrigation** *n.* The supplying of water to dry land

In dry areas of the country, you can see ditches all over the farmland for **irrigation**.

Parts of speech irrigate *v*

8. **obtain** *v.* To gain possession of; to get

After a series of difficult interviews, he finally was able to **obtain** the job.

9. **photosynthesis** *n.* The process by which green plants make their own food by combining water, salts, and carbon dioxide in the presence of light.

Oxygen is a by-product of the process of **photosynthesis**.

Parts of speech photosynthesize *v*

10. **precipitation** *n.* Water that falls to the Earth's surface

In the Pacific Northwest, the high level of **precipitation** ensures rich, green plant life.

TOEFL Prep 1-1 **Complete each sentence by filling in the blank with the best word from the list. Change the form of the word if necessary. Use each word only once.**

abandoned precipitation cultivation fertilize photosynthesis

1. Through_______, green plants create organic materials with the help of chlorophyll.
2. The coastal city gets half its_______during the rainy months of January, February, and March.
3. Farmers use various methods of land_______.
4. When they heard the hull crack, all but two of the sailors _______the ship.
5. Inexperienced gardeners may not realize how important it is that they_______their plants.

TOEFL Prep 1-2 **Find the word or phrase that is closest in meaning to the opposite of each word in the left-hand column. Write the letter in the blank.**

_______	1. obtain	(a) weaken
_______	2. intensify	(b) separate
_______	3. irrigation	(c) lose
_______	4. aggregate	(d) drainage
_______	5. adversely	(e) positively

TOEFL Success 1 **Read the passage to review the vocabulary you have learned. Answer the questions that follow.**

In countries like Niger and Mauritania, the *cultivation* of land has changed little in the past several centuries. Additionally, these countries' mono-modal rainfall pattern brings *precipitation* for only three months during the year. **As a result**, food production doesn't nearly meet demand.

TOEFL Prep 1-1 1. photosynthesis 2. precipitation 3. cultivation
4. abandoned 5. fertilize

Several agencies and organizations have *intensified* their efforts to increase the productivity of land in these countries. They have introduced new strains of seed, improved *irrigation* techniques, and introduced new methods of *fertilization* and soil management. With ample sunlight for *photosynthesis* and modern *irrigation* techniques, sustainable farming techniques should allow farmers to boost *aggregate* production in order to meet demand.

Still, crop revitalization faces an unexpected adversary: institutional incompetence. Where crop specialists have convinced individual farmers to *abandon* old farming techniques in place of new, they can't readily *obtain* the governmental cooperation they need. The biggest hurdles are political corruption, incompetence, and the absence of a marketing infrastructure.

Bonus Structure **As a result** means "therefore," "for this reason."

1. In this passage, the word adversary is closest in meaning to
   a. friend
   b. helper
   c. enemy
   d. leader

2. In the last paragraph, the word they refers to
   a. crop specialists
   b. farmers
   c. farming techniques
   d. adversaries

TOEFL Prep 1-2 1. c 2. a 3. d 4. b 5. e
TOEFL Success 1 1. c 2. a

自然
レッスン1

農作物

意味と例文

1 abandon（動詞） 置き去りにする／あきらめる

例文訳 自分たちの命を守るため、船乗りたちは沈みゆく船を置き去りにしなくてはならなかった。

関連語 abandonment（名詞）放棄

---

2 adversely（副詞） 有害な形で／否定的に

例文訳 春の早い時期に雨が降りすぎると、作物の植え付けに悪影響を及ぼす可能性がある。

ヒント 使い方 adverselyは後ろにaffect（影響を及ぼす）を伴うことが多い。

関連語 adversity（名詞）逆境、adverse（形容詞）有害な

---

3 aggregate（形容詞） 集められた、または全体の

例文訳 販売数の総計を知らないと、昨年の実績を評価することはできない。

ヒント 使い方 aggregateはsum（合計）、total（総計）やnumbers（数）といった単語を後ろに伴うことが多い。

関連語 aggregate（動詞）集める、aggregate（名詞）合計

---

4 cultivation（名詞） （作物を育てるため）土地を整えること／（農業のために）土地を改良すること

例文訳 農耕の発達によって、狩猟採集民は1カ所に定住できるようになった。

関連語 cultivate（動詞）耕す

---

5 fertilize（動詞） （土壌に有益な物質を加えて）作物に栄養を与える／肥やす

例文訳 トマトがここでよく育つのは、農家が土壌に窒素肥料を与え

ているからだ。

関連語 fertilizer（名詞）肥料、fertilization（名詞）肥やすこと

6 intensify（動詞） 力を増す／より強い力で行動する

例文訳 ジェイコブはローズと長く離れていたことで、彼女と結婚すべきだという確信を強めた。

関連語 intensification（名詞）強めること、intense（形容詞）強烈な、intensity（名詞）強烈さ

7 irrigation（名詞） （乾いた土地に）水を供給すること

例文訳 国内の乾燥した地域では、農地のあちこちに灌漑用の水路が見られる。

関連語 irrigate（動詞）水を引く

8 obtain（動詞） 手に入れる／得る

例文訳 一連の厳しい面接を経て、彼はついにその仕事を得ることができた。

9 photosynthesis（名詞） 緑色植物が光の下で、水、塩、二酸化炭素を結合させて養分をつくりだす過程（光合成）

例文訳 酸素は光合成の過程で発生する副産物である。

関連語 photosynthesize（動詞）光合成する

10 precipitation（名詞） 地表に降る水（降水量）

例文訳 太平洋岸北西部では、降水量が多いため緑豊かな植物が育つ。

TOEFL プレップ 1－1

リストの中から空欄に当てはまる適切な単語を選んで、各文を完成させなさい。必要に応じて単語を活用させること。なお、各単語は一度しか使用できません。

abandoned precipitation cultivation fertilize photosynthesis

1 緑色植物は＿＿＿＿＿＿により、葉緑素を使って有機物をつくりだす。

2 沿岸都市では、1月、2月、3月の雨季に＿＿＿＿＿＿の半分が降る。

3 農家はさまざまな方法で農地を＿＿＿＿＿＿。

4 船体の割れる音を聞いて、2人を除いたすべての船員が船を＿＿＿＿＿＿。

5 ガーデニングに慣れていない人は、植物を＿＿＿＿＿＿重要性を理解していないかもしれない。

TOEFL プレップ 1－2

左列の各単語の反対語に最も近い意味の単語や語句を選び、空欄にそのアルファベットを書きこみなさい。

＿＿＿＿＿＿	1. obtain	(a) 弱まる
＿＿＿＿＿＿	2. intensify	(b) 分ける
＿＿＿＿＿＿	3. irrigation	(c) 失う
＿＿＿＿＿＿	4. aggregate	(d) 排水
＿＿＿＿＿＿	5. adversely	(e) 前向きに

TOEFL サクセス 1

文章を読んで学んだ語彙を復習します。後に続く質問に答えなさい。

[例文訳]

ニジェールやモーリタニアのような国では、過去数世紀間、土地の耕作方法はほとんど変わっていない。さらにこれらの国では、一山型の降雨パターンにより、1年のうち3カ月しか雨が降らない。その結果、食料生産量が需要をほとんど満たしていない。

いくつかの機関や組織が、これらの国の土地の生産性を高める取り組みを強化している。新たな種子を導入し、灌漑技術を改良し、肥料を与えたり土壌を管理したりする新しい方法を取り入れた。光合成のための十分な日光と近代的な灌漑技術があれば、持続可能な農業技術によって、農家は需要を満たすために総生産量を増やすことができるはずだ。

しかし、農作物の再生は予期せぬ敵に直面する。その敵とは、制度の不十分さだ。農作物の専門家が、古い農法をやめて新しい農法に変えるよう個々の農家を説得しても、彼らが実際に必要な政府の協力を得ることは容易ではない。最大のハードルは、政治的な腐敗、不十分な制度、そしてマーケティング・インフラの欠如なのだ。

読解のポイント As a result は「だから」「このため」という意味。

1 この文章中の adversary という言葉に最も近い意味を持つのはどれか。

a. 友人
b. 協力者
c. 敵
d. リーダー

2 最後の段落で、they という言葉が指しているのはどれか。

a. 農作物の専門家
b. 農家
c. 農業技術
d. 敵

Disaster

Target Words

1. anticipate
2. catastrophic
3. collide
4. eruption
5. famine
6. flood
7. impact
8. persevere
9. plunge
10. unleash

Definitions and Samples

1. **anticipate** *v.* To expect; to sense something before it happens
By placing sensors in earthquake-prone areas, scientists can **anticipate** some tremors in time to warn the public.
Parts of speech anticipation *n*, anticipatory *adj*

2. **catastrophic** *adj.* Extremely harmful; causing financial or physical ruin
The architect died in a **catastrophic** elevator accident.
Parts of speech catastrophe *n*, catastrophically *adv*

3. **collide** *v.* To come together with great or violent force
As usual, their holiday was ruined when their in-laws' views on politics **collided** with their own.
Parts of speech collision *n*

4. **eruption** *n.* A sudden, often violent, outburst
The **eruption** of Mount St. Helens in 1980 caused 57 deaths and immeasurable change to the face of the mountain.
Usage tips *Eruption* is often followed by an *of* phrase.
Parts of speech erupt *v*

5. **famine** *n.* Severe hunger; a drastic food shortage
The potato **famine** in Ireland in the mid-nineteenth century caused large numbers of Irish people to emigrate to

America.

6. **flood** *n.* An overflowing of water; an excessive amount
The constant rain and poor drainage system caused a **flood** in town.
The political party sent out a **flood** of letters criticizing their opponents.
Parts of speech flood *v*

7. **impact** *n.* A strong influence
The speech about the importance of education made an **impact** on me.
Usage tips *Impact* is usually followed by *on* or *of*.
Parts of speech impact *v*

8. **persevere** *v.* To keep going, despite obstacles or discouragement; to maintain a purpose
The hikers **persevered** despite the bad weather and the icy trail.
Parts of speech perseverance *n*

9. **plunge** *v.* To go down suddenly; to decrease by a great amount in a short time
He jumped off the diving board and **plunged** into the pool.
The value of the company's stock **plunged** after its chief executive was arrested.
Usage tips *Plunge* is often followed by an *into* phrase.
Parts of speech plunge *n*

10. **unleash** *v.* To release a thing or an emotion
When they saw the strange man on their property, they **unleashed** their dogs.
He is from such an unemotional family, he will never learn to **unleash** his feelings.

TOEFL Prep 2-1 **Find the word or phrase that is closest in meaning to the opposite of each word in the left-hand column. Write the letter in the blank.**

________	1. persevere	(a) to pass by without hitting
________	2. anticipate	(b) to give up
________	3. famine	(c) to not see something coming
________	4. collide	(d) harmless
________	5. catastrophic	(e) excess of food

TOEFL Prep 2-2 **Circle the word that best completes each sentence.**

1. Residents of Hawaii must accept the possibility of a volcanic (eruption / perseverance).
2. Years after the accident, she was finally able to (anticipate / unleash) her feelings of anger.
3. Houses along the river often face (famine / flooding) during the rainy season.
4. Many people think it is cruel to (collide / plunge) live lobsters into boiling water.
5. A well-written essay should make some kind of (catastrophe / impact) on its readers.

TOEFL Success 2 **Read the passage to review the vocabulary you have learned. Answer the questions that follow.**

Nature challenges humans in many ways, through disease, weather, and *famine*. For those living along the coast, one unusual phenomenon capable of *catastrophic* destruction is the tsunami (pronounced "tsoo-NAH-mee"). A tsunami is a series of waves generated in a body of water by an impulsive disturbance. Earthquakes, landslides, volcanic *eruptions*, explosions, and even the *impact* of meteorites can generate

---

TOEFL Prep 2-1　1. b　2. c　3. e　4. a　5. d
TOEFL Prep 2-2　1. eruption　2. unleash　3. flooding　4. plunge　5. impact

tsunamis. Starting at sea, a tsunami slowly approaches land, growing in height and losing energy through bottom friction and turbulence. Still, just like any other water waves, tsunamis *unleash* tremendous energy as they *plunge* onto the shore. They have great erosion potential, stripping beaches of sand, undermining trees, and *flooding* hundreds of meters inland. They can easily crush cars, homes, vegetation, and anything they *collide* with. To minimize the devastation of a tsunami, scientists are constantly trying to *anticipate* them more accurately and more quickly. Because many factors come together to produce a life-threatening tsunami, foreseeing them is not easy. **Despite this**, researchers in meteorology *persevere* in studying and predicting tsunami behavior.

Bonus Structure **Despite this** means "even so; regardless."

1. Which sentence best expresses the essential information of this passage?
   a. Tsunamis could become a new source of usable energy in the next hundred years.
   b. Tsunamis do more damage to the land than flooding.
   c. Tsunamis can have an especially catastrophic impact on coastal communities.
   d. Scientists can predict and track tsunamis with a fair degree of accuracy, reducing their potential impact.

2. In the first sentence, why does the author mention weather?
   a. because tsunamis are caused by bad weather
   b. because tsunamis are more destructive than weather phenomena
   c. as an example of a destructive natural force
   d. as an introduction to the topic of coastal storms

TOEFL Success 2　1. c　2. c

自然
レッスン2

災害

意味と例文

1 anticipate （動詞） 予期する／（何かが起こる前に）それを感じる

例文訳 地震の発生しやすい地域にセンサーを設置することで、科学者はある程度の揺れを予測して、一般の人々に警告することができる。

関連語 anticipation （名詞） 予想、anticipatory （形容詞） 予期しての

2 catastrophic （形容詞） 極めて有害な／経済的または物理的な破壊を引き起こす

例文訳 その建築家はエレベーターの大事故で亡くなった。

関連語 catastrophe （名詞） 大災害、catastrophically （副詞） 壊滅的に

3 collide （動詞） （巨大な力または暴力的な力で）ぶつかる

例文訳 いつものように、義理の両親の政治観と自分たちの政治観がぶつかって、彼らの休日は台無しになってしまった。

関連語 collision （名詞） 衝突

4 eruption （名詞） （突然のしばしば激しい）爆発

例文訳 1980年に起きたセント・ヘレンズ山の噴火は、57名の死者を出し、山肌にはかりしれない変化をもたらした。

ヒント 使い方 eruption は後ろに of 句を伴うことが多い。

関連語 erupt （動詞） 噴火する

5 famine （名詞） 飢饉／深刻な食糧不足

例文訳 19世紀半ばに起きたアイルランドのジャガイモ飢饉により、多くのアイルランド人が米国に移住した。

6 flood （名詞） 水があふれ出すこと／過剰な量

例文訳 降り続く雨と、粗末な排水設備のために、町では洪水が発生した。
その政党は、政敵を批判する手紙を大量に送った。

関連語 flood （動詞） はんらんさせる

7 impact （名詞） 強い影響

例文訳 教育の重要性を説いたそのスピーチに、私は強い影響を受けた。

ヒント 使い方 impact は通常、後ろに on や of を伴うことが多い。

関連語 impact （動詞） 影響を及ぼす

8 persevere （動詞） （障害や妨害があるにもかかわらず）やり続ける／目的を貫く

例文訳 天候が悪く、道は凍っていたが、ハイカーたちは歩き通した。

関連語 perseverance （名詞） 根気

9 plunge （動詞） 急に下がる／（短期間に）大幅に減少する

例文訳 彼は飛び込み台からジャンプして、プールに飛び込んだ。
最高経営責任者が逮捕されると、同社の株価は急落した。

ヒント 使い方 plunge は後ろに into 句を伴うことが多い。

関連語 plunge （名詞） 飛び込むこと、急落

10 unleash （動詞） （物事や感情を）解放する

例文訳 見知らぬ男が敷地内にいるのを見て、彼らは犬たちを放した。
彼はあんなにも感情を表に出さない家庭で育ったので、自分の感情を解き放てるようには決してならないだろう。

TOEFL プレップ2-1

左列の各単語の反対語に最も近い意味の単語や語句を選び、空欄にそのアルファベットを書きこみなさい。

______	1. persevere	(a) ぶつからずに通り過ぎる
______	2. anticipate	(b) あきらめる
______	3. famine	(c) 何かがやってくるのが見えない
______	4. collide	(d) 無害である
______	5. catastrophic	(e) 食糧の過剰

TOEFL プレップ2-2

各文を完成させるのに最も適した単語を丸で囲みなさい。

1 ハワイに住んでいる人は、火山の（噴火／根気）の可能性を受け入れなければならない。

2 事故から何年も経ってから、彼女はようやく怒りの感情を（予測する／解き放つ）ことができた。

3 川沿いの家は、雨期になるとしばしば（飢饉／洪水）に見舞われる。

4 生きているロブスターを熱湯の中に（衝突する／沈める）のは残酷だと思う人は多い。

5 よくできたエッセイは、読者に何らかの（大災害／影響）を与えるはずだ。

TOEFL サクセス2

文章を読んで学んだ語彙を復習します。後に続く質問に答えなさい。

[例文訳]

自然は、病気や天候、飢饉といったさまざまな形で人間に挑戦してくる。海岸沿いに住んでいる人にとって、壊滅的な被害をもたらす異常現象の1つが津波（「tsoo-NAH-mee」と発音される）だ。津波とは、急激にかき乱されることによって水域に発生する一連の波である。地震、地滑り、火山の噴火、爆発、さらには隕石の衝突でさえ、津波を引き起こす可能性がある。海で生じた津波は、高さを増しながらゆっくりと陸地に近づき、海底との摩擦や乱流によってエネルギーを失う。しかし、他の水波と同じように、津波は海岸に衝突する際に途方もないエネルギーを放出する。津波は大きな侵食力を持っていて、砂浜から砂を奪い去り、樹木を根こそぎ破壊し、何百メートルも内陸部にまで勢いよく水を注ぐ。車や家や草木など、ぶつかったものすべてを簡単に潰してしまう。津波の被害を最小限に抑えるために、科学者たちは津波をより正確に、より早く予測しようと常に努力している。生命を脅かす津波の発生にはさまざまな要因が絡み合っているため、その予測は容易ではない。それでも、気象学者は、津波の動きを研究し、予測し続けている。

読解のポイント　Despite this **とは「それでもなお、～にもかかわらず」という意味。**

1　この文章の重要な情報を最もよく表しているのはどの文か。
- a. 津波は100年後には新しいエネルギー源になるかもしれない。
- b. 津波は洪水よりも大きな被害を土地に与える。
- c. 津波は、特に沿岸地域に壊滅的な影響を与える。
- d. 科学者は、津波をかなりの精度で予測・追跡することができ、その潜在的な影響を軽減することができる。

2　最初の文で、筆者はなぜ天候について言及しているのか？
- a. 津波は悪天候により引き起こされるから
- b. 津波は気象現象よりも大きな被害をもたらすから
- c. 自然災害の一例として
- d. 沿岸暴風雨の話題への導入として

Evolution and Migration

Target Words

1. adapt
2. diverse
3. evolve
4. feature
5. generation
6. inherent
7. migration
8. physical
9. process
10. survive

Definitions and Samples

1. adapt *v.* To adjust to the circumstances; to make suitable
Dinosaurs could not **adapt** to the colder temperatures.
The teacher **adapted** the exercises for his more advanced students.
Usage tips *Adapt* is often followed by *to*.
Parts of speech adaptation *n*, adapter *n*, adaptable *adj*

2. diverse *n.* Various; showing a lot of differences within a group
India is one of the most linguistically **diverse** countries in the world.
Usage tips An *-ly* adverb (e.g., *linguistically*) often comes before *diverse*.
Parts of speech diversify *v*, diversity *n*, diversification *n*

3. evolve *v.* To develop; to come forth
Modern-day sharks **evolved** from their ancestor Eryops, which lived more than 200 million years ago.
Usage tips *Evolve* is often followed by *into* or *from*.
Parts of speech evolution *n*, evolutionist *n*, evolutionary *adj*

4. feature *n.* Part; characteristic
The best **feature** of this car is its heated seats.
Usage tips *Feature* is often followed by *of*.
Parts of speech feature *v*

5. generation *n.* A group of people born at about the same time
As older managers retired, a new **generation** of leaders

took control of the company.

Usage tips Before *generation*, an adjective like *new*, *next*, *earlier*, or *older* is common. *Generation* is often followed by *of*.

Parts of speech generational *adj*

6. **inherent** *adj.* Naturally characteristic; always found within something, because it's a basic part of that thing

No job can be interesting all the time. Boredom is **inherent** in any kind of work.

Usage tips *Inherent* is often followed by *in*.

Parts of speech inherently *adv*

7. **migration** *n.* Movement from one place to another by a group of people or animals

The **migration** of farm workers from one state to the next depends primarily on the harvest.

Usage tips *Migration* is often followed by *to* or *from*.

Parts of speech migrate *v*, migrant *n*, migratory *adj*

8. **physical** *adj.* Related to the body; related to materials that can be seen or felt

Because of the shape of its throat, an ape does not have the **physical** ability to speak.

The mountains form a **physical** barrier between the west and the east.

Usage tips *Physical* usually comes before the noun it describes.

Parts of speech physically *adv*

9. **process** *n.* A series of steps leading to a result

To get a good job, most people go through a long **process** of letter-writing and interviews.

Usage tips *Process* is often followed by *of* plus the *-ing* form of a verb.

Parts of speech proceed *v*, process *v*

10. **survive** *v.* To continue living (despite some danger or illness)

After getting lost in the mountains, Gordon **survived** by eating wild plants and catching fish.

Usage tips *Survive* is often followed by a phrase with *by*.

Parts of speech survivor *n*, survival *n*

TOEFL Prep 3-1 Find the word or phrase that is closest in meaning to the opposite of each word in the left-hand column. Write the letter in the blank.

______	1. physical	(a) not an integral part
______	2. migration	(b) stay the same
______	3. adapt	(c) die
______	4. inherent	(d) staying in one place
______	5. survive	(e) mental

TOEFL Prep 3-2 Choose the word from the list that is closest in meaning to the underlined part of each sentence. Write it in the blank.

diverse evolved generation process survive

________ 1. Various languages are spoken on the Indian subcontinent.

________ 2. Making bread involves a sequence of steps that takes about three hours.

________ 3. Few sea turtles manage to live through their first year of life.

________ 4. This age group tends to support current educational policies.

________ 5. Her thinking about economics has changed slowly in the last several months.

TOEFL Success 3 Read the passage to review the vocabulary you have learned. Answer the questions that follow.

The *migration* from Asia to North America across the Bering Strait (perhaps by land bridge) was a *monumental* event in human history. The *process* of overspreading the Americas took more than 1,000 years, or 30 *generations*. This might

TOEFL Prep 3-1 1. e 2. d 3. b 4. a 5. c
TOEFL Prep 3-2 1. diverse 2. process 3. survive 4. generation 5. evolved

seem to confirm common sense—that slow travel was *inherent* in any great migration without wheeled vehicles across unknown terrain. **Further thought** shows that this process was remarkably fast—about 10 north-south miles per year, on average. The Americas were populated at an astounding pace, when one considers the *physical* limits of the human body and the physical *features* of the American continents. Legs of humans can move only so fast under the best of circumstances, and they work even slower over mountain passes or deserts. Populations spread through the *diverse* regions of the Americas (grasslands, eastern forests, coastal swamps) and needed to *adapt* to their new environments. The migrants' lifestyle had *evolved* over the years to that of professional nomads ensuring that they would find the resources needed to *survive*.

Bonus Structure **Further thought** means "looking deeper; thinking more."

1. Which sentence best expresses the essential information in this passage?
   a. Human migration across the Bering Strait was remarkably slow.
   b. Physical limitations made migration across the Bering Strait almost impossible.
   c. Humans readily adapted to life in the Bering Strait.
   d. The migration through the Americas was surprisingly fast.

2. In this passage, the word monumental is closest in meaning to
   a. disastrous
   b. evolving
   c. important
   d. physical

TOEFL Success 3 1. a 2. c

自然
レッスン3

進化と移動

意味と例文

1 adapt（動詞） 状況に合わせる／適したものにする

例文訳 恐竜は、気温の低下に適応できなかった。
教師は、より上級の生徒に合わせて練習問題をつくり直した。

ヒント 使い方 adapt は後ろに to を伴うことが多い。

関連語 adaptation（名詞）適応、適合、adapter（名詞）改作者、アダプター、adaptable（形容詞）適応できる

2 diverse（形容詞） いろいろな／（1つのグループの中で）多様性が見られる

例文訳 インドは世界で最も多様な言語を有する国の1つだ。

ヒント 使い方 diverse の前には～ ly の形の副詞がくることが多い（例：linguistically）。

関連語 diversify（動詞）多様化する、diversity（名詞）多様性、diversification（名詞）多様化

3 evolve（動詞） 発達する／前進する

例文訳 現在のサメは、2億年以上前に生息していたエリオプスを祖先として進化したものだ。

ヒント 使い方 evolve は後ろに into や from を伴うことが多い。

関連語 evolution（名詞）進化、発達、evolutionist（名詞）進化論者、evolutionary（形容詞）発展の、進化の

4 feature（名詞） 部分／特徴

例文訳 この車の一番の特徴は、ヒーター付きシートだ。

ヒント 使い方 feature は後ろに of を伴うことが多い。

関連語 feature（動詞）～を特徴づける、呼び物とする

5 generation（名詞） ほぼ同時期に生まれた人たちの集団

例文訳 年配の経営陣が退職すると、新しい世代のリーダーたちが会社を管理するようになった。

ヒント 使い方 generation の前には通常 new、next、earlier や older といっ

た形容詞がくる。また、generation は後ろに of を伴うことが多い。

関連語 generational (形容詞) 世代の

---

6 inherent (形容詞) 生まれながらに固有の／(ある物事の基本的部分なので) 常にその中に見られる

例文訳 常に面白い仕事というものはない。どんな仕事にも退屈はつきものである。

ヒント 使い方 inherent は後ろに in を伴うことが多い。

関連語 inherently (副詞) 本来的に、内在的に

---

7 migration (名詞) (人や動物の集団が) ある場所から別の場所へ移動すること

例文訳 農業従事者の州間移動は、主に収穫に左右される。

ヒント 使い方 migration は to または from を後ろに伴うことが多い。

関連語 migrate (動詞) 移住する、migrant (名詞) 移住者、migratory (形容詞) 移住性の

---

8 physical (形容詞) 身体に関連する／(見たり感じたりできる) 物質に関連する

例文訳 類人猿は、その喉の形のために、話すという身体能力を持たない。

その山々は、西と東を隔てる物理的な障壁となっている。

ヒント 使い方 physical は通常、それが説明する名詞の前に来る。

関連語 physically (副詞) 身体的に、物理的に

---

9 process (名詞) 結果に至るまでの一連の流れ

例文訳 いい仕事を得るためには、ほとんどの人は書類を書いたり面接を受けたりと長いプロセスを経る。

ヒント 使い方 process は「of ＋動詞の～ ing 形」を後ろに伴うことが多い。

関連語 proceed (動詞) 進む、process (動詞) 加工する、処理する

---

10 survive (動詞) (何らかの危険や病気があっても) 生き続ける

例文訳 山で遭難したゴードンは、野草を食べたり魚を捕ったりして生き延びた。

ヒント 使い方 survive は by 句を後ろに伴うことが多い。

関連語 survivor (名詞) 生存者、survival (名詞) 生き残ること

TOEFL プレップ 3-1

左列の各単語の反対語に最も近い意味の単語や語句を選び、空欄にそのアルファベットを書きこみなさい。

______ 1. physical (a) 不可欠な部分ではない
______ 2. migration (b) 変わらずにいること
______ 3. adapt (c) 死ぬ
______ 4. inherent (d) 1カ所にとどまること
______ 5. survice (e) 精神的な

TOEFL プレップ 3-2

各文の下線部に最も近い意味を持つ単語をリストから選んで、空欄に記入しなさい。

diverse evolved generation process survive

______ 1. インド亜大陸ではさまざまな言語が話されている。
______ 2. パンをつくるためには、3時間ほどかかる一連の工程が必要だ。
______ 3. 生まれてから1年生き延びられるウミガメはほとんどいない。
______ 4. この年齢層は現在の教育方針を支持する傾向にある。
______ 5. 彼女の経済学に対する考え方は、ここ数カ月で少しずつ変わってきた。

TOEFL サクセス 3

文章を読んで学んだ語彙を復習します。後に続く質問に答えなさい。

[例文訳]

ベーリング海峡を（おそらく陸伝いで）渡ったアジアから北アメリカへの移住は、人類史において大きな意義のある出来事だった。移住者がアメリカ大陸じゅうに広がっていく過程には、1000年以上、つまり30世代もかかった。このことは、車を使わずに未知の土地を横断して大移動をするのは、本来的に時間がかかるものだったという常識を裏付けているように思えるかもしれない。さらに見てみると、実はこの過程は驚くほどの速さで行われ、1年に平均して南北10マイルほど進んでいたことがわかる。人間の身体的な限界とアメリカ大陸の物理的な特徴を考えると、人々は驚異的なスピードでアメリカ大陸に住み着いていった。人間の脚ではどんなに良い条件下でもそんなに速く進むことはできず、山や砂漠ではさらに遅くなる。人々はアメリカ大陸の多様な地域（草原、東部森林地帯、海岸湿地帯）に広がっていき、それぞれの新しい環境に適応する必要があった。移住者たちは長い年月をかけて、その生活様式を、生き延びるために必要な資源を見つけることができるプロの遊牧民の生活様式へと進化させていった。

読解のポイント　Further thought とは「より深く見てみると、さらに考えると」という意味。

1　この文章の重要な情報を最もよく表しているのはどの文か。
a. ベーリング海峡を渡る人類の移動は驚くほど遅いものだった。
b. 身体的（物理的）な制約によりベーリング海峡を渡ることはほとんど不可能だった。
c. 人類はベーリング海峡での生活にあっさりと適応した。
d. アメリカ大陸での人類の移動は驚くほど速く行われた。

2　この文章中の monumental という言葉に最も近い意味を持つのはどれか。
a. 悲惨な
b. 発展する
c. 重要な
d. 物理的な

Petroleum Alternatives

Target Words

1. constraint
2. contamination
3. deplete
4. dispose of
5. elementally
6. emission
7. extinction
8. reservoir
9. shrink
10. stable

Definitions and Samples

1. **constraint** *n.* Something that restricts thought or action
The **constraints** of military life kept Eileen from seeing Private Morris more than once a month.
Parts of speech constrain *v*

2. **contamination** *n.* Being made less clean by a germ or hazardous substance
The **contamination** in the river came from the factory located just upstream.
Parts of speech contaminate *v*, contaminant *n*

3. **deplete** *v.* To greatly decrease the supply of a resource or material
The prolonged war **depleted** the country's national treasury.
Parts of speech depletion *n*

4. **dispose of** *v.* To throw away; to get rid of; to kill
She **disposed of** her unwanted possessions before moving.
The tyrant cruelly **disposed of** all his enemies.
Usage tips *Dispose of* should be learned as a unit. In this meaning, *dispose* does not occur without *of*.
Parts of speech disposal *n*, disposable *adj*

5. **elementally** *adv.* In terms of elements; basically

Elementally, coal and diamonds are the same.

Parts of speech element *n*, elemental *adj*

6. **emission** *n.* Sending out from a small space into the general environment; a substance discharged into the air

The Environmental Protection Agency regulates the **emission** of pollutants into the air.

Usage tips *Emission* is usually followed by an *of* phrase.

Parts of speech emit *v*

7. **extinction** *n.* Complete disappearance; the end of existence

Human beings have caused the **extinction** of many other species.

Usage tips *Extinction* implies an absolute end; an extinct species is gone and will not reappear (except if genetic scientists succeed with experimental "de-extinction" techniques).

Parts of speech extinct *adj*

8. **reservoir** *n.* A place where a liquid is collected and stored

Terrorists threatened to put poison in the town's **reservoir**.

Parts of speech reserve *v*

9. **shrink** *v.* To become reduced in size, amount, or value

If you dry your clothes on the "high heat" setting, they may **shrink**.

Parts of speech shrinkage *n*, shrinkable *adj*

10. **stable** *adj.* Firm and dependable; showing little change

He fell because the ladder wasn't **stable**.

Parts of speech stability *n*, stably *adv*, stabilize *v*

TOEFL Prep 4-1 **Find the word that is closest in meaning to the opposite of each word in the left-hand column. Write the letter in the blank.**

________	1. stable	(a) keep
________	2. contamination	(b) expand
________	3. extinct	(c) unsteady
________	4. dispose of	(d) existing
________	5. shrink	(e) purity

TOEFL Prep 4-2 **Circle the word that best completes each sentence.**

1. The (constraints / contamination) of being in prison made her hate society even more.
2. A recognition that the Earth is round was one of the (elemental / shrunken) advances in thought during the time period.
3. Mother Teresa, who helped the poorest of the poor, had a great (disposal / reservoir) of love within her spirit.
4. Automobiles are responsible for some (emissions / extinction) of greenhouse gases.
5. By the end of the storm, the hikers had (depleted / reserved) even their emergency stores.

TOEFL Success 4 **Read the passage to review the vocabulary you have learned. Answer the question that follows.**

Human consumption of fossil fuels is expected to fully *deplete* the Earth's crude oil reserves by the year 2060. As underground *reservoirs* of oil continue to *shrink*, we have no choice but to find alternatives. **One promising source**, with much cleaner *emissions*, is called bio-diesel. Bio-diesel is often made from soybean oil, although it can be made from any

---

TOEFL Prep 4-1 1. c 2. e 3. d 4. a 5. b
TOEFL Prep 4-2 1. constraints 2. elemental 3. reservoir 4. emissions 5. depleted

vegetable oil that is not *elementally* different from soy. Bio-diesel can even be made from used cooking oils that homes or restaurants would otherwise *dispose of*. Bio-diesel can be used without *constraint* in any vehicle that runs on diesel—no modifications are needed. Presently, diesel engines can take up to 20 percent soy in their soy-diesel blend. As the need for bio-diesel increases and the technology improves, we may soon witness the *extinction* of the fossil-fueled vehicle. This is good news for the planet, as bio-diesel is a more *stable* source of energy than petroleum, and it reduces *contamination* of our air and water.

Bonus Structure **One promising source** signals the point of this paragraph.

An introductory sentence for a brief summary of the passage is provided below. Complete the summary by selecting the three answer choices that express the most important ideas in the passage. In each blank, write the letter of one of your choices.

Bio-diesel is a promising alternative to fossil fuels.
•
•
•

a. Humans have shown little self-restraint in their consumption of fossil fuels.
b. Underground reservoirs of oil will soon be depleted.
c. Bio-diesel burns cleaner than fossil fuels.
d. Bio-diesel comes from a more stable source than petroleum.
e. Restaurants can save disposal fees on used cooking oil.

TOEFL Success 4 b, c, d

自然
レッスン4

石油代替エネルギー

意味と例文

1 constraint (名詞) (思考や行動を) 制限するもの

例文訳 軍隊生活の制約から、アイリーンはモリス1等兵と月に一度しか会うことができなかった。

関連語 constrain (動詞) 強制する、抑える

2 contamination (名詞) (細菌や有害物質によって) 清潔さが損なわれること

例文訳 川の汚染は、すぐ上流にある工場が原因だった。

関連語 contaminate (動詞) 汚染する、contaminant (名詞) 汚染物質

3 deplete (動詞) (資源や材料の供給を) 大幅に減らす

例文訳 長引く戦争で国庫は枯渇した。

関連語 depletion (名詞) 枯渇、消耗

4 dispose of (動詞) 捨てる／取り除く／殺す

例文訳 彼女は引っ越す前に不要な物を処分した。
その暴君は敵全員を残虐に殺した。

ヒント 使い方 dispose of はセットで覚えること。上記の意味において、dispose が of なしで使われることはない。

関連語 disposal (名詞) 処分、disposable (形容詞) 処分できる

5 elementally (副詞) 元素として、要素として／基本的に

例文訳 元素としては、石炭もダイヤモンドも同じだ。

関連語 element (名詞) 元素、要素、elemental (形容詞) 要素の、基本的な

6 emission (名詞) (小さな空間から広い環境へ) 送り出すこと／(空気中に) 放出される物質

例文訳 環境保護庁は、大気中への汚染物質の排出を規制している。

ヒント 使い方 emission は後ろに of 句を伴うことが多い。

関連語 emit (動詞) 放つ

7 extinction (名詞) 完全な消滅／存在が終わること

例文訳 人間は他の多くの種の絶滅を引き起こしてきた。

ヒント 使い方 extinction は絶対的な終わりを意味する。絶滅した種は消え、再び現れることはない（遺伝科学者が実験的な「絶滅種再生」技術を成功させないかぎりは）。

関連語 extinct (形容詞) 消滅した

8 reservoir (名詞) 液体を集めて保存する場所

例文訳 テロリストたちは、町の貯水所に毒を入れると脅した。

関連語 reserve (動詞) 予約する、取っておく

9 shrink (動詞) (大きさ、量、価値が) 減る

例文訳 服を「高温」設定で乾燥させると、縮むことがある。

関連語 shrinkage (名詞) 収縮、shrinkable (形容詞) 縮みやすい、収縮可能な

10 stable (形容詞) 堅固で信頼できる／ほとんど変化しない

例文訳 はしごが不安定だったので、彼は落ちてしまった。

関連語 stability (名詞) 安定性、stably (副詞) 安定して、stabilize (動詞) 安定させる

TOEFL プレップ４−１

左列の各単語に最も近い意味の単語を選び、空欄にそのアルファベットを書きなさい。

＿＿＿＿＿＿	1. stable	(a) 保持する
＿＿＿＿＿＿	2. contamination	(b) 拡大する
＿＿＿＿＿＿	3. extinct	(c) 安定しない
＿＿＿＿＿＿	4. dispose of	(d) 存在する
＿＿＿＿＿＿	5. shrink	(e) 純粋、清らかさ

TOEFL プレップ４−２

各文を完成させるのに最も適した単語を丸で囲みなさい。

1　刑務所の中にいるという（制約／汚染）によって、彼女は社会をより憎むようになった。

2　地球は丸いという認識は、その時代の思想における（基本的な／収縮した）進歩の１つだった。

3　極貧の人々を助けたマザー・テレサは、その精神の中に偉大な愛の（廃棄／蓄え）を持っていた。

4　自動車は、温室効果ガス（排出／消滅）の原因の１つだ。

5　嵐がやむまでに、ハイカーたちは非常用食料さえも（消費しつくして／保存して）いた。

TOEFL サクセス４

文章を読んで学んだ語彙を復習します。後に続く質問に答えなさい。

[例文訳]

人類による化石燃料の消費は、2060年までに地球に埋蔵されている原油を完全に枯渇させると予想されている。地下の原油の蓄えが減り続けているため、私たちは代わりになるものを探すほかない。有望なエネルギー源の１つは、排出ガスがよりクリーンな、バイオディーゼルと呼ばれるものだ。バイオディーゼルは、大豆油を原料とすることが多いが、大豆と基本要素が変わらなければ、どんな植物油からでもつくることができる。また、家庭やレストランでは廃棄するような使用済み食用油を原料とすることさえできる。ディーゼルエンジンで動く車両であれば、改造の必要なく、バイオディーゼルを制約なく使用できる。現在、ディーゼルエンジンには、大豆油由来のバイオディーゼルを最大20パーセントまで混合して使用できる。バイオディーゼルの需要が高まり、技術が向上すれば、化石燃料を使った車が消滅するのを目の当たりにする日も近いかもしれない。これは地球にとって朗報だ。バイオディーゼルは石油よりも安定したエネルギー源であり、大気や水の汚染を減らすからだ。

読解のポイント One promising source **は、この段落のポイントを示している。**

以下は、この文章の要約の導入である。選択肢の中から最も重要な考えを表している３つを選び、要約文を完成させなさい。それぞれの空欄に、選択したアルファベットを書くこと。

バイオディーゼルは、化石燃料の代替として期待されている。
・
・
・

a. 人類は、化石燃料の消費に関して、ほとんど自制をしてこなかった。
b. 地下の埋蔵石油は間もなく枯渇する。
c. バイオディーゼルは、化石燃料よりもクリーンに燃焼する。
d. バイオディーゼルは、石油よりも安定したエネルギー源に由来している。
e. レストランは、使用済み食用油を廃棄する費用を節約できる。

Time Efficiency

Target Words

1. adjust
2. arbitrary
3. denominator
4. exponentially
5. infinitesimal
6. maximize
7. parallel
8. proportion
9. rate
10. sequence

Definitions and Samples

1. adjust *v.* To change; to get accustomed to something

Travelers are advised to **adjust** their watches before arriving in the new time zone.

Parts of speech adjustment *n*, adjustable *adj*

2. arbitrary *adj.* Chosen simply by whim or chance, not for any specific reason

The decision to build a school in Blackberry Township was **arbitrary**, without any thought to future housing patterns.

Parts of speech arbitrate *v*, arbitrator *n*, arbitrarily *adv*

3. denominator *n.* The number written below the line in a fraction

In the fraction 1⁄2, the number 2 is the **denominator**.

Usage tips The phrase *lowest common denominator* means "the most basic and unsophisticated things that most people share."

Parts of speech denominate *v*, denomination *n*, denominational *adj*

4. exponentially *adv.* At a very fast rate

In Turkey, the value of the lira has decreased **exponentially** in the last several decades.

Usage tips *Exponentially* is taken from mathematics, where an exponent is a number indicating how many times something is multiplied by itself. For example, 4^3 contains the exponent "3," indicating $4 \times 4 \times 4$.

Parts of speech exponent *n*, exponential *adj*

5. infinitesimal *adj.* Immeasurably small

The number of contaminants in the water was **infinitesimal**, so the water was safe to drink.

Parts of speech infinitesimally *adv*

6. maximize *v.* To increase or make as great as possible

A coach helps each athlete **maximize** his or her potential.

Parts of speech maximum *n*, maximum *adj*

7. parallel *adj.* Being an equal distance apart everywhere

The street where I live runs **parallel** to the main road through town.

Usage tips *Parallel* is often followed by *to*.

Parts of speech parallel *n*, parallel *adv*

8. proportion *n.* A part in relation to the whole

The average employee spends a large **proportion** of each workday answering e-mails.

Usage tips *Proportion* is often followed by *of*.

Parts of speech proportionate *adj*, proportionally *adv*

9. rate *n.* The cost per unit of a good or service; the motion or change that happens in a certain time.

Postal **rates** in Japan are among the highest in the world.

Some grasses grow at the **rate** of one inch per day.

Parts of speech rate *v*, rating *n*

10. sequence *v.* To organize or arrange in succession

Volunteers have been asked to **sequence** the files and organize the boxes.

Parts of speech sequence *n*, sequentially *adv*

TOEFL Prep 5-1 **Complete each sentence by filling in the blank with the best word from the list. Change the form of the word if necessary. Use each word only once.**

adjust   arbitrary   denominator   infinitesimal   rate

1. Students felt that the exam was unfair and the grading system was rather______.
2. The______of increase in prices made it difficult for people to afford basic goods.
3. Politicians promised great changes in the coming year, but any improvement in people's lives was______.
4. She quickly overcame her culture shock and found it easy to______to the new country.
5. You can add two fractions that have the same______.

TOEFL Prep 5-2 **Find the word or phrase that is closest in meaning to the opposite of each word in the left-hand column. Write the letter in the blank.**

______	1. arbitrary	(a) mix up
______	2. maximize	(b) intersecting
______	3. sequence	(c) minimize
______	4. infinitesimal	(d) huge
______	5. parallel	(e) planned out

TOEFL Success 5 **Read the passage to review the vocabulary you have learned. Answer the questions that follow.**

Time is, **as we all know**, money. Such valuation of time leads people to extreme efforts to *maximize* their use of time. Some people obsess over knowing the exact time. They buy clocks and watches that automatically *adjust* themselves over the Internet or by radio waves. These measurements allow

---

TOEFL Prep 5-1   1. arbitrary   2. rate   3. infinitesimal   4. adjust   5. denominator
TOEFL Prep 5-2   1. e   2. c   3. a   4. d   5. b

them *infinitesimal* accuracy in dealing with time. Regardless of how one tracks time, most people share a common goal: They want to use time effectively. Since about 1982, this efficiency has increased *exponentially* each year, thanks to computers and their ability to multitask. In multitasking, a computer executes several different tasks in *parallel*. Rather than being set *arbitrarily*, each task is given a priority in the computer's operating system, and time is spent in *proportion* to the priority of the task. The computer executes different *sequences* of tasks at different clock cycles, thereby increasing the *rate* of output from a process.

Bonus Structure **As we all know** is a writer's device for appealing to common knowledge.

1. Why does the author mention computer multitasking in this article?
   a. because it is new
   b. because it measures time better than any clock
   c. because it helps people to arrange their activities sequentially
   d. because it is a good example of the efficient use of time

2. The underlined word *sequences* in the passage is closest in meaning to
   a. styles
   b. lengths
   c. orderings
   d. difficulty levels

TOEFL Success 5 1. d 2. c

科学
レッスン5

時間効率

意味と例文

1 adjust（動詞） 変更する／ある物事に慣れる

例文訳 旅行者は、新しいタイムゾーンに着く前に時計を調整することを勧められる。

関連語 adjustment（名詞）調整、調節、adjustable（形容詞）調整可能な

---

2 arbitrary（形容詞） （何らかの理由からではなく）気まぐれや偶然によって選ばれる

例文訳 ブラックベリー郡区に学校を建設するという決定は、将来の住宅パターンをまったく考慮することなく、独断的に下された。

関連語 arbitrate（動詞）仲裁する、arbitrator（名詞）調停者、仲裁人、arbitrarily（副詞）恣意的に、任意に、独断で

---

3 denominator（名詞） 分数の線の下に書かれている数字（分母）

例文訳 2分の1という分数では、数値2が分母だ。

ヒント▶使い方 lowest common denominator（最小公分母）という言葉は、「多くの人が共有する最も基本的で無難なもの」という意味。

関連語 denominate（動詞）呼ぶ、称する、denomination（名詞）単位名、名称、denominational（形容詞）名目上の、宗派の

---

4 exponentially（副詞） 非常に速いペースで

例文訳 トルコでは、ここ数十年の間にリラの価値が急激に下落した。

ヒント▶使い方 exponentiallyは数学に由来する言葉で、数学においてexponent（べき指数）とは、ある数字がそれ自体に何回掛け合わされるかを示す数字のこと。例えば、4^3にはべき指数「3」が含まれており、これは4×4×4を表す。

関連語 exponent（名詞）指数、べき指数、exponential（形容詞）指数の

---

5 infinitesimal（形容詞） はかりしれないほど小さい

例文訳 その水に含まれる汚染物質の数は限りなく少なかったので、

その水は安心して飲めるものだった。

関連語 infinitesimally（副詞）極めて小さく

---

6 maximize（動詞）（できるだけ）増やしたり、大きくしたりする

例文訳 コーチはアスリート一人ひとりの可能性を最大限に引き出す手助けをする。

関連語 maximum（名詞）最大量、最大限、maximum（形容詞）最大の

---

7 parallel（形容詞）（どこであっても）等しい間隔があいている

例文訳 私が住んでいる通りは、町を貫く幹線道路と平行に走っている。

ヒント 使い方 parallel は後ろに to を伴うことが多い。

関連語 parallel（名詞）平行線、parallel（副詞）平行に

---

8 proportion（名詞）（全体に対する）一部分

例文訳 一般的な会社員は、就業日の大部分をメールの返信に費やしている。

ヒント 使い方 proportion は後ろに of を伴うことが多い。

関連語 proportionate（形容詞）比例した、proportionally（副詞）比例して

---

9 rate（名詞）（商品やサービスの単位あたりの）コスト／（一定の時間内に起こる）動きや変化

例文訳 日本の郵便料金は世界で最も高い部類に入る。
草の中には1日1インチのペースで育つものもある。

関連語 rate（動詞）見積もる、（料金を）定める、rating（名詞）格付け

---

10 sequence（動詞）（順番に）並べたり、整理したりする

例文訳 ボランティアの人たちはファイルを順番に並べて箱を整理するよう頼まれている。

関連語 sequence（名詞）順序、連続、sequentially（副詞）連続して

TOEFL プレップ 5−1

リストの中から空欄に当てはまる適切な単語を選んで、各文を完成させなさい。必要に応じて単語を活用させること。なお、各単語は一度しか使用できません。

adjust arbitrary denominator infinitesimal rate

1 学生たちは、その試験は不公平であり採点システムがかなり＿＿＿＿＿＿＿＿＿＿＿＿感じた。

2 物価上昇の＿＿＿＿＿＿＿＿＿＿のために、人々は生活必需品を買うことが難しくなった。

3 政治家は、翌年の大きな変化を約束したが、人々の生活の改善は＿＿＿＿＿＿＿＿＿＿。

4 彼女はすぐにカルチャーショックを克服し、その新しい国に＿＿＿＿＿＿＿＿＿＿＿＿のは容易だとわかった。

5 同じ＿＿＿＿＿＿＿＿＿＿を持つ２つの分数は、足し合わせることができる。

TOEFL プレップ 5−2

左列の各単語の反対語に最も近い意味の単語や語句を選び、空欄にそのアルファベットを書きこみなさい。

＿＿＿＿＿＿＿＿	1. arbitrary	(a) ごちゃ混ぜにする
＿＿＿＿＿＿＿＿	2. maximize	(b) 交差する
＿＿＿＿＿＿＿＿	3. sequence	(c) 最小化する
＿＿＿＿＿＿＿＿	4. infinitesimal	(d) 巨大な
＿＿＿＿＿＿＿＿	5. parallel	(e) 計画された

TOEFL サクセス 5

文章を読んで学んだ語彙を復習します。後に続く質問に答えなさい。

［例文訳］

時は金なり――これは誰もが知っていることだ。このような時間についての価値観から、人々は時間を最大限に活用しようと極端に努力する。なかには、正確な時間を知ることに執着する人もいる。そういう人は、インターネットや電波によって自動的に時刻が調整される時計を買う。それらの計測によって、きわめて細かい精度で時間を使いこなせるようになる。どうやって時間を確認するかにかかわらず、たいていの人は共通の目標を持っている。それは、時間を有効に使いたい、ということだ。1982年頃から、コンピュータとそのマルチタスク能力のおかげで、作業効率は年々飛躍的に向上している。マルチタスクでは、コンピュータが複数の異なるタスクを並行して行う。各タスクは任意に設定されるのではなく、コンピュータのオペレーティングシステムで優先度を与えられ、その優先度に比例して時間が費やされる。コンピュータは、異なるタスクの連続を異なるクロックサイクルで行うことによって、プロセスの出力レートを向上させている。

読解のポイント as we all know **は一般常識に訴えかけるための筆者の工夫。**

1 この文章の中で筆者がコンピュータのマルチタスクについて言及しているのはなぜか？

a. 新しい事柄だから
b. どんな時計よりも正確に時間を計れるから
c. 人々が自分の活動を順序立てて調整するのに役立つから
d. 時間を効率的に使う良い例だから

2 この文章中の下線部 sequences という言葉に最も近い意味を持つのはどれか。

a. 方式
b. 長さ
c. 順序
d. 難易度

Ancient Life

Target Words

1. accuracy
2. adjacent
3. compress
4. feasibly
5. gut
6. integrally
7. overlap
8. retain
9. seep
10. structure

Definitions and Samples

1. accuracy *n.* Precision; exactness
The research department checks all our articles for **accuracy** of facts before we print them.
Usage tips *Accuracy* is often followed by *of*.
Parts of speech accurate *adj*, accurately *adv*

2. adjacent *adj.* Next to
Even though the villages are **adjacent** to each other, their residents speak different languages.
Usage tips *Adjacent* is often followed by *to*.
Parts of speech adjacency *n*

3. compress *v.* To press together
To make the foundation stronger, they **compressed** the soil before pouring the concrete.
Parts of speech compression *n*, compressed *adj*

4. feasibly *adv.* Practically; in a way that can work
Scientists can't **feasibly** bring energy from deep ocean currents to where it is needed—on land.
Parts of speech feasibility *n*, feasible *adj*

5. gut *v.* To empty or hollow out
In order to remodel the house, we must first **gut** it and throw away all the old fixtures.

Usage tips *Gut* also means "the stomach of an animal"; this verb makes an image, that the inside of a building is like the inside of an animal.

Parts of speech gut *n*, gutted *adj*

6. **integrally** *adv.* In a whole or complete manner
Writing and spelling are taught **integrally** as part of the reading program.
Parts of speech integrate *v*, integrity *n*, integral *n*, integral *adj*

7. **overlap** *v.* To lie over part of something; to have elements in common
One of the two assistants will likely get fired, since most of their duties in the office **overlap**.
Parts of speech overlap *n*

8. **retain** *v.* To keep or hold
The rain fell so heavily that the banks of the river could not **retain** all the water.
Parts of speech retainer *n*, retention *n*

9. **seep** *v.* To pass slowly for a long time, as a liquid or gas might
As the containers rusted, the toxic waste **seeped** into the ground.
Usage tips *Seep* is often followed by *into* or *through*.

10. **structure** *n.* Something constructed, such as a building
Most companies have a social **structure** that can't be understood by outsiders.
Parts of speech structure *v*, structural *adj*, structurally *adv*

TOEFL Prep 6-1 **Complete each sentence by filling in the blank with the best word from the list. Change the form of the word if necessary. Use each word only once.**

accuracy adjacent feasibly integrally structure

1. She had no idea how they could ______ take a big vacation and remodel their house in the same year.
2. Three things have equal roles in the recovery program and are used ______—daily meditation, massage, and herbal medicines.
3. The rival politicians were raised in ______ counties.
4. If you build a ______ next to this river, you must be sure it is safe against floods.
5. After making a few mistakes, the politician understood the importance of checking his public statements for ______.

TOEFL Prep 6-2 **Find the word or phrase that is closest in meaning to the opposite of each word in the left-hand column. Write the letter in the blank.**

______	1. seep	(a) fill
______	2. gut	(b) separate
______	3. retain	(c) stay contained
______	4. compress	(d) loosen
______	5. overlap	(e) throw away

TOEFL Success 6 **Read the passage to review the vocabulary you have learned. Answer the questions that follow.**

Organic products from ancient life are an *integral* part of the Earth's resources, offering scientists a more *accurate* picture of ancient life-forms. One key to ancient life comes in the form of petrified matter. Petrifaction is a process that slowly turns the remains of a living object into stone. In this process, minerals *seep* into a mass of organic matter. After the organic matter has been replaced, a mineral version of the living object is left. Petrifaction often occurs in trees that

TOEFL Prep 6-1 1. feasibly 2. integrally 3. adjacent 4. structure 5. accuracy
TOEFL Prep 6-2 1. c 2. a 3. e 4. d 5. b

are found *adjacent* to rivers, floodable areas, and volcanoes, which provide the mud or ash that initially covers the organic matter. Some pieces of petrified wood *retain* the original cellular *structure* of the wood and the grain can be easily seen. **Today**, it is *feasible* to petrify wood in a simple laboratory process.

Fossils are another way that ancient life is preserved. Most fossils include an animal's hard parts, such as teeth and bones. One type of fossil, called a trace fossil, may also include eggs, tooth marks, contents of the *guts*, and fossil excrement. Some products from ancient life offer us more than scientific knowledge. One such product is coal, a solid fuel of plant origin. It develops over millions of years, during which swamp vegetation is submerged in water, depleted of oxygen, and covered by layers and layers of sand and mud. These *overlapping* layers settle with the Earth's movements and are *compressed* over time.

Bonus Structure In this context, **today** means "at present; at this time in history."

1. Which sentence best expresses the essential information of this passage?
   a. Preserved life-forms, including petrified matter and fossils, teach us about ancient life.
   b. The primary function for preserved life-forms is scientific discovery.
   c. Scientists try to replicate natural processes that preserve ancient life-forms.
   d. Ancient organic matter provides the most concentrated forms of energy known to humans.

2. In the passage, the words submerged in are closest in meaning to
   a. made wet
   b. completely covered by
   c. adjacent to
   d. depleted of

TOEFL Success 6 1. a 2. b

科学
レッスン6

古代の生命

意味と例文

1 accuracy（名詞） 正確さ／精度

例文訳 調査部門は、印刷する前にすべての記事の事実の正確さをチェックする。

ヒント 使い方 accuracy は後ろに of を伴うことが多い。

関連語 accurate（形容詞）正確な、accurately（副詞）正確に

---

2 adjacent（形容詞） 隣の

例文訳 その村々は互いに隣接しているが、住民は異なる言語を話している。

ヒント 使い方 adjacent は後ろに to を伴うことが多い。

関連語 adjacency（名詞）近隣、隣接

---

3 compress（動詞） 圧する

例文訳 基礎をより強固にするため、コンクリートを流し込む前に土を押し固めた。

関連語 compression（名詞）圧縮、compressed（形容詞）圧縮された

---

4 feasibly（副詞） 現実的に／うまくいく方法で

例文訳 科学者は、実際には深海の海流からエネルギーを必要とされる場所、つまり陸に運ぶことができない。

関連語 feasibility（名詞）実現可能性、feasible（形容詞）実現可能な

---

5 gut（動詞） 空っぽにする、またはくり抜く

例文訳 家を改築するには、まず家の中を空にして、それから古い設備をすべて処分しなければならない。

ヒント 使い方 gut には「動物の胃」という意味もある。この動詞は、建物の内部は動物の体内のようだというイメージを表している。

関連語 gut（名詞）胃腸、gutted（形容詞）ひどく破壊された、打ちひしがれた

---

6 integrally（副詞） 全部そろって、または完全な形で

例文訳 ライティングとスペリングは、リーディングプログラムの一部として統合的に教えられる。

関連語 integrate（動詞）統合する、まとめる、integrity（名詞）完全、高潔、integral（名詞）全体、積分、integral（形容詞）完全な、不可欠な

---

7 overlap（動詞） （何かの一部を）覆う／共通の要素を持つ

例文訳 オフィスでの職務のほとんどが重なるため、2人のアシスタントのうち1人がおそらく解雇されるだろう。

関連語 overlap（名詞）重複

---

8 retain（動詞） 保持する、または抱える

例文訳 雨が激しく降ったので、その川の堤防はすべての水をとどめることはできなかった。

関連語 retainer（名詞）保持者、retention（名詞）保有

---

9 seep（動詞） （液体や気体のように）時間をかけてゆっくりと移動する

例文訳 コンテナが錆びるにつれ、有毒な廃棄物が地中にしみ出した。

ヒント 使い方 seep は into や through を後ろに伴うことが多い。

---

10 structure（名詞） （建物のように）組み立てられたもの

例文訳 たいていの企業は、外部の人には理解できないような集団的構造を持っている。

関連語 structure（動詞）組み立てる、構築する、structural（形容詞）構造上の、structurally（副詞）構造上は

TOEFL プレップ 6-1

リストの中から空欄に当てはまる適切な単語を選んで、各文を完成させなさい。必要に応じて単語を活用させること。なお、各単語は一度しか使用できません。

accuracy　adjacent　feasibly　integrally　structure

1 彼女は、彼らがどうやって同じ年に長期休暇の取得と家の改築を＿＿＿＿＿＿できたのかわからなかった。
2 回復プログラムでは、3つのものが同等の役割を持ち、＿＿＿＿＿＿用いられている。その3つとは、毎日の瞑想、マッサージ、そしてハーブ療法だ。
3 そのライバル政治家たちは＿＿＿＿＿＿の郡で育った。
4 この川のそばに＿＿＿＿＿＿を建てるのなら、洪水対策が確実なものでなければならない。
5 何度か失敗したのち、その政治家は自分の公の発言の＿＿＿＿＿＿を確かめることの重要性を理解した。

TOEFL プレップ 6-2

左列の各単語の反対語に最も近い意味の単語や語句を選び、空欄にそのアルファベットを書きこみなさい。

＿＿＿＿＿＿	1. seep	(a) 満たす
＿＿＿＿＿＿	2. gut	(b) 別々にする
＿＿＿＿＿＿	3. retain	(c) 入ったままでいる
＿＿＿＿＿＿	4. compress	(d) 緩める
＿＿＿＿＿＿	5. overlap	(e) 捨てる

TOEFL サクセス 6

文章を読んで学んだ語彙を復習します。後に続く質問に答えなさい。

［例文訳］

古代の生命体の有機物は、地球の資源に不可欠な一部であり、古代の生命体のより正確なイメージを科学者に示している。古代の生命体を知る鍵の１つが石化した物質だ。石化とは、生物の残骸がゆっくりと石に変わる過程のことだ。この過程の中では、鉱物が有機物の塊の中にしみこんでいく。有機物と置き換わることで、生物の残骸は鉱物の形で残るのである。石化は、川や浸水しやすい地域や火山の近くにある木の中でよく起こる。そういう場所には、石化が始まる時点で有機物を覆う泥や灰があるからだ。石化した木片の中には元の細胞構造をとどめていて、その木目を容易に見ることができるものもある。今日では、簡単な実験プロセスで木材を石化することも実現可能である。

化石は、古代の生物が保存されたもう１つの方法だ。たいていの化石は、歯や骨などの動物の硬い部分を含んでいる。生痕化石と呼ばれる種類には、卵、歯形、胃腸の内容物、排泄物などが含まれていることもある。古代生命による生成物の中には、私たちに科学的知識以上のものを与えてくれるものがある。その１つが、植物由来の固形燃料である石炭だ。石炭は何百万年もかけて出来上がっていくもので、その年月の間に、湿地の植物は水に浸かり、酸素を失い、砂や泥で何層にも覆われる。これらの何重にもなった層は地球の動きに合わせて沈んでいき、時間とともに圧縮されていく。

読解のポイント この文脈の today は「現在、歴史上の今この時期に」という意味。

1　この文章の重要な情報を最もよく表しているのはどの文か。

a. 石化した物質や化石を含む保存された生命体は、私たちに古代の生命について教えてくれる。

b. 保存された生命体の主要な役割は科学的発見だ。

c. 科学者たちは、古代の生命体を保存する自然のプロセスを再現しようとしている。

d. 古代の有機物は、人類が知る限り最も濃縮されたエネルギーを供給している。

2　この文章中の下線部submerged inに最も近い意味を持つのはどれか。

a. 濡れて

b. ～に完全に覆われて

c. ～と隣接して

d. ～が枯渇して

LESSON 7 Science

Computers

Target Words

1. circulate
2. corrode
3. derive
4. detection
5. expeditiously
6. implement
7. innovative
8. installation
9. maintenance
10. simulation

Definitions and Samples

1. circulate *v.* To move throughout an area or group; to move along a somewhat circular route

The gossip **circulated** quickly through the small town.

Blood **circulates** more quickly during physical exercise.

Usage tips *Circulate* is often followed by *through*.

Parts of speech circulation *n*

2. corrode *v.* To be slowly weakened by chemical reactions

Sitting in salt water, the old coins **corroded** and became very easy to break.

Usage tips A familiar kind of corrosion produces rust, the reddish coating on iron or steel that has been exposed to air and water.

Parts of speech corrosion *n*, corrosive *adj*

3. derive *v.* To come from, usually through a long, slow process

The Cyrillic alphabet was **derived** from the Greek alphabet.

Usage tips *Derive* is often followed by *from*.

Parts of speech derivation *n*, derivative *adj*

4. detection *n.* Discovering something that cannot easily be found

With new medical technology, the **detection** of cancer is much easier nowadays.

Usage tips *Detection* is often followed by an *of* phrase.

Parts of speech detect *v*, detectable *adj*

5. **expeditiously** *adv.* Quickly and efficiently

Using carrier pigeons, the military commanders exchanged messages **expeditiously**.

Parts of speech expedite *v*, expedition *n*, expeditious *adj*

6. **implement** *v.* To make use of; to carry out

Not until after the new software was installed could we **implement** the new filing system.

Parts of speech implement *n*, implementation *n*

7. **innovative** *adj.* Ahead of the times; novel

The **innovative** use of props and lighting at the experimental theater drew many favorable comments.

Parts of speech innovation *n*

8. **installation** *n.* Setting something into position for use

Installation of the new software takes only four minutes.

Parts of speech install *v*

9. **maintenance** *n.* The act of keeping something in good condition

The only problem with living in such a big house is that it requires a lot of **maintenance**.

Parts of speech maintain *v*

10. **simulation** *n.* An imitation or representation

To test car safety, automobile makers study crash **simulations**.

Parts of speech simulate *v*, simulator *n*

TOEFL Prep 7-1 **Circle the most likely meaning of the word part that is shared within each set of words.**

1. circulate, circumnavigate, circuit
   The root *circ* / *circum* probably means
   a. around
   b. broken
   c. fair
   d. straight
2. innovative, novel, renovate
   The root *nov* probably means
   a. clear
   b. old
   c. new
   d. sweet
3. installation, implement, imprison
   The prefix *in-* / *im-*probably means
   a. aside
   b. behind
   c. in
   d. out

TOEFL Prep 7-2 **Circle the word that best completes each sentence.**

1. Please make sure this information (circulates / derives) throughout the office quickly.
2. The (installation / simulation) of the new telephones took three days.
3. In order to stay on schedule, we need to complete this project as (expeditiously / innovatively) as possible.
4. The smuggler moved cautiously through the airport to avoid (detection / maintenance).
5. Years of neglect had caused the building's water pipes to (corrode / implement).

TOEFL Success 7 **Read the passage to review the vocabulary you have learned. Answer the questions that follow.**

TOEFL Prep 7-1 1. a 2. c 3. c
TOEFL Prep 7-2 1. circulates 2. installation 3. expeditiously 4. detection 5. corrode

As dependence on computers increases, so does the need for technical support. From *installation* of software to *detection* of viruses, computers require constant vigilance. Most larger companies find it most *expeditious* to maintain in-house computer staff. Many smaller companies, however, can't fund their own full-time, in-house technical help. Instead, many of them assign the task of computer *maintenance* to a current employee who may not have any formal training. Rather, these "computer buffs" have *derived* their skills through practice and self-training. These self-appointed tech specialists, however, often cannot solve bigger problems. What's more, they may see their office relations *corrode* when they are swamped with basic user questions that they simply don't have time to address. For these reasons, many small companies choose to employ a freelance technical assistant who *circulates* among clients on an as-needed basis. With their professional training, these consultants may propose *innovative* solutions to users' unique needs, which could vary from tracking inventory to *simulating* mechanized processes. They can *implement* new programs, train personnel, and escape the workplace before being asked, "How can I cut and paste this text?"

1. Which sentence best expresses the essential information of this passage?
   a. Larger companies are better off using freelance technical consultants.
   b. Computer maintenance and troubleshooting cut into employee productivity.
   c. Self-trained technical support personnel are often as effective as trained professionals.
   d. Smaller companies may benefit from hiring occasional technical support.

2. The article implies that the question *How can I cut and paste this text?* is
   a. a waste of the professional technician's time
   b. a good question to give to in-house tech support
   c. appropriate for a freelancer to address
   d. too difficult for the freelance technical assistant

TOEFL Success 7 1. d 2. a

科学
レッスン7

コンピュータ

意味と例文

1 circulate（動詞） ある場所や集団の中をくまなく移動する／円形に近いルートに沿って移動する

例文訳 その噂話は小さな町にすぐに広まった。
血液は、運動中にはより速く循環する。

ヒント 使い方 circulate は後ろに through を伴うことが多い。

関連語 circulation（名詞）循環

---

2 corrode（動詞） （化学反応で）徐々に弱くなる

例文訳 塩水に浸かっていたので、その古いコインは腐食して非常にもろくなっていた。

ヒント 使い方 身近な腐食の生成物に、空気や水に触れた鉄や鋼鉄につく赤みがかった被覆物である錆がある。

関連語 corrosion（名詞）腐食、corrosive（形容詞）腐食性の

---

3 derive（動詞） （通常、長くゆっくりとしたプロセスを経て）生じる

例文訳 キリル文字は、ギリシャ文字から派生した。

ヒント 使い方 derive は後ろに from を伴うことが多い。

関連語 derivation（名詞）由来、派生 derivative（形容詞）由来した、派生的な

---

4 detection（名詞） （簡単には見つけられないものを）発見すること

例文訳 新しい医療技術により、現在ではがんの発見はずっと容易になっている。

ヒント 使い方 detection は後ろに of 句を伴うことが多い。

関連語 detect（動詞）見つける、検出する、detectable（形容詞）見つけられる、検出できる

---

5 expeditiously (副詞) 素早くかつ効率的に

例文訳 伝書鳩を使い、軍司令官たちは迅速に連絡をとった。

関連語 expedite (動詞) 促進する、迅速に処理する、expedition (名詞) 探検、迅速、expeditious (形容詞) 迅速な

6 implement (動詞) 利用する／実行する

例文訳 新しいソフトウェアをインストールして初めて、その新しいファイリングシステムを使えるようになった。

関連語 implement (名詞) 道具、implementation (名詞) 実行

7 innovative (形容詞) 時代に先駆けている／斬新な

例文訳 その実験的な劇場での、小道具や照明の革新的な使い方は、多くの好意的な反響を呼んだ。

関連語 innovation (名詞) 革新

8 installation (名詞) (あるものを) 使える状態にすること

例文訳 その新しいソフトウェアのインストールには、たった4分しかかからない。

関連語 install (動詞) 取りつける、インストールする

9 maintenance (名詞) (あるものを) よい状態に保つ行為

例文訳 こんなに大きな家に住むことの唯一の問題点は、多くのメンテナンスを必要とすることだ。

関連語 maintain (動詞) 維持する

10 simulation (名詞) 模倣または模写

例文訳 自動車の安全性をテストするため、自動車メーカーは衝突シミュレーションを研究する。

関連語 simulate (動詞) 振りをする、模擬実験をする、simulator (名詞) 模擬実験装置

TOEFL プレップ 7−1

各単語に共通する部分の意味として、最も当てはまるものを丸で囲みなさい。

1　circulate, circumnavigate, circuit
　語根 circ / circum が意味すると思われるのは、次のうちどれか。
　a. ぐるっと回って
　b. 壊れた
　c. 公正な
　d. まっすぐな

2　innovative, novel, renovate
　語根 nov が意味すると思われるのは、次のうちどれか。
　a. はっきりした
　b. 古い
　c. 新しい
　d. 甘い

3　installation, implement, imprison
　接頭語 in- / im- が意味すると思われるのは、次のうちどれか。
　a. わきに
　b. 後ろに
　c. 中に
　d. 外に

TOEFL プレップ 7−2

各文を完成させるのに最も適した単語を丸で囲みなさい。

1　この情報が素早くオフィス全体に（行き渡る／派生する）ようにしてください。
2　新しい電話機の（設置／シミュレーション）には3日かかった。
3　予定通りに進めるためには、このプロジェクトをできるだけ（迅速に／革新的に）完了させる必要がある。
4　密輸業者は（探知／メンテナンス）を避けるため、空港内を慎重に移動した。
5　長年放置されていたため、その建物の水道管は（腐食／実行）していた。

TOEFL サクセス 7

文章を読んで学んだ語彙を復習します。後に続く質問に答えなさい。

［例文訳］

コンピュータへの依存度が大きくなるにつれ、テクニカルサポートの必要性も高まっている。ソフトウェアのインストールからウイルスの検出まで、コンピュータには常に警戒する必要がある。ほとんどの大企業では、社内にコンピュータの専門スタッフを置くことが最も手っとり早いと考えられている。しかし、多くの中小企業では、自社で常勤のテクニカルスタッフを雇うことができない。代わりに、そういう企業の多くは、コンピュータのメンテナンスを、正規のトレーニングを受けていないような一般社員に任せている。このような「コンピュータ通」は、実践と独学でスキルを身につけてきた。しかしながら、このような自称「技術専門家」は、大きな問題になると解決できないことが多い。さらには、対応する時間を見つけられないほど多くの、ユーザーからの基本的な質問に忙殺されているうちに、職場での自分の人間関係が悪くなっているということもある。これらの理由から、多くの中小企業では、必要に応じて取引先を回るフリーランスのテクニカルアシスタントを雇うことを選んでいる。専門的なトレーニングを受けたこれらのコンサルタントは、在庫の追跡から機械化されたプロセスのシミュレーションまで多岐に渡る、ユーザーそれぞれのニーズに合わせた革新的な解決策を提案してくれるだろう。彼らは新しいプログラムを実行したり、社員をトレーニングしたり、さらには、「このテキストをカット&ペーストするにはどうすればいいですか？」などときかれる前に職場から脱出することもできるのだ。

1　この文章の重要な情報を最もよく表しているのはどの文か。

a. 大企業はフリーのテクニカルコンサルタントを使うほうが賢明だ。

b. コンピュータのメンテナンスやトラブルシューティングは、従業員の生産性を低下させる。

c. 独学で学んだテクニカルサポート要員は、トレーニングを受けた専門家と同じくらい有能であることが多い。

d. 中小企業では、臨時のテクニカルサポートを雇うと得になる可能性がある。

2　この文章中の「このテキストをカット&ペーストするにはどうしたらいいですか？」という質問が示唆しているのは、次のうちどれか？

a. プロ技術者の時間の無駄遣い

b. 社内の技術サポートに相談するのに適した質問

c. フリーランスが対応するのに適している

d. フリーランスの技術アシスタントには難しすぎる

Energy

Target Words

1. combustion
2. component
3. convey
4. discretely
5. nucleus
6. permeate
7. rotate
8. solar
9. source
10. trigger

Definitions and Samples

1. combustion *n.* The process of burning

When air quality is poor, **combustion** of materials in a fireplace is prohibited.

Usage tips *Combustion* is often followed by *of*.

Parts of speech combust *v*, combustible *adj*

2. component *n.* One part of a system or whole

Their home theater system has a number of separate **components**.

Usage tips *Component* is often followed or preceded by *of*.

3. convey *v.* To transport from one place to another; to transmit or make known

A messenger **conveyed** the prince's letter to the commander of the army.

The worst part about being a doctor was when she had to **convey** bad news to a family.

Parts of speech conveyance *n*, conveyor *n*

4. discretely *adv.* Separately; distinctly

In order to understand how the engine worked, each component needed to be studied **discretely**.

Parts of speech discrete *adj*

5. nucleus *n.* A central or essential part around which other parts are gathered; a core

The **nucleus** of many European cities is the town square.

Usage tips *Nucleus* is often followed by *of*.

Parts of speech nuclear *adj*

6. **permeate** *v.* To spread or flow throughout; to pass through or penetrate

The smell of cooking **permeated** the entire apartment building.

Parts of speech permeation *n*, permeable *adj*

7. **rotate** *v.* To turn around; to take turns in sequence

The planet **rotates** on its axis once every 14 Earth days.

The children **rotate** classroom responsibilities on a weekly basis.

Parts of speech rotation *n*, rotator *n*, rotor *n*

8. **solar** *adj.* Of, or relating to, the sun

The ancient society kept time with a **solar** calendar.

9. **source** *n.* The point of origin or creation

The reporter was unable to identify the **source** of the information for his story.

Parts of speech source *v*

10. **trigger** *v.* To set off or initiate

I was certain any mention of politics would **trigger** a big argument.

Parts of speech trigger *n*

TOEFL Prep 8-1 **Complete each sentence by filling in the blank with the best word from the list. Change the form of the word if necessary. Use each word only once.**

combustion convey permeate source trigger

1. It is often difficult to ______ the meaning of a poem to a large audience.
2. The ______ of the gossip was someone inside this office.
3. Her bad mood that day ______ the atmosphere in the laboratory.
4. The internal ______ engine revolutionized the way automobiles run.
5. A cigarette ______ the explosion.

TOEFL Prep 8-2 **Find the word or phrase that is closest in meaning to each word in the left-hand column. Write the letter in the blank.**

______	1. rotate	(a) separately, as an individual part
______	2. solar	(b) spin on an axis
______	3. component	(c) sun
______	4. discretely	(d) center
______	5. nucleus	(e) part

TOEFL Success 8 **Read the passage to review the vocabulary you have learned. Answer the questions that follow.**

Most of the electricity in the United States is produced in steam turbines. There are many *discrete* steps in this process. In a steam turbine, *combustion* of coal, petroleum, or natural gas heats water to make steam. The steam *rotates* a shaft that is connected to a generator that produces electricity. Finally, that electricity is converted by a transformer and *conveyed*

TOEFL Prep 8-1 1. convey 2. source 3. permeated 4. combustion 5. triggered
TOEFL Prep 8-2 1. b 2. c 3. e 4. a 5. d

from the turbine to its place of use. Many *sources* can provide energy to heat the water in a steam turbine. Coal is primary, producing 51 percent of the country's electricity. Another common way to heat water for steam turbines is through *nuclear* power. In nuclear fission, atoms of uranium fuel are hit by neutrons, *triggering* a continuous chain of fission that releases heat. In 2001, nuclear power generated 21 percent of the electricity in the United States. *Solar* power produces less than 1 percent of the United States' electricity needs, because it is not regularly available and harnessing it is more expensive than using fossil fuels. Dependence on electricity *permeates* daily life in the United States. **Still**, few people are aware of the many *components* of electricity production.

Bonus Structure In this context, **still** means "even so; despite this."

1. What does the author say about solar power?
   a. It produces more electricity than any other source.
   b. It is a relatively small source of energy for heating water in steam turbines.
   c. Electricity producers are trying to use it more regularly.
   d. Researchers are trying to make it cheaper to use.

2. In the passage, the word transformer probably refers to a
   a. truck
   b. generator that produces electricity
   c. type of turbine
   d. device that changes electric currents

TOEFL Success 8 1. b 2. d

科学
レッスン8

エネルギー

意味と例文

1 combustion（名詞） 燃える過程（燃焼）

例文訳 空気の質が悪いときは、暖炉で何かを燃焼させることは禁止されている。

ヒント 使い方 combustion は後ろに of を伴うことが多い。

関連語 combust（動詞）燃焼する、燃焼させる、combustible（形容詞）可燃性の

---

2 component（名詞） （システムまたは全体の）一部分

例文訳 彼らのホームシアターシステムには、いくつかの独立したパーツがある。

使い方 component は of を後ろや前に伴うことが多い。

---

3 convey（動詞） （ある場所から別の場所へ）運ぶ／伝達する、または知らせる

例文訳 使いの者が王子の手紙を軍の司令官に届けた。
彼女が医者として一番辛かったのは、患者の家族に悪い知らせを伝えなければならないときだった。

関連語 conveyance（名詞）運搬、conveyor（名詞）運搬する人、コンベアー

---

4 discretely（副詞） 別々に／はっきり分かれて

例文訳 エンジンがどのように動くのか理解するためには、それぞれの部品を別々に研究する必要があった。

関連語 discrete（形容詞）別々の、分離した

---

5 nucleus（名詞） （他の部分が集まる）中心的または重要な部分／核心

例文訳 ヨーロッパの多くの都市の中心は、街の広場だ。

使い方 nucleus は後ろに of を伴うことが多い。

関連語 nuclear（形容詞）核エネルギーの、原子力の

---

6 permeate（動詞） 全体に広がる、または流れる／通過する、または浸透する

例文訳 料理の匂いがアパート全体に行き渡っていた。

関連語 permeation（名詞）浸透、permeable（形容詞）通すことができる

---

7 rotate（動詞） 回転する／順番通りに交代する

例文訳 その惑星は地球の 14 日に一度自転する。
子どもたちは 1 週間ごとに教室の係を交代する。

関連語 rotation（名詞）回転、ローテーション、rotator（名詞）回転するもの、rotor（名詞）回転部、ローター

---

8 solar（形容詞） 太陽の、または太陽に関連する

例文訳 その古代社会は、太陽暦で時間を記録していた。

---

9 source（名詞） 起源または創造の起点

例文訳 その記者は彼の話の情報源を特定することができなかった。

関連語 source（動詞）出所が明らかになる、手に入れる

---

10 trigger（動詞） 引き起こす、または開始する

例文訳 政治について少しでも触れれば大論争が引き起こされるだろうと私は確信していた。

関連語 trigger（名詞）引き金

TOEFL プレップ8－1

リストの中から空欄に当てはまる適切な単語を選んで、各文を完成させなさい。必要に応じて単語を活用させること。なお、各単語は一度しか使用できません。

combustion　convey　permeate　source　trigger

1　詩の意味を多くの人に__________のは、たいていの場合難しい。
2　その噂話の__________は、このオフィスの中にいる誰かだった。
3　その日の彼女の機嫌の悪さは、研究室の雰囲気にも__________。
4　内部で__________させる機関は、自動車の走り方に大変革をもたらした。
5　タバコが爆発を__________。

TOEFL プレップ8－2

左列の各単語に最も近い意味の単語や語句を選び、空欄にそのアルファベットを書きなさい。

__________	1. rotate	(a) 別々に、個別の部分として
__________	2. solar	(b) 軸を中心にして回転する
__________	3. component	(c) 太陽
__________	4. discretely	(d) 中心
__________	5. nucleus	(e) 部分

TOEFL サクセス8

文章を読んで学んだ語彙を復習します。後に続く質問に答えなさい。

[例文訳]

米国では電力の大部分は蒸気タービンでつくられている。このプロセスには多くの個別の段階がある。蒸気タービンでは、石炭、石油、天然ガスなどの燃焼により水が加熱されて蒸気が発生する。その蒸気が発電機に接続されたシャフトを回転させ、電気を生み出す。最後に、その電気は変圧器で変換され、タービンから電気が使用される場所に運ばれる。蒸気タービンの水を加熱するエネルギーは、さまざまな供給源からもたらされる。石炭が最も主要な電力源で、米国内電力の51%を生産している。蒸気タービンの水を加熱する別の一般的な方法は、原子力を使うものだ。核分裂では、ウラン燃料の原子に中性子が当たることで核分裂の絶え間ない連鎖が生じ、熱が放出される。2001年には、米国の電力の21%が原子力により生み出された。太陽光発電は米国の電力需要の1%にも満たないが、それは太陽光が安定的に利用できず、化石燃料を使うよりもコストが高いからだ。電気への依存は、米国の日常生活にすっかり浸透している。にもかかわらず、発電にはたくさんの構成要素があることを知っている人はほとんどいない。

読解のポイント **この文脈では、still は「たとえそうであっても、にもかかわらず」という意味。**

1 太陽光発電について、筆者はなんと言っているか？

a. 他のどの電力源よりも多くの電力を生産する。

b. 蒸気タービンで水を加熱するためのエネルギー源としては比較的小さい。

c. 電力メーカーは、より安定的に使用しようとしている。

d. 研究者は、より安く使えるように試しているところだ。

2 この文章の中で、下線部の transformer という言葉が意味すると思われるのは、次のうちどれか？

a. トラック

b. 電気をつくりだす発電機

c. タービンの種類

d. 電流を変える装置

Memory

Target Words

1. acquisition	6. indisputable
2. anomaly	7. intervene
3. consciously	8. intuitively
4. degrade	9. recede
5. gap	10. retrieve

Definitions and Samples

1. **acquisition** *n.* The act of taking possession of something
Our recent **acquisition** of over 2,000 books makes ours the biggest library in the region.
Usage tips *Acquisition* is often followed by *of*.
Parts of speech acquire *v*, acquisitive *adj*

2. **anomaly** *n.* Something unusual
White tigers get their beautiful coloring from a genetic **anomaly**.
Parts of speech anomalous *adj*

3. **consciously** *adv.* With awareness of one's actions
He may have hurt her feelings, but he never would have done so **consciously**.
Parts of speech consciousness *n*, conscious *adj*

4. **degrade** *v.* To reduce in value or strength
The roads in cold or wet areas of the United States **degrade** faster than those in warm, sunny regions.
Parts of speech degradation *n*, degradable *adj*

5. **gap** *n.* Opening; a big difference in amount or quality
The small **gap** between the walls in the old house caused cold drafts to come in.

6. **indisputable** *adj.* Beyond doubt; unquestionable
The members of the jury found her guilty because they found the facts of the case **indisputable**.
Parts of speech indisputably *adv*

7. **intervene** *v.* To come between
A good mediator **intervenes** only as much as necessary to settle a dispute between other parties.
Parts of speech intervention *n*

8. **intuitively** *adv.* By means of a natural sense about things that are hard to observe
Many mothers know **intuitively** when something is wrong with their children.
Parts of speech intuition *n*, intuitive *adj*

9. **recede** *v.* To move back or away from
After the age of 30, his hairline began to **recede** further back from his forehead.
Parts of speech recession *n*, recessive *adj*

10. **retrieve** *v.* To bring or get back
Most dogs can be trained to **retrieve** objects that their owners have thrown.
Parts of speech retriever *n*, retrievable *adj*

TOEFL Prep 9-1 **Find the word or phrase that is closest in meaning to the opposite of each word in the left-hand column. Write the letter in the blank.**

______	1. degrade	(a) stay out of a dispute
______	2. anomaly	(b) improve
______	3. recede	(c) questionable
______	4. intervene	(d) the norm
______	5. indisputable	(e) come forward

TOEFL Prep 9-2 **Circle the word that best completes each sentence.**

1. A huge (anomaly / gap) between the wealthy and the working class often leads to social unrest.
2. The new computers enable us to (intervene / retrieve) information more quickly.
3. Although she wasn't qualified for the job, she (indisputably / intuitively) felt that she should apply.
4. Before he joined the military, he didn't know that officers routinely (degrade / recede) and insult new soldiers.
5. The art in the foyer was an important (acquisition / consciousness) for the museum.

TOEFL Success 9 **Read the passage to review the vocabulary you have learned. Answer the question that follows.**

Like other functions of the human mind, perception and memory are imperfect. When we tell a story about something that we witnessed, we may *intuitively* believe that our recollection is accurate. However, several factors bias our memories of events. To study this *anomaly*, let us look at the three steps of memory creation: *acquisition* of memory, storing of memory, and *retrieval*. At every stage of memory formation, distortion can occur. At the first stage, acquisition of memory, events are perceived and bits of information are prepared for storage in the brain. However, it is impossible

---

TOEFL Prep 9-1 1. b 2. d 3. e 4. a 5. c
TOEFL Prep 9-2 1. gap 2. retrieve 3. intuitively 4. degrade 5. acquisition

for us to remember every single thing we observe. Through processes that are both *conscious* and unconscious, people determine which details they will focus on.

In its second stage, storage, memories can become further distorted. Over time, our memories *degrade*, as we forget portions of events. To compensate, we may even creatively fill in the *gap* created by the *recession* of long-term memory. Additionally, an individual's memory can be altered during the storage stage by *intervening* occurrences, which can be subconsciously combined with previously stored memories. Last but not least, we search our memory to locate information. During recall, emotion also seems to play a part in memory distortion. **In sum**, our memories may not be the *indisputable* source of information that we would like them to be.

Bonus Structure **In sum** means "to summarize; to give a short version of what has been stated."

An introductory sentence for a brief summary of the passage is provided below. Complete the summary by selecting the three answer choices that express the most important ideas in the passage. In each blank, write the letter of one of your choices.

Memory provides an imperfect record of events.
•
•
•

a. People purposefully present a slanted version of events.
b. Memories can be altered at any point in memory creation.
c. People naturally cannot recall everything they observe.
d. Memories are an indisputable source of fact.
e. Time and emotion contribute to memory degradation.
f. Past occurrences often displace current memories.

TOEFL Success 9 b, c, e

心と体
レッスン9

記憶

意味と例文

1 acquisition（名詞） （何かを）手に入れる行為

例文訳 最近2,000冊以上の本を手に入れたことで、私たちの図書館はこの地方で最大の図書館になる。

ヒント 使い方 acquisitionは後ろにofを伴うことが多い。

関連語 acquire（動詞）得る、acquisitive（形容詞）欲深い

2 anomaly（名詞） 普通ではないもの

例文訳 ホワイトタイガーは、遺伝子の異常によって美しい色をしている。

関連語 anomalous（形容詞）異常な

3 consciously（副詞） （自分の行動を）意識して

例文訳 彼は彼女の気持ちを傷つけたかもしれないが、決して意識的にそうしたわけではなかっただろう。

関連語 consciousness（名詞）意識、conscious（形容詞）意識している

4 degrade（動詞） （価値や強さが）減少する

例文訳 米国の寒冷地や雨の多い地域の道路は、温暖で晴天の多い地域の道路よりも早く劣化する。

関連語 degradation（名詞）低下、悪化、degradable（形容詞）分解できる

5 gap（名詞） すき間／（量や質の）大きな差

例文訳 その古い家には、壁の間にわずかなすき間があるせいで冷たい風が入ってきた。

6 indisputable (形容詞) 疑いのない／議論の余地がない

例文訳 陪審員たちは、その事件の事実関係が疑問の余地のないものであるとわかったので、彼女を有罪とした。

関連語 indisputably (副詞) 疑いの余地なく

7 intervene (動詞) 間に入る

例文訳 優れた調停者は、当事者間の争いを解決するために、必要なぶんしか介入しないものだ。

関連語 intervention (名詞) 仲裁、介入

8 intuitively (副詞) （気づきにくいものに対して）自然な感覚を使って

例文訳 多くの母親は、自分の子どもに何か問題が起きたとき、直感的にそれがわかるものだ。

関連語 intuition (名詞) 直感、intuitive (形容詞) 直感的な

9 recede (動詞) 後ろに下がる／離れる

例文訳 30歳を過ぎてから、彼の髪の生え際は額からさらに後退し始めた。

関連語 recession (名詞) 後退、一時的な不況、recessive (形容詞) 退行の、劣性の

10 retrieve (動詞) 持ってくる、または取り戻す

例文訳 たいていの犬は、飼い主が投げたものを取ってくるよう訓練することができる。

関連語 retriever (名詞) 取り戻す人、レトリーバー、retrievable (形容詞) 取り戻せる、検索可能な

TOEFL プレップ9-1

左列の各単語の反対語に最も近い意味の単語や語句を選び、空欄にそのアルファベットを書きこみなさい。

________	1. degrade	(a) 争いと関わらない
________	2. anomaly	(b) 改善する
________	3. recede	(c) 疑わしい
________	4. intervene	(d) 標準
________	5. indisputable	(e) 前に出る

TOEFL プレップ9-2

各文を完成させるのに最も適した単語を丸で囲みなさい。

1 富裕層と労働者層の間の大きな（例外／隔たり）はしばしば社会不安をもたらす。

2 その新しいコンピュータによって、私たちはより速く情報を（介入する／検索する）ことができる。

3 彼女はその仕事をするための資格を満たしていなかったが、自分は応募すべきだと（議論の余地なく／直感的に）感じた。

4 彼は軍隊に入る前は、将校が日常的に新兵を（はずかしめて／後退して）侮辱するということを知らなかった。

5 ロビーにある美術品は、その美術館にとって重要な（入手品／意識）だった。

TOEFL サクセス9

文章を読んで学んだ語彙を復習します。後に続く質問に答えなさい。

[例文訳]

人間の精神の他の機能と同様に、知覚と記憶もまた、不完全だ。私たちは自分の目で見たものについて語るとき、自分の記憶は正確だと直感的に信じているかもしれない。しかし、複数の要因が、私たちの記憶を偏らせている。この特殊性について学ぶために、記憶をつくりあげる3つのステップ、つまり「記憶の獲得」「記憶の保存」そして「想起」について見てみよう。記憶はつくられるすべての段階で、歪みが起こりうる。最初の段階である「記憶の獲得」では、出来事が知覚され、情報の断片が脳に保存される準備が整う。しかし、見たものすべてを記憶することは不可能だ。人は、意識的であれ無意識であれ、記憶のプロセスを通してどの細部に注目するかを決めているのである。

第二段階の「保存」では、記憶がさらに歪められることがある。時間が経って出来事の部分部分を忘れるにつれ、記憶は劣化する。それを補おうとして、私たちは長期記憶の後退によって生じたギャップを創造的に埋めることさえある。さらに、個人の記憶は保存段階で起きた別の出来事によって変えられることがある。その出来事が過去に保存された記憶と潜在意識下で結びつけられるのだ。最後に、私たちは情報を見つけ出すために記憶を探る。何かを思い出すときには、感情も記憶の歪みに加担しているようである。つまり記憶とは、私たちが期待するほどに疑う余地のない情報源ではないのかもしれない。

読解のポイント In sum は「要約すると、述べられていることを短く説明すると」という意味。

以下は、この文章の要約の導入である。選択肢の中から最も重要な考えを表している３つを選び、要約文を完成させなさい。それぞれの空欄に、選択したアルファベットを書くこと。

記憶は出来事の不完全な記録である。
・
・
・

a. 人間は意図的に、出来事の偏った解釈を示す。
b. 記憶は、それがつくりあげられるどの時点でも変えられる可能性がある。
c. 人間は当然ながら、見たものすべてを思い出すことはできない。
d. 記憶は疑う余地のない事実の源である。
e. 時間と感情は記憶の劣化に加担する。
f. 過去の出来事がしばしば現在の記憶に置き換えられる。

Spirituality

Target Words

1. agnostic
2. animism
3. atheist
4. be inclined to
5. contemplate
6. deify
7. ecclesiastical
8. exalt
9. pious
10. sacrifice

Definitions and Samples

1. agnostic *adj.* Believing that humans cannot know whether there is a god

His devoutly Christian parents had problems with his **agnostic** beliefs.

Parts of speech agnostic *n*, agnosticism *n*

2. animism *n.* The belief that natural objects, such as trees, have souls

Desert cultures that practice **animism** often believe that winds contain spirits.

Parts of speech animistic *adj*, animist *n*

3. atheist *n.* One who does not believe in the existence of a supreme being

He argued that his scientific training made it impossible for him to be anything but an **atheist**.

Parts of speech atheistic *adj*, atheism *n*

4. be inclined to *v.* To favor an opinion or a course of action

He couldn't say which candidate he favored, but he had always **been inclined to** vote Republican.

Parts of speech incline *n*, inclination *n*

5. contemplate *v.* To consider thoughtfully

If you **contemplate** each step for so long, we will never complete this project on time.

Parts of speech contemplation *n*, contemplative *adj*

6. **deify** *v.* To worship as a god

When people **deify** the leader of their country, he or she is able to abuse power more easily.

Parts of speech deity *n*, deification *n*

7. **ecclesiastical** *adj.* Relating to a church

He was looking specifically for a university where he could study **ecclesiastical** history.

Parts of speech ecclesiastic *n*, ecclesiastically *adv*

8. **exalt** *v.* To praise or honor

He would often **exalt** the virtues of his new wife.

Parts of speech exaltation *n*

9. **pious** *adj.* Having or exhibiting religious reverence

Sometimes she was so **pious** that the rest of us felt like heathens.

Parts of speech piousness *n*, piety *n*, piously *adv*

10. **sacrifice** *v.* Anything offered to a deity as a religious thanksgiving; giving up something in order to have something more valuable later on

Every harvest time, the Fadeloni people **sacrificed** vegetables to their gods as a show of thanks.

In order to succeed in his career, he had to **sacrifice** his private life and his leisure time.

Parts of speech sacrifice *n*, sacrificial *adj*, sacrificially *adv*

TOEFL Prep 10-1 **Complete each sentence by filling in the blank with the best word or phrase from the list. Change the form of the word if necessary. Use each word or phrase only once.**

be inclined to *contemplate* *deify* *exalted* *sacrifice*

1. Traditionally, the Camerian society______its leaders, considering them to be sent from the land of the gods.
2. To do well in his university courses, he had to______a lot of his personal time.
3. The generation of American leaders known as "the Founders" are______by many scholars for their wisdom and courage.
4. She knew she would always______agree with what her mother said, so she struggled to remain unbiased.
5. The human resources department______whether they should let Mary go.

TOEFL Prep 10-2 **Circle the likely meaning of the word part that is shared within each set of words.**

1. animism, animal, animation
   The root *anima* probably means
   a. color
   b. death
   c. many
   d. life
2. atheistic, amoral, apathetic
   The prefix *a* probably means
   a. not
   b. loving
   c. excessive
   d. surely

TOEFL Success 10 **Read the passage to review the vocabulary you have learned. Answer the questions that follow.**

TOEFL Prep 10-1 1. deifies 2. sacrifice 3. exalted 4. be inclined to 5. contemplated
TOEFL Prep 10-2 1. d 2. a

In Russia, several religions coexist, including Christianity, Judaism, Islam, and *animism*. The most common religion is Christianity, and most Christians are members of the Russian Orthodox Church. The Church has existed for over 1,000 years, surviving even the official *atheism* of the Soviet era and the *agnosticism* that may have been even more prominent at the time. During the communist years, many Russians who practiced Orthodoxy *sacrificed* career and educational opportunities. The tenacity of Russian Orthodoxy may explain why even nonreligious Russians *are inclined to* call themselves Russian Orthodox. That same staying power drives the Church today, which is run by Kirill of Leningrad. Born Vladimir Mikhailovich Gundyayev, the future patriarch was from a very *pious* family. Both his father and grandfather were priests, and as a boy he must have begun *contemplation* of the religious way of life he was to choose. **As patriarch,** Kirill is *exalted* in Church governance, but he is not *deified*. He has closely aligned the church with recent secular leaders of Russia, such as Vladimir Putin. In addition to his *ecclesiastical* accomplishments, he has a strong reputation as a geologist.

Bonus Structure Here **As patriarch** means "while working in the position of church leader."

1. Which sentence best expresses the essential information of this passage?
   a. The Russian Orthodox Church was banned under Soviet control.
   b. Few Russians believe in a god.
   c. Aleksey II has updated the church's image.
   d. The Russian Orthodox Church has a long history of strong membership in Russia.

2. According to the passage, Kirill is
   a. a god
   b. a high Church official
   c. a secular leader
   d. an atheist

TOEFL Success 10 1. d 2. b

心と体
レッスン10

精神性

意味と例文

1 agnostic（形容詞） 人間は神が存在するかどうかを知ることはできないと信じている

例文訳 敬虔なキリスト教徒である彼の両親は、彼の不可知論的な考えに困っていた。

関連語 agnostic（名詞）不可知論者、agnosticism（名詞）不可知論

---

2 animism（名詞） （樹木などの）自然物に魂があると信じること

例文訳 精霊崇拝（アニミズム）を実践している砂漠の文化では、風に魂が宿っていると信じることが多い。

関連語 animistic（形容詞）精霊崇拝の、animist（名詞）精霊崇拝者

---

3 atheist（名詞） 神の存在を信じない人

例文訳 彼は、科学を学んでいると無神論者以外にはなりえないと主張した。

関連語 atheistic（形容詞）無神論者の、atheism（名詞）無神論

---

4 be inclined to（動詞） （ある意見や策などを）支持する

例文訳 彼は、どの候補者を支持しているかは言えなかったが、ずっと共和党に投票したいと思っていた。

関連語 incline（名詞）傾斜、inclination（名詞）意向、好み

---

5 contemplate（動詞） 深く考える

例文訳 一つひとつのステップをそんなに長く熟考していては、このプロジェクトを予定通りには終わらせることは決してできないだろう。

関連語 contemplation（名詞）熟慮、contemplative（形容詞）熟慮する

---

6 deify（動詞） 神として崇める

例文訳 人々が国の指導者を神格化すると、その指導者は権力をより簡単に乱用できるようになる。

関連語 deity（名詞）神、神性、deification（名詞）神格化

7 ecclesiastical（形容詞） 教会に関係した

例文訳 彼はとりわけ、教会史を学べる大学を探していた。

関連語 ecclesiastic（名詞）聖職者、ecclesiastically（副詞）教会に関して

8 exalt（動詞） 褒める、または称える

例文訳 彼はよく自分の新しい妻の美点を褒め称えていた。

関連語 exaltation（名詞）有頂天、賞賛

9 pious（形容詞） 宗教的な畏敬の念を持っている、または示している

例文訳 時には彼女があまりにも敬虔なので、私たちは自分を異教徒のように感じるほどだった。

関連語 piousness（名詞）信心深さ、piety（名詞）信心、piously（副詞）信心深く

10 sacrifice（動詞） (宗教的な感謝の気持ちとして)神に捧げる／(後でより価値のあるものを手に入れるために何かを）あきらめる

例文訳 収穫のたびごとに、ファデローニの人々は、感謝のしるしとして野菜を神に捧げた。
仕事で成功するために、彼は私生活や余暇を犠牲にしなければならなかった。

関連語 sacrifice（名詞）いけにえ、犠牲、sacrificial（形容詞）いけにえの、犠牲の、sacrificially（副詞）犠牲的に

TOEFL プレップ 10－1

リストの中から空欄に当てはまる適切な単語や語句を選んで、各文を完成させなさい。必要に応じて単語を活用させること。なお、各単語は一度しか使用できません。

be inclined to　contemplate　deify　exalted　sacrifice

1　伝統的に「カメリア会」では、自らの指導者たちを＿＿＿＿＿＿＿＿、神の国から送られてきた存在とみなしている。

2　大学の授業で良い成績を収めるため、彼はプライベートな時間をたくさん＿＿＿＿＿＿＿＿にしなければならなかった。

3　「建国者」として知られる米国の指導者の世代は、多くの学者からその知恵と勇気のために＿＿＿＿＿＿＿＿。

4　彼女は、母の言うことには必ず同意＿＿＿＿＿＿＿＿とわかっていたので、公平性を保つのに苦労していた。

5　人事部は、メアリーを解雇すべきかどうかを＿＿＿＿＿＿＿＿。

TOEFL プレップ 10－2

各単語に共通する部分の意味として、最も当てはまるものを丸で囲みなさい。

1　animism, animal, animation

語根 anima が意味すると思われるのは、次のうちどれか。

a. 色

b. 死

c. たくさんの

d. 生命

2　atheistic, amoral, apathetic

接頭語 a が意味すると思われるのは、次のうちどれか。

a. （否定の）ない

b. 愛する

c. 過剰な

d. 確かに

TOEFL サクセス 10

文章を読んで学んだ語彙を復習します。後に続く質問に答えなさい。

[例文訳]

ロシアでは、キリスト教、ユダヤ教、イスラム教やアニミズムなどいくつもの宗教が共存している。最も一般的な宗教はキリスト教であり、キリスト教徒のほとんどはロシア正教会の信者である。正教会は1000年以上も前から存在し、ソビエト時代の公的な無神論政策や、当時はさらに際立っていたと思われる不可知論のもとでさえも生き延びてきた。共産主義の時代には、正教を信仰する多くのロシア人は仕事や教育の機会を犠牲にした。ロシア正教会が生き延びてきた力は、無宗教のロシア人でさえ自分をロシア正教徒と呼びがちであることの理由だと言えるかもしれない。その同じ持久力が、レニングラードのキリルによって運営されている現在の正教会の原動力となっている。ウラジーミル・ミハイロヴィチ・グンヂャエフとして生まれたのちの総主教は、非常に敬虔な家庭で育った。父も祖父も神父だったので、少年時代には自分が選ぶべき宗教的な生き方について熟慮し始めていたに違いない。キリルは総主教として、教会の統治において称賛されているものの、神格化されてはいない。彼は、ウラジーミル・プーチンのような、最近のロシアの世俗的指導者と教会を密接に関わらせてきた。教会に関する実績に加えて、地質学者としても高い評価を得ている。

読解のポイント ここでの As patriarch は「教会の指導者の立場で働きながら」という意味。

1　この文章の最も重要な情報を表しているのはどの文か。

a. ロシア正教会はソ連の統治下で禁止されていた。

b. 神を信じているロシア人はほとんどいない。

c. アレクセイ２世は教会のイメージを一新した。

d. ロシア正教会は、強力な信者による長い歴史を持っている。

2　この文章によると、キリルとは次のうちどれか。

a. 神

b. 教会の高位の幹部

c. 世俗的なリーダー

d. 無神論者

Illness

Target Words

1. aggravate
2. decrepit
3. disease
4. fatally
5. forensics
6. persist
7. prognosis
8. terminal
9. vein
10. wound

Definitions and Samples

1. **aggravate** *v.* To make worse; to anger or intensify
Running will **aggravate** your sore knees.
Parts of speech aggravation *n*

2. **decrepit** *adj.* Weakened or worn out because of age, illness, or excessive use
The once-beautiful building was now dirty, **decrepit**, and roofless.

3. **disease** *n.* An unhealthful condition caused by an infection or a long-term physical problem
Thanks to developments in medicine, many once-fatal **diseases** can now be cured.

4. **fatally** *adv.* Causing death or disaster
The soldier was **fatally** wounded in the battle.
Parts of speech fatality *n*, fatal *adj*

5. **forensics** *n.* The use of science and technology to investigate facts in criminal cases
Advances in the study of **forensics** have made it much easier to identify criminals from very small traces of evidence.
Parts of speech forensic *adj*

6. **persist** *v.* To continue to exist; to hold to a purpose, despite any obstacle

If your symptoms **persist**, you should go see a doctor.

Lola **persisted** in her efforts to become a lawyer.

Parts of speech persistence *n*, persistent *adj*

7. **prognosis** *n.* An educated guess of how something will develop, especially a disease

The room fell silent when the doctor gave Senator Grebe a grim **prognosis** of months of treatment.

8. **terminal** *adj.* Located at an end; approaching death

The cancer ward at the hospital held both **terminal** and recovering patients.

Parts of speech terminate *v*, terminally *adv*

9. **vein** *n.* Any of the tubes that form a branching system, especially those that carry blood to the heart

She became fascinated with human anatomy, especially when she learned how **veins** transport oxygen.

10. **wound** *v.* To inflict an injury on

Sometimes he didn't realize his sharp humor could **wound** as well as entertain.

Parts of speech wound *n*

TOEFL Prep 11-1 **Choose the word from the list that is closest in meaning to the underlined part of each sentence. Write it in the blank.**

disease fatal persist prognosis wound

__________ 1. He sustained a serious <u>injury</u> in the war, so he was sent home immediately.

__________ 2. Her <u>sickness</u> was so rare, doctors weren't certain how to treat it.

__________ 3. His motto was to <u>keep trying</u>, no matter what happened.

__________ 4. The medical staff could not know for sure whether the treatment would work, but they made a confident <u>prediction</u> that the patient would recover.

__________ 5. The airplane crash was tragic, killing many people immediately and inflicting injuries on others that would eventually prove <u>deadly</u>.

TOEFL Prep 11-2 **Next to each definition, write the word that most closely fits it.**

aggravate decrepit forensics terminal vein

__________ 1. the science involved in solving crimes

__________ 2. a vessel for carrying blood

__________ 3. to make worse

__________ 4. unable to be cured

__________ 5. in very bad condition

TOEFL Success 11 **Read the passage to review the vocabulary you have learned. Answer the questions that follow.**

The man was *decrepit*. With high blood pressure, cancer,

TOEFL Prep 11-1 1. wound 2. disease 3. persist 4. prognosis 5. fatal
TOEFL Prep 11-2 1. forensics 2. vein 3. aggravate 4. terminal 5. decrepit

and liver *disease*, he *aggravated* his situation by smoking. His *prognosis* was death. His advanced lung cancer was *terminal*, and his family members knew that he would pass away soon. So no one was surprised to find him dead on that sharp winter Thursday, no one, that is, except one sharp-eyed detective, who noticed the bedroom window ajar on the morning of the old man's death. Would a *fatally* ill person be likely to sleep with the window open on a freezing cold night?

This question occupied *forensic* specialists from the medical examiner's office. There, an autopsy revealed an unlikely *wound* on the victim's thigh. Such a wound could easily have been inflicted by someone administering medicine . . . or poison. From there, the poison could travel hrough the *veins*, shutting down vital organs and causing death within seconds.

Indeed, the death turned out to be murder in the first degree. Criminal investigators *persisted* in their questioning of friends and family, only later finding the motive: money. Two distant relatives who stood to inherit large sums from the old man's estate plotted the death, believing that the old man's death would not be questioned.

Bonus Structure **Indeed** indicates that an idea in an earlier paragraph was actually true.

1. Why does the author mention a wound?
   a. The wound caused the death.
   b. It was evidence of a struggle.
   c. It was suspicious.
   d. It was predictable, considering the man's disease.

2. In the passage, the word inherit is closest in meaning to
   a. lose
   b. gain
   c. earn
   d. want

TOEFL Success 11 1. c 2. b

心と体
レッスン11

病気

意味と例文

1 aggravate（動詞） 悪化させる／怒らせる、またはさらに重くする

例文訳 走ることは膝の痛みを悪化させるだろう。

関連語 aggravation（名詞）悪化

---

2 decrepit（形容詞） （加齢や病気、過度の使用によって）弱っている、または消耗している

例文訳 かつては美しかったその建物が、今では汚れ、ぼろぼろになり、屋根もなくなってしまった。

---

3 disease（名詞） （感染や長期にわたる身体的不調によって引き起こされる）不健康な状態

例文訳 医学の発展のおかげで、かつては致命的だった多くの病気が、今では治るようになった。

---

4 fatally（副詞） 死や災害を引き起こす

例文訳 その兵士は戦闘で致命的な傷を負った。

関連語 fatality（名詞）不慮の死、致死性、fatal（形容詞）致命的な

---

5 forensics（名詞） （刑事事件の事実関係を捜査するために）科学技術を用いること

例文訳 犯罪科学研究の進歩により、証拠となる非常に小さな痕跡から犯人を特定することがずっと簡単にできるようになった。

関連語 forensic（形容詞）犯罪科学の、法廷の

---

6 persist（動詞） 存在し続ける／（どんな障害があっても目的に）固執する

例文訳 症状が続くようなら、医者に診てもらったほうがいい。
ローラは弁護士になるために努力し続けた。

関連語 persistence（名詞）固執、持続性、persistent（形容詞）しつこい、持続する

---

7 prognosis（名詞） （あるもの、特に病気がどのように推移するかについての知識や経験に基づく）推測

例文訳 医師がグリーブ上院議員に、数カ月の治療を要するという厳しい予測を伝えると、部屋は静まりかえった。

---

8 terminal（形容詞） 終わりにある／死に近づいている

例文訳 その病院の癌病棟には、末期の患者と回復期の患者がいた。

関連語 terminate（動詞）終わらせる、terminally（副詞）末期的に

---

9 vein（名詞） （枝分かれした組織を構成する）管状のもの、特に心臓に血液を運ぶ管（静脈）

例文訳 とりわけ血管がどのように酸素を送るのかを知ったとき、彼女は人体解剖学に夢中になった。

---

10 wound（動詞） 傷を負わせる

例文訳 彼は、自分の鋭いユーモアが人を楽しませるだけでなく、傷つける可能性もあることに気づいていないときがあった。

関連語 wound（名詞）傷

TOEFL プレップ 11–1

各文の下線部に最も近い意味を持つ単語をリストから選び、空欄に記入しなさい。

disease　fatal　persist　prognosis　wound

______ 1. 彼は戦争で深い傷を負ったので、すぐに帰国させられた。

______ 2. 彼女の病気は大変珍しいものだったので、医師たちはどのように治療すべきか確信が持てなかった。

______ 3. 彼のモットーは、どんなことがあっても努力し続けることだった。

______ 4. 医療スタッフは、その治療がうまくいくかどうかはっきりとはわからなかったが、患者は回復するだろうと自信に満ちた予測をした。

______ 5. その飛行機の墜落事故は悲劇的で、多くの人が即死し、他の人にも最終的には致命的と判明する傷を負わせた。

TOEFL プレップ 11–2

それぞれの意味に最も当てはまる単語を以下から選んで書きなさい。

aggravate　decrepit　forensics　terminal　vein

______ 1. 犯罪の解決に関わる科学

______ 2. 血液を運ぶための管

______ 3. 悪化させる

______ 4. 治らない

______ 5. 非常に悪い状態である

TOEFL サクセス 11

文章を読んで学んだ語彙を復習します。後に続く質問に答えなさい。

［例文訳］

その男は老衰していた。高血圧症、癌、肝臓病を患いながら、喫煙によって体調を悪化させていた。彼の予後は死であった。肺がんはすでに進行して末期状態にあり、家族は彼が間もなく亡くなるだろうとわかっていた。したがって、その寒さ厳しい冬の木曜日、彼が死んでいるのを見つけても誰も驚かなかった。ただ1人、目ざとい刑事を除いては。その刑事は、老人が死んだ朝、寝室の窓が少し開いていたことに気がついた。凍えるような寒さの夜に、命に関わる病気の人間が窓を開けて寝るなどということがあるのだろうか？

この問題は、検視局の犯罪科学捜査の専門家の注意をひいた。検視局では、検視の結果、被害者の太ももに普通ではありえない傷があることが明らかになった。こういう傷はおそらく、何者かが薬・・・あるいは毒を注入したときについたものだと考えられる。そこから毒が血管を伝わって、重要な器官を停止させ、数秒で死に至らしめたのかもしれない。

実際、その老人の死は第一級殺人であることが判明した。犯罪捜査官は、友人や家族への聴取を粘り強く続け、のちにようやく動機がわかった。金目当てだった。老人の遺産の多くを相続する予定だった2人の遠い親戚が、老人の死に疑問を抱かれることはないと考え、殺人を企てたのだ。

読解のポイント Indeed **は前の段落の話が実際にあったことを示している。**

1 なぜ筆者は傷について述べているのか。

a. その傷が死をもたらしたから。

b. もみ合いがあった証拠だから。

c. 不審なものだったから。

d. 男の病気を考えれば、予測できたことだから。

2 文章の中で、inheritという言葉に最も近い意味を持つのは、次のうちどれか。

a. 失う

b. 得る

c. 稼ぐ

d. 欲する

Surgery

Target Words

1. anesthesia
2. augment
3. certifiably
4. complication
5. cure
6. implant
7. inject
8. obese
9. procedure
10. scar

Definitions and Samples

1. anesthesia *n.* Techniques for reducing sensation and feeling, especially to control pain

The Civil War was the first American war when **anesthesia** was widely used in surgery on soldiers.

Usage tips *Anesthesia* and *anesthetic* are often used interchangeably.

Parts of speech anesthetic *n*, anesthetic *adj*

2. augment *v.* To make bigger or better by adding to

In some types of popular cosmetic surgery people **augment** parts of their bodies.

The college **augmented** its course offerings because students complained that there were too few choices.

Parts of speech augmentation *n*

3. certifiably *adv.* In a manner that is officially recognized

He couldn't be institutionalized until he was declared **certifiably** insane.

Parts of speech certify *v*, certification *n*, certificate *n*, certifiable *adj*

4. complication *n.* A factor that makes something more difficult or complex

The surgeons could not easily stop the bleeding because of **complications** related to the patient's diabetes.

Parts of speech complicate *v*

5. **cure** *v.* To restore to health
They say laughter can help **cure** many illnesses.
Parts of speech cure *n*, curable *adj*

6. **implant** *v.* To set in firmly; to insert in the body surgically
The doctor **implanted** some tissue into the actress's cheeks to make her face look fuller.
Parts of speech implantation *n*, implant *n*

7. **inject** *v.* To insert a liquid by means of a syringe
The doctor used a needle to **inject** the medicine slowly into her arm.
Parts of speech injection *n*

8. **obese** *adj.* Excessively overweight
More Americans are **obese** now because U.S. culture encourages overeating and discourages exercise.
Parts of speech obesity *n*

9. **procedure** *n.* A specific way of performing or doing something
The flight attendant explained the emergency evacuation **procedure**.
Parts of speech proceed *v*, procedural *adj*

10. **scar** *n.* A mark on the skin left after a wound has healed; a lasting sign of damage, either mental or physical
The surgery was successful, but it left a large **scar** across her abdomen.
Parts of speech scar *v*

TOEFL Prep 12-1 **For each word, choose the word or phrase that has the most similar meaning. Write the letter of your choice on the line.**

1. scar______
   (a) bandage (b) mark (c) shine (d) cover
2. augment______
   (a) take away (b) discuss (c) use (d) add to
3. complication______
   (a) added difficulty (b) improved performance
   (c) method of training (d) prediction about results
4. obese______
   (a) attractive (b) healthy (c) very overweight (d) high
5. cure______
   (a) heal (b) study (c) diagnose (d) tie up

TOEFL Prep 12-2 **Circle the word that best completes each sentence.**

1. The (procedure / scar) to prepare for the surgery took four hours.
2. Only seriously (certifiable / obese) people should get their stomachs surgically reduced.
3. He almost died during the operation because the doctors did not give him the right kind of (anesthesia / complication).
4. Doctors are now able to (cure / implant) many types of sickness that were usually fatal in the past.
5. Before (augmenting / injecting) a painkiller, the dentist rubbed cloves on the woman's gums to numb them.

TOEFL Success 12 **Read the passage to review the vocabulary you have learned. Answer the questions that follow.**

TOEFL Prep 12-1 1. b 2. d 3. a 4. c 5. a
TOEFL Prep 12-2 1. procedure 2. obese 3. anesthesia 4. cure 5. injecting

Since 1992, the number of cosmetic surgery *procedures* has risen 175 percent in the United States. Two of the most popular are liposuction and breast *augmentation*. In liposuction, the doctor *inserts* a small tube into the skin that sucks fat from the body. And while it may sound easy, it isn't. Liposuction is so painful that people are often given *anesthesia*. **What's more**, liposuction is not really a *cure* for *obesity*. Rather, it should be used when diet and exercise do not reduce fat in certain "trouble spots." Another common cosmetic procedure is breast augmentation. In this procedure, an *implant* is inserted through the armpit, making the breasts appear larger. Breast augmentation usually leaves only a small *scar*. Some common *complications* include the effects of anesthesia, infection, swelling, redness, bleeding, and pain. To reduce these risks, consumers are advised to be sure that their surgeon is board-*certified*.

Bonus Structure **What's more** means "in addition; even more importantly."

1. Which sentence best expresses the essential information of this passage?
   a. Cosmetic surgery is dangerous.
   b. Many people do not have cosmetic surgery because of the pain.
   c. Cosmetic surgery is increasing in popularity in the United States.
   d. Breast reduction is almost as popular as breast augmentation.

2. In the underlined sentence, *trouble spots* refers to
   a. places where people are commonly overweight
   b. methods of exercise that aren't effective
   c. parts of the body where liposuction doesn't work
   d. specific areas on the body where fat is hard to minimize

TOEFL Success 12 1. c 2. d

心と体
レッスン12

手術

意味と例文

1 **anesthesia**（名詞） 特に痛みを抑えるために感覚や意識を弱める技術（麻酔）

例文訳 南北戦争は、兵士の手術に麻酔が広く使われた米国での最初の戦争だった。

ヒント 使い方 anesthesia（麻酔）と anesthetic（麻酔剤）はしばしば同義語として使われる。

関連語 anesthetic（名詞）麻酔剤、（形容詞）麻酔の

---

2 **augment**（動詞） （加えることによって）より大きくしたり、よりよくしたりする

例文訳 人気のある美容整形手術の中には、体の一部を大きくするタイプの手術がある。
選択肢が少なすぎると学生から苦情があったため、その大学は提供する講座を増やした。

関連語 augmentation（名詞）増加

---

3 **certifiably**（副詞） 公式に認められている方法で

例文訳 精神に異常があると正式に認定されるまで、彼は施設に入ることができなかった。

関連語 certify（動詞）証明する、認定する、certification（名詞）証明、certificate（名詞）証明書、certifiable（形容詞）証明できる

---

4 **complication**（名詞） あるものをより難しく、あるいはより複雑にする要因（合併症）

例文訳 その患者には糖尿病に関連した合併症があったため、外科医は容易には止血できなかった。

関連語 complicate（動詞）複雑にする

---

5 cure（動詞） 健康な状態に戻す

例文訳 笑いは多くの病気を治すのに役立つと言われている。

関連語 cure（名詞）治癒、curable（形容詞）治療できる

6 implant（動詞） しっかりと固定する／（手術によって）体内に挿入する

例文訳 医師はその女優の顔をふっくらと見せるため、頬に詰めものを注入した。

関連語 implantation（名詞）移植、注入、implant（名詞）移植されたもの、インプラント

7 inject（動詞） （注射器を使って）液体を注入する

例文訳 医師は針を使って彼女の腕にゆっくりと薬を注入した。

関連語 injection（名詞）注射

8 obese（形容詞） 過度に太っている

例文訳 米国の文化が食べすぎを促し、運動を妨げているために、現在ではより多くの米国人が肥満になっている。

関連語 obesity（名詞）肥満

9 procedure（名詞） あることを実行すること、または行うための特定の方法

例文訳 客室乗務員が緊急避難の手順を説明した。

関連語 proceed（動詞）続ける、手続きをする、procedural（形容詞）手続き上の

10 scar（名詞） （傷が治った後に皮膚に残る）痕／（精神的または肉体的なダメージの後々まで残る）痕跡

例文訳 手術は成功したが、彼女の腹部に横方向の大きな傷跡が残った。

関連語 scar（動詞）跡を残す

TOEFL プレップ 12-1

各単語に最も近い意味を持つ単語や語句を選び、線の上に選んだアルファベットを書きなさい。

1 scar __________

(a) 包帯 (b) 跡 (c) 輝き (d) 覆い

2 augment __________

(a) 取り去る (b) 話し合う (c) 使う (d) 増やす

3 complication __________

(a) 追加された困難 (b) 向上したパフォーマンス

(c) 訓練方法 (d) 結果予測

4 obese __________

(a) 魅力的な (b) 健康的な (c) とても太っている (d) 高い

5 cure __________

(a) 治す (b) 勉強する (c) 診断する (d) 縛る

TOEFL プレップ 12-2

各文を完成させるのに最も適した単語を丸で囲みなさい。

1 手術の準備をするための（手順／傷跡）に4時間かかった。

2 深刻な（証明可能な／肥満の）人だけが胃を手術で小さくするべきだ。

3 医師が適切な（麻酔／合併症）を投与しなかったため、彼は手術中に死ぬところだった。

4 医師たちは今では、以前はたいていは死に至ってしまった多くの種類の病気を（治す／移植する）ことができるようになった。

5 痛み止めを（増大させる／注入する）前に、歯科医は女性の歯茎にクローブを擦りつけて麻痺させた。

TOEFL サクセス 12

文章を読んで学んだ語彙を復習します。後に続く質問に答えなさい。

［例文訳］

米国では1992年以来、美容整形手術の件数が175％増加した。その中でも最も人気が高い2つが、脂肪吸引と豊胸手術だ。脂肪吸引では、医師が皮膚に小さな管を挿入し、体から脂肪を吸引する。簡単そうに聞こえるかもしれないが、そうではない。脂肪吸引はあまりに強い痛みを伴うため、しばしば麻酔が使われる。さらに言うと、脂肪吸引は実際には肥満の治療ではない。治療のためではなくむしろ、食事制限や運動をしても特定の「難しい場所」の脂肪が減らないときに用いられるべきだ。もう1つのよく行われている美容整形の処置は、豊胸手術だ。この処置では、脇の下からインプラントを挿入して、胸が大きく見えるようにする。豊胸手術では通常、小さな傷跡しか残らない。併発する一般的な症状としては、麻酔の影響、感染症、腫れ、赤み、出血、痛みなどがある。このようなリスクを軽減するため、手術を受ける人は、担当外科医が医師会認定であることを確認するよう勧められている。

読解のポイント What's more **は「加えて、さらに重要なことに」の意味。**

1　この文章の重要な情報を最もよく表しているのはどの文か。

a. 美容整形手術は危険である。
b. 多くの人は、痛みがあるために美容整形手術をしない。
c. 米国では美容整形手術の人気が高まっている。
d. 乳房縮小術は豊胸手術と同じくらい人気がある。

2　下線部で *trouble spots* が意味するのは、次のうちどれか。

a. 人々が一般的に太りすぎている場所
b. 効果のない運動方法
c. 脂肪吸引が効かない体の部位
d. 脂肪を減らすのが難しい体の特定の部位

Ghosts

Target Words

1. astrological
2. divination
3. haunt
4. horror
5. intermediary
6. invoke
7. meditate
8. phantom
9. psychic
10. self-perpetuating

Definitions and Samples

1. astrological *adj.* Related to the study of the position of stars, the sun, and the planets in the belief that they influence earthly events

Every day, Mona read her **astrological** forecast in the newspaper, and she was careful if the horoscope predicted trouble.

Parts of speech astrology *n*, astrologer *n*, astrologically *adv*

2. divination *n.* Foretelling the future by finding patterns in physical objects

In Turkey, women offer **divinations** by reading the dregs from a coffee cup.

Parts of speech divine *v*

3. haunt *v.* To continually appear (in the form of a ghost) in the same place or to the same person

Some say the ghost of Princess Hilda **haunts** this castle, appearing as a headless form while she plays the piano.

The pictures of children dying in war have **haunted** me for a long time.

4. horror *n.* Strong fear mixed with disgust

On Halloween night, all the **horror** movies were rented out.

Parts of speech horrify *v*, horrific *adj*

5. intermediary *n.* Acting as an agent between people or things

The plaintiff's lawyer suggested that they hire an **intermediary** to help them discuss their case.

Usage tips *Intermediary* comes from the Latin words meaning "between the ways."

Parts of speech intermediary *adj*

6. **invoke** *v.* To call on for support

In many religions, believers **invoke** their god by holding out their hands.

Parts of speech invocation *n*

7. **meditate** *v.* To reflect; to think quietly and deeply for a long time

Every morning, the monks **meditated** for three hours in complete silence.

Parts of speech meditation *n*, meditative *adj*

8. **phantom** *n.* A dimly visible form, usually thought to be the spirit of a dead person, a sunken ship, etc.

Many visitors reported seeing a **phantom** who appeared around the lake.

Usage tips *Phantom* originates in a word meaning "dream"; like a dream, a phantom leaves an observer wondering whether it's real or not.

9. **psychic** *adj.* Relating to the supposed ability of the human mind to sense things that cannot be observed

The governor's assistant claimed to have unique **psychic** abilities enabling him to read people's minds.

Parts of speech psychic *n*, psychically *adv*

10. **self-perpetuating** *adj.* Having the power to renew oneself for an indefinite period of time

It is difficult to escape from a lie, as they are often **self-perpetuating**.

Parts of speech self-perpetuation *n*

TOEFL Prep 13-1 **For each word, choose the word or phrase that has the most similar meaning. Write the letter of your choice on the line.**

1. divination______
   (a) demand (b) prediction (c) problem (d) route
2. haunt______
   (a) dry out (b) fail to show up
   (c) continue to disturb (d) search desperately
3. meditate______
   (a) clarify (b) expose (c) purge (d) think
4. invoke______
   (a) call (b) cry (c) inspire (d) reject
5. psychic______
   (a) empty (b) mental (c) powerful (d) vague

TOEFL Prep 13-2 **Circle the word that best completes each sentence.**

1. The leaders of the religious group are said to have (astrological / psychic) powers that allow them to move objects just by the power of their thoughts.
2. For years after the earthquake, she was disturbed by the (haunting / self-perpetuating) memories of destruction.
3. The boys told their new friend that they had seen (intermediaries / phantoms) in the cemetery at night.
4. During the scuffle, the citizens were prepared to (invoke / meditate) the right of citizen's arrest because no police officers were present.
5. Even people who don't believe in (divination / horror) were impressed by her ability to predict future events.

TOEFL Success 13 **Read the passage to review the vocabulary you have learned. Answer the questions that follow.**

Some say that sailors are a superstitious group. Long nights of watching stars predispose them to a belief in *astrology*.

TOEFL Prep 13-1 1. b 2. c 3. d 4. a 5. b
TOEFL Prep 13-2 1. psychic 2. haunting 3. phantoms 4. invoke 5. divination

Long periods of isolation lead them to believe in *psychic* phenomena that others would laugh at. This may explain sailors' frequent reports of seeing *phantom* ships. From the Gulf of Mexico, across the Atlantic, and to the South China Sea, sailors often claim that such vessels *haunt* the seas. One of the most famous stories of ghost ships is the *Flying Dutchman*, which sailed in 1680 from Amsterdam to Dutch East India under Hendrick Vanderdecken. When the captain ignored the danger warnings of a storm, his ship was smashed and the crew was lost. According to legend, his arrogance *invoked* the wrath of God, who condemned the lost crew-members to battle the waters off the Cape of Good Hope for eternity. Since then, there have been repeated sightings of the *Flying Dutchman*, one as recent as 1939. Many sightings of phantom ships occur in areas where vessels are known to have sunk. Sailors can never *divine* when or where they will next encounter a phantom ship. Rather, most of their sightings occur randomly, only later to bring forth information of a former sea *horror*. Some say that ghosts aboard a phantom ship are trying to use living sailors as their *intermediaries*. Still others think that the existence of phantom ships is merely a *self-perpetuating* myth for bored sailors who are prone to too much idle *meditation* about the meaning of life and death on the high seas.

1. How would the author explain phantom ships?
   a. Their appearance is tied to the stars.
   b. Sailors at sea have little to do.
   c. Fog and high waves can distort one's vision.
   d. Shipwreck remains haunt oceans around the world.

2. Why does the author mention the *Flying Dutchman*?
   a. as the basis of primitive navigation systems
   b. as an example of a commonly sighted phantom ship
   c. as the reason why many sailors have mental problems
   d. as an explanation for sightings of phantom ships

TOEFL Success 13 1. b 2. b

心と体
レッスン13

幽霊

意味と例文

1 astrological (形容詞) 星や太陽、惑星が地球上の出来事に影響を与えているとの考えに基づきそれらの位置の研究に関連している（占星術の）

例文訳 モナは毎日、新聞の星座占いを読んで、その占いがトラブルを予言していたら注意していた。

関連語 astrology (名詞) 占星術、astrologer (名詞) 占星術師、astrologically (副詞) 占星術で

---

2 divination (名詞) （物理的なものにパターンを見つけて）未来を予知する占い

例文訳 トルコでは、女性がコーヒーカップの残りかすを読み取って占いをする。

関連語 divine (動詞) 占う、推測する

---

3 haunt (動詞) （幽霊の形で同じ場所や同じ人の前に）継続的に現れる

例文訳 この城にはヒルダ姫の亡霊が出没し、首のない姿で現れピアノを弾くと言われている。
戦争で死んでいく子どもたちの写真が、ずっと私を苦しめてきた。

---

4 horror (名詞) （嫌悪感の混じった）強い恐怖心

例文訳 ハロウィンの夜には、すべてのホラー映画が貸し出された。

関連語 horrify (動詞) 怖がらせる、horrific (形容詞) 恐ろしい

---

5 intermediary (名詞) （人やものの間で）仲介する存在

例文訳 原告側の弁護士は、原告たちが事件について話し合う手助けとなるように仲介者を雇うことを提案した。

ヒント 使い方 intermediary は、「道と道の間」を意味するラテン語に由来している。

関連語 intermediary (形容詞) 仲介の、間の

---

6 invoke (動詞) 支援を求める

例文訳 多くの宗教で、信者は手を差し出して神に助けを求める。

関連語 invocation (名詞) 祈り、嘆願

7 meditate (動詞) 熟考する／（長い間）静かに深く考える

例文訳 毎朝、その僧侶たちは3時間、完全に沈黙して瞑想した。

関連語 meditation (名詞) 瞑想、meditative (形容詞) 瞑想にふける、考え込んだ

8 phantom (名詞) ぼんやりと見える形をしているもの（通常は、死者や沈没船などの霊、幻だと考えられている）

例文訳 多くの訪問者が、湖の周りに現れる幽霊を見たと報告した。

ヒント 使い方 phantom は「夢」を意味する言葉に由来している。phantom は夢と同じように、見る人にそれが現実なのかどうかを考えさせる。

9 psychic (形容詞) （人間が持つとされる）目に見えないものを感知する心の能力に関連する

例文訳 その知事補佐官は、自分は人の心が読める特異な超自然的能力を持っていると主張した。

関連語 psychic (名詞) 超能力者、霊能者、psychically (副詞) 心霊的に

10 self-perpetuating (形容詞) （無期限に）自身の存在を継続させる力を持っている

例文訳 嘘というのは多くの場合、いつまでも存在し続けるので、それから逃れるのは難しい。

関連語 self-perpetuation (名詞) 居座り続けること、無期限に継続すること

TOEFL プレップ 13-1

各単語に最も近い意味を持つ単語や語句を選び、線の上に選んだアルファベットを書きなさい。

1 divination ____________

(a) 要求 (b) 予言 (c) 問題 (d) 道筋

2 haunt ____________

(a) 干上がる (b) 姿を現さない (c) 悩ませ続ける (d) 必死に探す

3 meditate ____________

(a) 明確にする (b) あらわにする (c) 追放する (d) 考える

4 invoke ____________

(a) 呼び起こす (b) 泣く (c) 鼓舞する (d) 拒絶する

5 psychic ____________

(a) 空っぽな (b) 精神的な (c) 強力な (d) 曖昧な

TOEFL プレップ 13-2

各文を完成させるのに最も適した単語を丸で囲みなさい。

1 その宗教団体の指導者たちは、思考の力だけで物体を動かすことを可能にする（占星術的な／超自然的な）力を持っていると言われている。

2 震災後何年もの間、彼女は（絶えず思い出される／無期限に存在し続ける）破壊の記憶に悩まされていた。

3 その少年たちは新しい友人に、夜の墓地で（仲介者／幽霊）を見たことがあると話した。

4 市民たちはその小競り合いの間、その場に警察官がいなかったので、私人逮捕権を（行使する／瞑想する）準備をしていた。

5 （占い／恐怖）を信じていない人でも、未来の出来事を予言する彼女の能力に感心した。

TOEFL サクセス 13

文章を読んで学んだ語彙を復習します。後に続く質問に答えなさい。

［例文訳］

船乗りは迷信深い集団だと言う人がいる。彼らは夜通し星を見ていることで、占星術を信じるようになる。孤独な時間が長く続くため、他の人なら笑いとばすような心霊現象を信じるようになる。こういったことが、船乗りたちが幽霊船を見たと頻繁に報告する理由かもしれない。メキシコ湾から大西洋を渡り、南シナ海にいたるまで、船乗りたちはよく、そういった船が海に出没すると主張する。幽霊船で最も有名な話は、1680 年にアムステルダムからオランダ領東インドに向けてヘンドリック・ファン・デル・デッケンの指揮のもと航海したフライング・ダッチマン号である。船長が嵐の危険な兆候を無視すると、船は大破し、乗組員たちは行方不明になった。言い伝えによると、船長の傲慢さが神の怒りを呼び起こし、神は、亡くなった乗組員たちが喜望峰沖で永遠に水と戦い続ける運命を与えたのだという。それ以来、フライング・ダッチマン号は繰り返し目撃されていて、直近では 1939 年に目撃例がある。幽霊船は、船が沈んだと知られる場所で多く目撃される。船乗りは、次にいつ、どこで幽霊船に遭遇するかを知ることは決してできない。むしろ、目撃されるのは予測不可能な場合がほとんどで、あとになって過去の海の恐怖の情報がもたらされるばかりなのである。幽霊船に乗っている幽霊は、生きている船員を仲介者として使おうとしていると言う人もいる。また一方で、幽霊船の存在は、外洋で生と死の意味についてとりとめもなく考え込みすぎている退屈な船乗りのための、永遠に存在し続ける神話に過ぎないとする人もいる。

1　筆者は幽霊船をどのように説明しているか。

a. その姿は星と結びついている。

b. 海にいる船員たちにはほとんどできることがない。

c. 霧や高波が視界を歪ませる可能性がある。

d. 難破船の残骸が世界中の海に出没する。

2　なぜ筆者はフライング・ダッチマン号について述べているのか。

a. 原始的な航海システムの基礎として

b. よく目撃される幽霊船の一例として

c. 多くの船員が精神的な問題を抱えている理由として

d. 幽霊船の目撃例の説明として

Anthropology

Target Words

1. assimilate
2. cremation
3. domesticate
4. folklore
5. fossilize
6. relic
7. rite
8. ritually
9. saga
10. vestige

Definitions and Samples

1. **assimilate** *v.* To consume and incorporate; to become similar

Not all of the overseas students could **assimilate** into the rigidly controlled school.

Usage tips *Assimilate* is often followed by *into*.

Parts of speech assimilation *n*

2. **cremation** *n.* The act of burning the dead

Cremation is particularly common in Japan, where land for burial is very limited.

Parts of speech cremate *v*

3. **domesticate** *v.* To make something suitable for being in a home

The Barnes family hoped to **domesticate** the tiger, but their neighbors were skeptical.

Usage tips The object of *domesticate* is usually a plant or animal.

Parts of speech domestic *adj*

4. **folklore** *n.* Traditional myths of a people transmitted orally

Through **folklore**, archaeologists have learned about the migration of Native Americans in North America.

Parts of speech folkloric *adj*

5. **fossilize** *v.* To become preserved in clay or stone or ash after death, so that a natural record is left of the original organism; to become rigid and stuck in old ways
The dinosaur eggs had **fossilized** over thousands of years.
Parts of speech fossilization *n*, fossil *n*

6. **relic** *n.* Something left from a long-ago culture, time period, or person
Relics of the war can still be found in the sand dunes along this shore.

7. **rite** *n.* A ceremony meant to achieve a certain purpose
Many cultures have fertility **rites** that supposedly make it more likely for women to bear children.

8. **ritually** *adv.* As part of a formal ceremony involving a required sequence of actions
The children **ritually** kissed their parents on the cheek before bed.
Parts of speech ritual *n*, ritual *adj*

9. **saga** *n.* A long story about important events long ago
Many American families tell **sagas** about their ancestors' arrival in the United States.

10. **vestige** *n.* A visible trace that something once existed
The wilted flowers were the only **vestige** of their romantic weekend.
Parts of speech vestigial *adj*

TOEFL Prep 14-1 **Choose the word from the list that is closest in meaning to the underlined part of each sentence. Write it in the blank.**

assimilate cremation domesticate folklore ritually

__________ 1. Many cultures around the world have "manhood" traditions in which a boy ceremonially becomes a man in front of a whole community.

__________ 2. It is difficult to tame a bird that was born in the wild.

__________ 3. Based on the oral legends about the fire, researchers estimate that about half of the townspeople died in the blaze.

__________ 4. After the burning of the body, the remaining bits of bone are transferred to a large urn.

__________ 5. Her husband could never fit into her family's way of life.

TOEFL Prep 14-2 **Write the best word next to each definition. Use each word only once.**

fossilize relic rite saga vestige

__________ 1. to harden after death
__________ 2. a customary act
__________ 3. a memento
__________ 4. something remaining from the past
__________ 5. a long story

TOEFL Success 14 **Read the passage to review the vocabulary you have learned. Answer the questions that follow.**

The aborigines of Australia may have been some of the first people on the planet. Recent discoveries of *relics*, including stone tools, show that humans lived near Penrith, New South Wales, about 47,000 years ago. Australian aborigines migrated from northern lands by sea, when the water passages were narrower than they are today. This is the first evidence of

TOEFL Prep 14-1 1. ritually 2. domesticate 3. folklore 4. cremation 5. assimilate
TOEFL Prep 14-2 1. fossilize 2. rite 3. relic 4. vestige 5. saga

sea travel by prehistoric humans. The *saga* of this water passing survives in modern-day aboriginal *folklore*. **To put this in perspective**, remember that 50,000 years ago, humans were nomadic. Early aborigines did not cultivate crops, and in Australia at the time there were no animals that could be *domesticated*. No one knows how long it took aboriginal people to reach Australia, but archaeologists are searching through ancient campsites for *vestiges* of their early lifestyle. *Fossilized* remains indicate that these nomadic people not only gathered food from the land, but they also subsisted on meat from large animals that no longer exist today. As part of their hunting tradition, aborigines *ritually* covered themselves in mud to mask their own scent or for camouflage. Aboriginal society marked the major events of life with *rites* such as circumcision, marriage, and *cremation*. Older people were revered and cared for as great sources of wisdom. When Westerners arrived in Australia in 1788, the 300,000 aborigines who lived there were not eager to *assimilate* into Europe-based society. In the following years, disease, loss of land, and loss of identity shaped the aborigines' history perhaps as much as their first prehistoric crossing from the north.

Bonus Structure **To put this in perspective** means "to give some background information."

1. Which sentence best expresses the essential information in this passage?
   a. Australian aborigines were some of the Earth's first people.
   b. White explorers did not respect aboriginal culture.
   c. Australian aborigines probably migrated from Africa.
   d. The organization and functioning of aboriginal society is mostly unknown.

2. In this passage, the word *ritually* is closest in meaning to
   a. regularly
   b. ignorantly
   c. superstitiously
   d. dramatically

TOEFL Success 14 1. a 2. a

社会
レッスン14

人類学

意味と例文

1 assimilate（動詞） 摂取して取り込む／同様のものになる

例文訳 すべての留学生が、その厳格に管理された学校にとけこめたわけではなかった。

ヒント 使い方 assimilate は後ろに into を伴うことが多い。

関連語 assimilation（名詞）同化、吸収

---

2 cremation（名詞） 死者を焼く行為（火葬）

例文訳 火葬は、埋葬するための土地が非常に限られている日本で、特に一般的である。

関連語 cremate（動詞）火葬する

---

3 domesticate（動詞） （あるものを）家に置くのに適した状態にする

例文訳 バーンズ家は、そのトラを飼いならしたがっていたが、近所の人々はそんなことができるのかと懐疑的だった。

使い方 domesticate の目的語は通常、植物や動物である。

関連語 domestic（形容詞）国内の、家庭の

---

4 folklore（名詞） 口頭で伝えられた伝統的な民族神話

例文訳 考古学者は、民間伝承を通して、北米のネイティブアメリカンの移住について学んできた。

関連語 folkloric（形容詞）民間伝承の

---

5 fossilize（動詞） 死後に土や石、灰の中に保存されて元の有機体の自然な記録が残る／融通がきかず昔のやり方のままになる

例文訳 その恐竜の卵は何千年もかけて化石化した。

関連語 fossilization（名詞）化石化、形骸化、fossil（名詞）化石、時代遅れのもの

---

6 relic（名詞）（遠い昔の文化や時代、人から）残されたもの

例文訳 この海岸沿いの砂丘には、今でも戦争の遺物が見られる。

---

7 rite（名詞）（特定の目的を達成するための）儀式

例文訳 多くの文化では、女性が子どもを産みやすくなるとされる豊穣の儀式が行われている。

---

8 ritually（副詞）（必要な一連の動作を伴う）正式な儀式の一部として

例文訳 子どもたちは寝る前に、両親の頬にお決まりのキスをした。

関連語 ritual（名詞）儀式、習慣的行為、ritual（形容詞）儀式の、儀礼的な

---

9 saga（名詞）（遠い昔の重要な出来事についての）長い物語

例文訳 米国の多くの家庭では、先祖が米国に到着したときの物語が語られている。

---

10 vestige（名詞）（あるものがかつて存在したことの目に見える）痕跡

例文訳 そのしおれた花は、彼らのロマンチックな週末の唯一の痕跡だった。

関連語 vestigial（形容詞）痕跡の

TOEFL プレップ 14-1

各文の下線部に最も近い意味を持つ単語をリストから選び、空欄に記入しなさい。

assimilate　cremation　domesticate　folklore　ritually

______ 1. 世界中の多くの文化には、コミュニティ全体の前で少年が儀式的に男になる、という「大人」になるための伝統がある。

______ 2. 野生で生まれた鳥を飼いならすのは難しい。

______ 3. その火事にまつわる口承の伝説をもとに、研究者たちはその火災によって町民の約半数が亡くなったと推定している。

______ 4. 遺体を燃やした後、残った骨のかけらは大きな骨壷に移される。

______ 5. 彼女の夫は彼女の家族の生活様式にとけこむことがどうしてもできなかった。

TOEFL プレップ 14-2

以下の定義に最も当てはまる単語を記入すること。各単語は一度しか使えません。

fossilize　relic　rite　saga　vestige

______ 1. 死後に固まること

______ 2. 慣習的な行為

______ 3. 記念の品、遺品

______ 4. 過去から残っているもの

______ 5. 長い物語

TOEFL サクセス 14

文章を読んで学んだ語彙を復習します。後に続く質問に答えなさい。

［例文訳］

オーストラリアのアボリジニの人々は、地球上に最初に存在した人々の一部であったかもしれない。近年、石器などの遺物が発見されたことで、約 47,000 年前にニューサウスウェールズ州のペンリス付近に人類が住んでいたことが判明した。オーストラリアのアボリジニは、現在よりも水路が狭かった時代に、北方の土地から海路で移住してきた。これは先史時代の人類が海を渡ったことを示す最初の証拠である。このときの海を渡った物語は、現代のアボリジニの民間伝承に残っている。ここで広い視野に立ち、5 万年前に人類は遊牧民だったということを思い起こそう。初期のアボリジニは作物を栽培しておらず、当時のオーストラリアには家畜化できる動物もいなかった。アボリジニの人々がオーストラリアに到着するまでどのくらいかかったのかは不明だが、彼らの初期の生活様式の痕跡を求めて、考古学者たちは古代の居住地を調査している。化石化した遺物は、遊牧民が土地から食料を集めるだけでなく、今日ではもう存在しない大型動物の肉を食べて生きていたことを示している。アボリジニは狩猟の伝統の一部として、自分の匂いを消したりカモフラージュしたりするために、しきたりとして自分の身体を泥で覆っていた。アボリジニの社会では、人生の重要な行事は、割礼、結婚、火葬などの儀式とともに行われた。年長者は偉大な知恵の源としてあがめられ、大切にされていた。1788 年に西洋人がオーストラリアに到着したとき、そこに住んでいた 30 万人のアボリジニは、ヨーロッパ型社会に同化したがらなかった。その後の病気、土地の喪失、アイデンティティの喪失は、おそらく先史時代に彼らが北から渡ってきたことと同じくらい、アボリジニの歴史を形成するものとなった。

読解のポイント　To put this in perspective は「背景情報を与える」という意味。

1　この文章の重要な情報を最もよく表しているのはどの文か。

a. オーストラリアのアボリジニは、地球上に最初に存在した人類の一部だった。

b. 白人の探検家は、アボリジニの文化を尊重しなかった。

c. オーストラリアのアボリジニは、おそらくアフリカから移住してきた。

d. アボリジニ社会の組織や機能はほとんど知られていない。

2　この文章中の ritually という言葉に最も近い意味を持つのは、次のうちどれか？

a. いつも決まって

b. 知らないで

c. 迷信的に

d. 劇的に

Social Inequality

Target Words

1. amend
2. biased
3. burden
4. counter
5. de facto
6. discriminate
7. notion
8. oppress
9. paradigm
10. prejudiced

Definitions and Samples

1. amend *v.* To change for the better

The residents voted to **amend** their neighborhood policy on fences.

Parts of speech amendment *n*

2. biased *adj.* Leaning unfairly in one direction

Her newspaper article was criticized for being heavily **biased** toward the mayor's proposal.

Parts of speech bias *n*

3. burden *n.* Something that is carried; a source of stress or worry

The donkey walked slowly under the **burden** of its heavy load.

The failing company faced the **burden** of bad debts and a poor reputation.

Parts of speech burden *v*

4. counter *v.* To act in opposition to; to offer in response

The hockey player **countered** the punch with a smashing blow from his hockey stick.

Jane **countered** every accusation with a specific example of her achievements.

Parts of speech counter *n*, counter *adj*

5. **de facto** *adj.* Truly doing a job, even if not officially
After the president's death, the country had no official leader, but the powerful army had **de facto** control of the government.
Parts of speech de facto *adv*

6. **discriminate** *v.* To choose carefully among options
The governor wisely **discriminated** between urgent issues and those that could wait.
Usage tips If you *discriminate against* someone, you treat him/her unfairly because of ethnicity, sex, religion, or some other characteristic.
Parts of speech discriminatory *adj*, discriminate *adj*

7. **notion** *n.* A belief; a fanciful impulse
The **notion** that older office equipment is unreliable is inaccurate.
One morning, she suddenly took the **notion** to paint her kitchen red.
Usage tips *Notion* can be followed by a *that* clause or a *to* phrase.

8. **oppress** *v.* To keep down by force; to weigh heavily on
Factory management **oppressed** workers through intimidation.
Parts of speech oppression *n*

9. **paradigm** *n.* A pattern or model; a set of assumptions
The usual **paradigm** for economic growth in developed countries does not apply to some poor nations.
Usage tips *Paradigm* is often followed by *for*.

10. **prejudiced** *adj.* Causing to judge prematurely and unfairly
Many consumers are **prejudiced** against commercial goods made in third-world countries.
Parts of speech prejudice *v*, prejudice *n*

TOEFL Prep 15-1 **Complete each sentence by filling in the blank with the best word from the list. Change the form of the word if necessary. Use each word only once.**

biased counter de facto notion paradigm

1. During the trial, the defense lawyer_______each claim with an opposite charge.
2. The basketball coach was naturally_______toward the taller players.
3. After we saw the fancy car that the Jacobses bought, we gave up the_______that they could not afford the basic things in life.
4. The battle was successful, as judged by the prevailing_______of that era.
5. Even though Jovie was a cleaner, not a nanny, she was the baby's_______caregiver because his parents worked so many hours.

TOEFL Prep 15-2 **Find the word or phrase that is closest in meaning to the opposite of each word in the left-hand column. Write the letter in the blank.**

_______	1. amend	(a) relieve
_______	2. burden	(b) allow to operate freely
_______	3. oppress	(c) leave as is
_______	4. indiscriminately	(d) unbiased
_______	5. prejudiced	(e) by making careful choices

TOEFL Success 15 **Read the passage to review the vocabulary you have learned. Answer the questions that follow.**

Nelson Mandela devoted his life to fighting *prejudice* in South Africa. Mandela traveled his state, organizing a fight against *discriminatory* laws and racial *bias*. He encouraged civil disobedience as a tool against the *oppression* of Blacks. As

TOEFL Prep 15-1 1. countered 2. biased 3. notion 4. paradigm 5. de facto
TOEFL Prep 15-2 1. c 2. a 3. b 4. e 5. d

deputy president of the African National Congress, Mandela encouraged his fellow citizens to challenge the prevailing *paradigm* of power. Mandela believed that prejudice *burdened* not only the oppressed, but also the oppressors.

The government *countered* Mandela's activities with a criminal conviction. Still, Mandela's *de facto* leadership gained him respect and authority among his fellow citizens. Mandela's courage and popularity worried **the ruling class**, who did not want to share power. What's more, they refused to *amend* the state's laws. So when Mandela returned from an overseas trip to gain support for his cause in 1962, he was arrested, jailed, and sentenced to life in prison for various crimes.

This only fueled Mandela's *notions* about inequality and justice. He took his demands to jail, where he demanded the same dress and safety gear for Black prisoners as for White prisoners. After 28 years in prison, Mandela was released, returning immediately to public life. In 1994, he was elected the president of South Africa.

Bonus Structure **The ruling class** means those who held power mostly because of the families they were born into.

1. Which of the following best expresses the essential information of this passage?
   a. Nelson Mandela used illegal means to achieve his ends.
   b. Nelson Mandela fought prejudice in South Africa.
   c. Nelson Mandela inspired Blacks around the world.
   d. Nelson Mandela was driven primarily by his religious beliefs.

2. In the passage, the word *amend* is closest in meaning to
   a. ignore
   b. write down
   c. change
   d. discuss

TOEFL Success 15 1. b 2. c

社会
レッスン 15

社会的不平等

意味と例文

1 amend（動詞） よい方向に変える

例文訳 住民たちは、柵に関するその地域の方針を改正することを投票で決めた。

関連語 amendment（名詞）改正、修正

---

2 biased（形容詞） （ある方向に）不公平に偏っている

例文訳 彼女の新聞記事は、市長の提案に大きく偏っていると批判された。

関連語 bias（名詞）偏見、先入観

---

3 burden（名詞） 運ばれるもの／ストレスや心配の源

例文訳 ロバは重い荷物を背負ってゆっくりと歩いた。
その倒産しかけている会社は、不良債権と悪評という苦しみに直面した。

関連語 burden（動詞）負担をかける、悩ます

---

4 counter（動詞） 反対して行動する／反応して答える

例文訳 そのホッケー選手は、ホッケースティックを一撃してパンチに反撃した。
ジェーンはすべての非難に対して、自分の業績の具体例を挙げて反論した。

関連語 counter（名詞）反撃、反論 、counter（形容詞）反対の

---

5 de facto（形容詞） 公式ではないとしても実際には役目を果たしている（事実上の）

例文訳 大統領の死後、その国には公式な指導者はいなかったが、強力な軍隊が事実上、政府をコントロールしていた。

関連語 de facto（副詞）事実上

6 discriminate（動詞） （選択肢の中から）慎重に選ぶ

例文訳 知事は、緊急性の高い問題と後回しにできる問題を賢明に区別した。

ヒント 使い方 人に対して「discriminate against（差別する）」というと、民族、性別、宗教、その他の特徴のためにその人を不当に扱う、という意味になる。

関連語 discriminatory（形容詞）差別的な、discriminate（形容詞）識別された、差別的な

7 notion（名詞） 考え／気まぐれな衝動

例文訳 より古いオフィス機器はそれだけあてにならないという考えは間違っている。

ある朝、彼女は突然、キッチンを赤く塗りたいという気持ちになった。

使い方 notion の後には、that 節や to 不定詞句が続くことがある。

8 oppress（動詞） 力ずくで抑え込む／重くのしかかる

例文訳 工場の経営者は脅迫によって労働者を抑圧した。

関連語 oppression（名詞）抑圧

9 paradigm（名詞） 典型または模範／一連の前提

例文訳 先進国の経済成長のための通常のパラダイムは、一部の貧しい国には当てはまらない。

使い方 paradigm は後ろに for を伴うことが多い。

10 prejudiced（形容詞） 早すぎる、または不公平な判断の原因となる（偏見のある）

例文訳 多くの消費者は、第三世界の国々でつくられた商品に対して偏見を持っている。

関連語 prejudice（動詞）偏見を持たせる、prejudice（名詞）偏見

TOEFL プレップ 15－1

リストの中から空欄に当てはまる適切な単語を選んで、各文を完成させなさい。必要に応じて単語を活用させること。なお、各単語は一度しか使用できません。

biased　counter　de facto　notion　paradigm

1　裁判で、被告側の弁護士は一つひとつの主張に対して反論とともに______________。

2　そのバスケットボールのコーチは、自然と背の高い選手たちに______________。

3　ジェイコブス家が購入した高級車を見てから、私たちは彼らが生活必需品も買うゆとりがないという______________を捨てた。

4　その戦いは、その時代の一般的な______________から判断すると、成功であった。

5　ジョービーは子守ではなく清掃員だったが、赤ちゃんの両親があまりにも長い時間働いていたため、その子の______の世話係であった。

TOEFL プレップ 15－2

左列の各単語の反対語に最も近い意味の単語や語句を選び、空欄にそのアルファベットを書きこみなさい。

______________	1. amend	(a) 苦痛を和らげる
______________	2. burden	(b) 自由に動けるようにする
______________	3. oppress	(c) そのままにしておく
______________	4. indiscriminately	(d) 偏見のない
______________	5. prejudiced	(e) 慎重に選択して

TOEFL サクセス 15

文章を読んで学んだ語彙を復習します。後に続く質問に答えなさい。

［例文訳］

ネルソン・マンデラは、南アフリカにおける偏見と戦うことに人生を捧げた。マンデラは国内を回って、差別的な法律や人種的偏見に反対する闘争を組織した。彼は黒人への抑圧に対抗する手段として、市民的不服従を奨励した。マンデラは、アフリカ民族会議の副議長として、広くはびこる権力の既成概念に挑戦するよう仲間である市民に呼びかけた。マンデラは、偏見というのは抑圧される側だけでなく、抑圧する側にも重荷を負わせるものだと考えていた。

政府は、刑事上の有罪判決を下すことでマンデラの活動に反撃した。しかし、彼は事実上のリーダーシップによって、仲間の市民から尊敬と権威を獲得した。マンデラの勇気と人望は、支配者層を不安にさせた。彼らは権力を共有したくなかったのだ。その上、彼らは国家の法律を改正することを拒んだ。そのため、1962年にマンデラは運動の支持を得るための海外旅行から戻ってくると、さまざまな罪で逮捕、投獄され、終身刑を宣告されたのである。

この出来事は、不平等や正義についてのマンデラの考えをさらに強めただけだった。彼は自分の要求を刑務所に持ち込み、黒人の囚人にも白人の囚人と同じ服装や安全装備を求めた。28年間を刑務所で過ごしたのちにマンデラは釈放され、すぐに公の場に復帰した。そして1994年には南アフリカ共和国の大統領に選ばれた。

読解のポイント The ruling class **は、主に生まれた家柄によって権力を握った人たちのこと。**

1 この文章の最も重要な情報を表しているのはどの文か。

a. ネルソン・マンデラは、目的を達成するために違法な手段を使った。
b. ネルソン・マンデラは、南アフリカで偏見と戦った。
c. ネルソン・マンデラは、世界中の黒人を鼓舞した。
d. ネルソン・マンデラは、主に宗教的信念につき動かされていた。

2 この文章中の単語 *amend* に最も近い意味を持つのは、次のうちどれか。

a. 無視する
b. 書き留める
c. 変える
d. 話し合う

Expertise

Target Words

1. curriculum
2. distinctly
3. erudite
4. fortify
5. implicitly
6. parochial
7. rigor
8. roster
9. secular
10. suspend

Definitions and Samples

1. curriculum *n.* The courses of study offered by an educational institution

The teachers met to design a new **curriculum** for the Intensive English Program.

2. distinctly *adv.* Clearly

I **distinctly** remember saying that we would meet at noon.

Parts of speech distinction *n*, distinct *adj*

3. erudite *adj.* Highly educated

Even though Stella was only a freshman, she was considered **erudite** by both her classmates and her professors.

4. fortify *v.* To strengthen

The high-priced drink had extra vitamins and minerals to **fortify** the body.

Parts of speech fortification *n*

5. implicitly *adv.* Without being stated; unquestioningly

By joining the competition, she agreed **implicitly** to the rules.

Parts of speech implicit *adj*

6. parochial *adj.* Restricted in outlook; relating to the local parish

Marla moved from her rural community to get away from its **parochial** thinking.

Sending your children to a **parochial** school can cost as much as sending them to college.

7. **rigor** *n.* Strictness; difficult situations that come from following rules strictly

The wrestler followed his diet with **rigor**.

The **rigors** of military life toughened the young men quickly.

Parts of speech rigorous *adj*

8. **roster** *n.* A list, especially of names

Two of the names on the **roster** were misspelled.

9. **secular** *adj.* Worldly rather than spiritual; not related to religion

Originally, the university was related to a church, but that connection is gone and it's now totally **secular**.

10. **suspend** *v.* To cause to stop for a period; to hang as to allow free movement

The trial was **suspended** when the judge learned that one of the jury members knew the defense lawyer.

The circus acrobat was **suspended** in midair.

Parts of speech suspension *n*, suspensory *adj*

TOEFL Prep 16-1 **For each word, choose the word that has the most similar meaning. Write the letter of your choice on the line.**

1. distinctly______
   (a) clearly (b) fully (c) softly (d) aggressively
2. erudite______
   (a) strong (b) wise (c) complicated (d) plain
3. fortify______
   (a) weaken (b) contemplate (c) strengthen (d) reshape
4. rigor______
   (a) strictness (b) talent (c) peace (d) recklessness
5. suspend______
   (a) tie (b) fill (c) hang (d) throw

TOEFL Prep 16-2 **Choose the word from the list that is closest in meaning to the underlined part of each sentence. Write it in the blank.**

curriculum implicitly parochial roster secular

__________ 1. The class list showed that only 12 students had enrolled for spring quarter.
__________ 2. Many parents feel that public schools are as good as private, religious schools.
__________ 3. The principal requested parents' feedback on the new set of math classes.
__________ 4. In the United States, many private grade schools are not affiliated with a religion.
__________ 5. The janitor agreed indirectly not to turn in the students.

TOEFL Success 16 **Read the passage to review the vocabulary you have learned. Answer the questions that follow.**

In the last three decades, universities across the United States have attempted to adapt their *curriculums* to meet the changing purposes of higher education. University education

TOEFL Prep 16-1 1. a 2. b 3. c 4. a 5. c
TOEFL Prep 16-2 1. roster 2. parochial 3. curriculum 4. secular 5. implicitly

was also once considered an exclusive opportunity, with *erudite* scholars establishing courses based on the goal of training a *distinctly* academic "elite." These days, not every undergraduate is destined to become a scholar, and the *roster* of students represents a more complete cross section of society, including minorities, women, and returning students. These days, most learners attend university to *fortify* basic skills, primarily learning how to learn and how to express themselves. Far from its earlier religious or *elitist* image, the university is seen increasingly as a *secular* center for career development, where students know they will graduate into a competitive job market. Most professors have embraced this evolution in the university's role, letting go of the traditional, *parochial* view of higher education. **On the other hand**, many feel that while they want to accommodate an adaptable curriculum, universities must not *suspend* their obligation of establishing *rigorous* requirements for education and graduation. *Implicit* in their stance is support for the traditional liberal arts curriculum with a core of classes required across disciplines.

Bonus Structure **On the other hand** introduces an opposing point.

1. According to information in the reading, which of the following sentences would the author be most likely to agree with?
   a. Universities are becoming increasingly exclusive.
   b. A curriculum needs to be completely adaptable to students' needs.
   c. The role of higher education is changing, and so is the university curriculum.
   d. The cost of university puts it out of reach of many populations.

2. In this passage, the word elitist is closest in meaning to
   a. superior
   b. academic
   c. populist
   d. elegant

TOEFL Success 16 1. c 2. a

社会
レッスン16

専門的知識

意味と例文

1 curriculum （名詞） （教育機関が提供する）学習課程

例文訳 集中英語プログラムの新しいカリキュラムを作成するため、教師たちが集まった。

---

2 distinctly （副詞） 明確に

例文訳 私は正午に会おうと言ったことをはっきりと覚えている。

関連語 distinction（名詞）区別、distinct（形容詞）はっきりわかる

---

3 erudite （形容詞） 高い教養のある

例文訳 ステラはまだ1年生だったが、クラスメートからも教授たちからも博識だとみなされていた。

---

4 fortify （動詞） 強化する

例文訳 その高価な飲み物には、体を強化するためのビタミンやミネラルが添加されていた。

関連語 fortification（名詞）強化、補強設備

---

5 implicitly （副詞） はっきりと述べられずに／絶対的に

例文訳 その競技に参加することで、彼女は無条件にルールに同意した。

関連語 implicit（形容詞）暗黙の、絶対的な

---

6 parochial （形容詞） ものの見方が制限されている／地元の教区に関する

例文訳 マーラは、その偏狭な考え方から逃れるために、田舎町から引っ越してきた。

子どもを教区学校に通わせると、大学に通わせるのと同じく

らいの費用がかかることがある。

---

7 rigor（名詞） 厳しさ／（ルールを厳守することで生じる）困難な状況

例文訳 そのレスラーは厳格に食事制限を守った。

軍隊生活の厳しさにより、その若者たちはすぐにたくましくなった。

関連語 rigorous（形容詞）厳密な、厳格な

---

8 roster（名詞） 一覧表（特に名前の一覧表）

例文訳 その名簿に載っている名前のうち２つに、つづりの間違いがあった。

---

9 secular（形容詞） （宗教的というよりも）世俗的な／宗教とは関係がない

例文訳 元々その大学は教会と関係があったが、そのつながりがなくなり、今では完全に宗教色のないものになっている。

---

10 suspend（動詞） 一定期間停止させる／自由に動けるように吊るす

例文訳 陪審員の１人が被告側の弁護士を知っていると裁判官が知ったとたん、その裁判は一時中断された。

サーカスの曲芸師は空中に吊るされた。

関連語 suspension（名詞）一時的停止、suspensory（形容詞）一時的に停止させる、吊っている

TOEFL プレップ 16－1

各単語に最も近い意味を持つ単語を選び、線の上に選んだアルファベットを書きなさい。

1　distinctly ＿＿＿＿＿＿
(a) はっきりと　(b) 十分に　(c) 柔らかく　(d) 攻撃的に

2　erudite ＿＿＿＿＿＿
(a) 強い　(b) 賢い　(c) 複雑な　(d) 明白な

3　fortify ＿＿＿＿＿＿
(a) 弱める　(b) 熟考する　(c) 強くする　(d) つくり変える

4　rigor ＿＿＿＿＿＿
(a) 厳しさ　(b) 才能　(c) 平和　(d) 無謀さ

5　suspend ＿＿＿＿＿＿
(a) 縛る　(b) 満たす　(c) 吊るす　(d) 投げる

TOEFL プレップ 16－2

各文の下線部に最も近い意味を持つ単語をリストから選び、空欄に記入しなさい。

curriculum　implicitly　parochial　roster　secular

＿＿＿＿＿＿ 1. そのクラス名簿によると、春学期に入学した学生はわずか 12 人だった。

＿＿＿＿＿＿ 2. 多くの親は、公立学校は私立の宗教系の学校と同じくらい良いと感じている。

＿＿＿＿＿＿ 3. 校長は、その新しい数学の教育課程について保護者の意見を求めた。

＿＿＿＿＿＿ 4. 米国では、多くの私立小学校は宗教と結びついていない。

＿＿＿＿＿＿ 5. 守衛はその生徒たちを引き渡さないことに遠まわしに同意した。

TOEFL サクセス 16

文章を読んで学んだ語彙を復習します。後に続く質問に答えなさい。

［例文訳］

過去30年間、米国じゅうの大学では、高等教育の目的の変化に応じるためカリキュラムを修正する試みが行われてきた。大学教育もかつては、博識な学者が明らかに学術的に優れた「エリート」を育成することを目的とした課程を持ち、一部の人にしか開かれていない機会とみなされていた。現在では、すべての大学生が必ず学者になるわけではない。また、学生名簿は、マイノリティ、女性、復学した学生などを含み、以前よりも社会全体を横断的に表している。今日では、大半の学生は、主には学び方や自己表現の仕方といった基本的なスキルを身につけるために大学に通っている。大学は、以前の宗教的、エリート主義的なイメージとは大きく異なり、ますます、キャリア開発のための世俗的なセンターとして見られるようになっている。そこで学生たちは、卒業後には競争の激しい就職市場に参入することを知るのである。大半の教授は、このような大学の役割の進化を好意的に受け入れ、高等教育に対する従来の偏狭な考え方を手放している。一方で、変化に適応させたカリキュラムを受け入れたいと思ってはいるものの、大学は教育や卒業について厳格な要件を打ちたてるという義務をうやむやにしてはならないと考える人もたくさんいる。彼らの立場においてはっきりしているのは、学問分野を越えて必修とされるクラスを中核とした、伝統的なリベラルアーツのカリキュラムを支持しているということだ。

読解のポイント On the other hand は、反対の意見を紹介するときに使用される表現。

1 この文章の情報によれば、次のどの文に筆者は最も同意するだろうか。
- a. 大学はますます排他的になっている。
- b. カリキュラムは、学生のニーズに完全に対応できるものでなければならない。
- c. 高等教育の役割は変化しており、大学のカリキュラムもまた変化している。
- d. 大学の費用は、多くの人々にとって手の届かないものである。

2 この文章で、elitist という言葉に最も近い意味を持つのは次のうちどれか。
- a. より優れている
- b. 学問的な
- c. 庶民派の
- d. 優雅な

Military Operations

Target Words

1. allegiance
2. artillery
3. battle
4. cease
5. hierarchy
6. in the trenches
7. mobilize
8. rank
9. ratio
10. strategic

Definitions and Samples

1. **allegiance** *n.* Loyalty
My **allegiance** to my country is based on respect for its principles.
Usage tips *Allegiance* is commonly followed by a *to* phrase.

2. **artillery** *n.* Large guns that shoot powerful shells; army units that handle such guns
An **artillery** barrage broke down the city's thick walls within seconds.
The 47th **Artillery** fired on rebels camped in the city center.
Usage tips When it means a part of an army, *artillery* is sometimes plural.

3. **battle** *v.* To fight against
The Viet Minh **battled** French forces at Dien Bien Phu for nearly two months in 1954.
Parts of speech battle *n*

4. **cease** *v.* Stop
The lightning continued even after the thunder had **ceased.**
Usage tips *Cease* is found in official statements, not usually in everyday speech.
Parts of speech cessation *n*, ceaseless *adj*

5. **hierarchy** *n.* A system of levels that places people high or low according to their importance

Starting as a lowly private, Burt Jones gradually rose through the **hierarchy** of the army.

Usage tips *Hierarchy* is often followed by an *of* phrase.

Parts of speech hierarchical *adj*, hierarchically *adv*

6. **in the trenches** *adv'l.* In the middle of the hardest fighting or work

With their unrealistic view of this war, our generals don't know what things are like out **in the trenches**.

Usage tips Creates an image of soldiers fighting in a long, dug-out place in the battlefield.

7. **mobilize** *v.* To put members of a group into motion

After a terrible storm, the governor **mobilized** the National Guard to rescue victims.

Parts of speech mobilization *n*

8. **rank** *v.* To put into a many-leveled order, depending on importance or achievement

The Marines **ranked** Jim Hurst highest among all their officer candidates.

Parts of speech rank *n*

9. **ratio** *n.* The relationship of one number or amount to another

Military analysts say that the **ratio** of attackers to defenders in a battle should be about three to one for the attackers to win.

Usage tips *Ratio* is very often followed by an *of . . . to* structure.

10. **strategic** *adj.* Related to long-term plans for achieving a goal

The United States has formed **strategic** friendships with Tajikistan and Mongolia to have Central Asian bases in the future.

Usage tips *Strategic* is often used with nouns for plans.

Parts of speech strategy *n*, strategize *v*, strategically *adv*

TOEFL Prep 17-1 **Find the word or phrase that is closest in meaning to the opposite of each word or phrase in the left-hand column. Write the letter in the blank.**

________	1. cease	(a) stay still
________	2. artillery	(b) not in the fighting
________	3. mobilize	(c) continue
________	4. battle	(d) make peace
________	5. in the trenches	(e) light guns

TOEFL Prep 17-2 **Choose the word from the list that is closest in meaning to the underlined part of each sentence. Write it in the blank.**

allegiance   hierarchy   ranked   rati   strategy

__________ 1. Destruction of the enemy's radar defenses was rated very high in the plan of attack.

__________ 2. The president's constant mistakes weakened the army's loyalty to him.

__________ 3. Eventually, Gordon reached the highest level in the military's system of positions, that of five-star general.

__________ 4. The planet Mercury is so small that the proportion of its volume to Earth's is only about 1 to 20.

__________ 5. While other officers worried about day-to-day operations, General Helvetski kept his eye on long-term plans.

TOEFL Success 17 **Read the passage to review the vocabulary you have learned. Answer the questions that follow.**

Until a century ago, military medicine was poor at *battling* disease. The *ratio* of soldiers killed by diseases to those killed in combat was probably at least two to one. For *strategic*

TOEFL Prep 17-1 1. c 2. e 3. a 4. d 5. b
TOEFL Prep 17-2 1. ranked 2. allegiance 3. hierarchy 4. ratio 5. strategy

reasons, military camps were often set up near a body of water. This gave some protection from enemy *artillery*, but it exposed soldiers to disease-carrying mosquitoes. Mosquitoes also plagued troops *in the trenches*. Low-*ranking* troops suffered the most. Officers who were advanced enough in the *hierarchy* slept in separate tents on high ground.

The long-held belief that disease resulted from evil spirits or bad air eventually *ceased* to rule military medicine. The germ theory *mobilized* actual science against disease. General George Washington ordered that his men be vaccinated against smallpox. Their *allegiance* to him can be measured by the fact that they obeyed, for Washington's doctors used the actual smallpox virus, not the safer vaccination that Edward Jenner would introduce in 1798.

Bonus Structure **Until a century ago** indicates that the condition to be described stopped about 100 years ago.

1. Which sentence best expresses the essential information of this passage?
   a. Army officers were far healthier than common foot soldiers.
   b. For a long time, a soldier was more likely to die of disease than in battle.
   c. Armies should camp on dry ground, not near water.
   d. Diseases are caused by viruses and spread by mosquitoes.

2. Why does the author mention that military camps were often set up near water?
   a. to explain why soldiers were not usually killed by artillery
   b. to show that officers and men did not mix
   c. to explain how soldiers came into contact with disease-carrying mosquitoes
   d. to show that water was valuable in treating "camp fever"

TOEFL Success 17 1. b 2. c

社会
レッスン17

軍事作戦

意味と例文

1 allegiance（名詞） 忠誠

例文訳 母国に対する私の忠誠は、その主義への敬意に基づいている。

ヒント 使い方 allegiance は一般的に to 不定詞句を後ろに伴う。

---

2 artillery（名詞） （強力な砲弾を発射する）大型の銃／（そのような銃を扱う）軍隊

例文訳 大砲による集中砲撃により、その都市の厚い壁は数秒で破壊された。

第47砲兵隊は市の中心部に野営する反乱軍を砲撃した。

ヒント 使い方 軍隊の一部を意味する場合、artillery は複数形になることがある。

---

3 battle（動詞） 対抗して戦う

例文訳 ベトミン（ベトナム独立同盟会）は、1954年にディエンビエンフーでフランス軍と2カ月間近く戦った。

関連語 battle（名詞）戦闘

---

4 cease（動詞） 終わる

例文訳 雷が止んだ後でも稲妻は続いた。

ヒント 使い方 cease は公式発表で使われる言葉で、日常会話では通常は使わない。

関連語 cessation（名詞）休止、ceaseless（形容詞）絶え間ない

---

5 hierarchy（名詞） （人をその重要度に応じて高く、または低く位置づける）階級の制度

例文訳 バート・ジョーンズは下級の2等兵としてスタートし、軍隊の階級制をだんだんと上っていった。

ヒント 使い方 hierarchy は後ろに of 句を伴うことが多い。

関連語 hierarchical（形容詞）階級制の、階層制の、hierarchically（副詞）階層的に

---

6 in the trenches（副詞句）最も困難な戦いや仕事の真っただ中に

例文訳 わが軍の将官たちは、この戦争に対して非現実的な見解を持っていて、前線の状況をわかっていない。

ヒント 使い方 この表現は、戦場の長い塹壕で戦う兵士たちのイメージをもたらす。

---

7 mobilize（動詞）ある集団のメンバーを動かす

例文訳 ひどい嵐の後、知事は被災者を救助するために州兵を動員した。

関連語 mobilization（名詞）動員

---

8 rank（動詞）（重要度や実績に応じて）何段階もの等級づけをする

例文訳 海兵隊は、ジム・ハーストを全士官候補生の中で最も高い階級にした。

関連語 rank（名詞）階級

---

9 ratio（名詞）ある数字や量と他の数字や量との関係（比率）

例文訳 軍事アナリストによると、戦闘において攻撃側が勝つためには、攻撃側対防御側の比率は約３対１であるべきだという。

ヒント 使い方 ratio の後には、「of ～ to」の構造が続くことが非常に多い。

---

10 strategic（形容詞）（目標達成のための）長期的な計画に関連している

例文訳 米国は将来中央アジアに基地を持つために、タジキスタンやモンゴルと戦略的な友好関係を結んでいる。

ヒント 使い方 strategic は計画を表す名詞と一緒に使われることが多い。

関連語 strategy（名詞）戦略、strategize（動詞）戦略を立てる、strategically（副詞）戦略的に

TOEFL プレップ 17−1

左列の各単語の反対語に最も近い意味の単語や語句を選び、空欄にそのアルファベットを書きこみなさい。

________	1. cease	(a) 動かないでいる
________	2. artillery	(b) 戦闘中ではない
________	3. mobilize	(c) 続く
________	4. battle	(d) 和解する
________	5. in the trenches	(e) 軽い銃

TOEFL プレップ 17−2

各文の下線部に最も近い意味を持つ単語をリストから選び、空欄に記入しなさい。

allegiance　hierarchy　ranked　ratio　strategy

________ 1. 敵のレーダー防御を破壊することは、攻撃計画の中で非常に高く<u>位置づけられていた</u>。

________ 2. 大統領が失敗を繰り返すことで、軍の大統領への<u>忠誠</u>は薄れた。

________ 3. 最終的にゴードンは、軍の<u>地位制度</u>における最高位にあたる、五つ星将軍の階級に達した。

________ 4. 水星は非常に小さく、水星の体積対地球の体積の<u>割合</u>はわずか1対20程度である。

________ 5. 他の将校たちが日々の業務に気を揉む一方で、ヘルヴェツキ将軍は<u>長期的な計画</u>に目を配っていた。

TOEFL サクセス 17

文章を読んで学んだ語彙を復習します。後に続く質問に答えなさい。

［例文訳］

1世紀前まで、軍の医療は病気との戦いが苦手だった。病気で死んだ兵士と戦闘で死んだ兵士の比率は、おそらく少なくとも2対1であった。戦略上の理由から、軍の野営地はしばしば水域の近くに設置された。これにより、敵の大砲からはある程度守られたが、兵士は病気を媒介する蚊にさらされた。蚊は、前線にいる兵士たちも悩ませた。最も被害を受けたのは下級兵たちであった。階級が十分に高い将校たちは、高台で個別のテントで寝ていた。

長い間悪霊や悪い空気のせいで病気になると信じられていたが、そういう考えは、ついに軍隊の医療を支配するものではなくなった。病原菌の理論が、病気に対して実際の科学を動員したのだ。ジョージ・ワシントン司令官は、部下に天然痘の予防接種を受けるように命じた。部下たちがそれに従ったという事実によって、彼らのワシントンへの忠誠心を推し量ることができる。このときに使用されたのは、1798年にエドワード・ジェンナーが導入した、より安全なワクチンではなく、実際の天然痘ウイルスだったからだ。

読解のポイント Until a century ago は、続いて説明される状態が約100年前に終わったことを示している。

1 この文章の重要な情報を最もよく表しているのはどの文か？

a. 陸軍将校は、一般の歩兵に比べてはるかに健康であった。
b. 長い間、兵士は戦闘で死ぬよりも病気で死ぬことのほうが多かった。
c. 軍隊は水辺ではなく、乾いた土地で野営するべきである。
d. 病気はウイルスによって引き起こされ、蚊によって広がる。

2 なぜ筆者は、軍の野営地が水辺に設置されることが多いと言っているのか？

a. 兵士がたいていの場合大砲で殺されない理由を説明するため。
b. 将校と兵士は混ざらないことを示すため。
c. 兵士が病気を運ぶ蚊とどのように接触したかを説明するため。
d. 「キャンプ熱」の治療には水が有益だったことを示すため。

War and Conquest

Target Words

1. annex
2. apex
3. collapse
4. conquest
5. devise
6. invasive
7. prevailing
8. resist
9. severely
10. violation

Definitions and Samples

1. annex *v.* To make something (usually land) part of another unit

Bardstown grew by **annexing** several farms at the north edge of town.

Parts of speech annexation *n*, annex *n*

2. apex *n.* The highest point

Gregory knew that his running skills had to be at their **apex** during the tournament.

Usage tips *Apex* is often used to describe the high point of someone's abilities.

3. collapse *v.* To fall down, usually because of weakness

Parts of speech collapse *n*, collapsible *adj*

4. conquest *n.* A takeover by force or continued effort

The first recorded **conquest** of Mt. Everest was by Tensing Norgay and Sir Edmund Hilary.

Usage tips *Conquest* is usually followed by an *of* phrase.

Parts of speech conquer *v*

5. devise *v.* To find an original way to make an object or a plan

The soldiers **devised** a way to cross the river into enemy territory without being seen.

Parts of speech device *n*

6. **invasive** *adj.* Aggressively entering into someone else's territory
Surgery with a laser is less **invasive** than surgery with a knife or scalpel.
Parts of speech invade *v*, invasion *n*, invader *n*

7. **prevailing** *adj.* Strongest or most common
The **prevailing** attitude among our neighbors is to be friendly but not too friendly.
Parts of speech prevail *v*, prevalence *n*

8. **resist** *v.* To refuse to give in to a strong force or desire
Although many native nations **resisted**, the U.S. government eventually took over almost all Indian land.
Parts of speech resistance *n*, resistant *adj*

9. **severely** *adv.* Harshly; extremely
Commanders **severely** punished any soldier who criticized the battle plan.
Parts of speech severity *n*, severe *adj*

10. **violation** *n.* An action that breaks a law or agreement; mistreatment of something that deserves respect
The army's testing of new weapons was a **violation** of the cease-fire agreement.
The sculptures at Mt. Rushmore may be a **violation** of sacred Indian land.
Usage tips *Violation* is often followed by an *of* phrase.
Parts of speech violate *v*, violator *n*

TOEFL Prep 18-1 **Find the word or phrase that is closest in meaning to each word in the left-hand column. Write the letter in the blank.**

______	1. severely	(a) invent
______	2. prevailing	(b) fall down
______	3. devise	(c) add on
______	4. collapse	(d) extremely
______	5. annex	(e) most common

TOEFL Prep 18-2 **Circle the word that best completes each sentence.**

1. The judge ruled that Harry was guilty of a (violation / conquest) of the seat-belt law.
2. Because Dalmatia was protected by high mountains, the empire could not (apex / annex) it.
3. We have to (conquest / devise) a way to fight this new disease.
4. Several armed groups joined together to (resist / collapse) the foreign invaders.
5. The (prevailing / invasive) belief held that the enemy's peace moves were not sincere.

TOEFL Success 18 **Read the passage to review the vocabulary you have learned. Answer the questions that follow.**

The Roman *conquest* of North Africa is, in the *prevailing* view, less interesting than Rome's European adventures. In truth, one of the first lands Rome *annexed* beyond the Italian peninsula was the area around Carthage in North Africa. Carthage and Rome had been in conflict (called the Punic Wars) since 264 BCE for control of trade along the Mediterranean coast. In 202 BCE, during the Second Punic

---

TOEFL Prep 18-1 1. d 2. e 3. a 4. b 5. c
TOEFL Prep 18-2 1. violation 2. annex 3. devise 4. resist 5. prevailing

War, the Carthaginian general Hannibal *devised* a clever plan, in *violation* of most military wisdom, to march through the high Alps to attack the Roman heartland. The cold weather and steep terrain *severely* stressed Hannibal's forces, many of whom rode elephants. The Romans *resisted* Hannibal's attacks, and his bold *invasion* force *collapsed*. **In the end**, Rome finished off Carthage in the Third Punic War (149–146 BCE). At its *apex* in 117 CE, Rome controlled all of North Africa and territories from the Persian Gulf to Britain.

Bonus Structure **In the end** introduces the last stage of a long process.

1. Which sentence best expresses the essential information of this passage?
   a. Romans were very successful at resisting invaders.
   b. Hannibal tried crossing the Alps on elephants to invade Rome.
   c. Rome and Carthage fought three wars, known as the Punic Wars.
   d. One of Rome's first overseas conquests was of the North African state of Carthage.

2. The author of this passage believes that Hannibal's attack on Rome by crossing the Alps was______.
   a. not what most military commanders would do
   b. exactly what the Roman army used to do
   c. cruel to elephants
   d. impractical because elephants can't cross mountains

TOEFL Success 18 1. d 2. a

社会
レッスン18

戦争と征服

意味と例文

1 annex （動詞） あるもの（通常は土地）を他の（場所の）一部にする

例文訳 バーズタウンは、町の北端にあるいくつかの農場を併合して発展した。

関連語 annexation（名詞）併合、annex（名詞）建て増し、付帯物

2 apex （名詞） 頂点

例文訳 グレゴリーは、大会中に自分の走力が最高の状態でなければならないとわかっていた。

ヒント 使い方 apex は、人の能力の最高点を表すのによく使われる。

3 collapse （動詞） （通常は弱さが原因で）崩れ落ちる

関連語 collapse（名詞）崩壊、collapsible（形容詞）折りたためる

4 conquest （名詞） （力や継続的な努力によって）奪い取ること

例文訳 記録に残る初めてのエベレスト山征服は、テンジン・ノルゲイとエドモンド・ヒラリー卿によるものだった。

ヒント 使い方 conquest は通常 of 句を後ろに伴う。

関連語 conquer（動詞）征服する

5 devise （動詞） （ものや計画をつくりだすための）独自の方法を見つける

例文訳 兵士たちは、姿を見られずに川を渡って敵の領地に入る方法を考え出した。

関連語 device（名詞）装置

6 invasive（形容詞）（他人の領域に）積極的に入り込んでいる

例文訳 レーザーを使った手術は、ナイフやメスを使った手術ほど侵襲的ではない。

関連語 invade（動詞）侵入する、侵略する、invasion（名詞）侵入、侵略、invader（名詞）侵入者、侵略者

7 prevailing（形容詞）最も強い、または最も一般的な

例文訳 私たちの近所の人の間で最もよく見られる態度は、親しみはあるが、馴れ馴れしすぎないというものだ。

関連語 prevail（動詞）普及する、打ち勝つ、prevalence（名詞）普及、流行

8 resist（動詞）（強い力や願望に）屈することを拒む

例文訳 多くの先住民族が抵抗したにもかかわらず、最終的には米国政府は先住民のほとんどの土地を奪った。

関連語 resistance（名詞）抵抗、resistant（形容詞）抵抗する

9 severely（副詞）厳しく／極端に

例文訳 指揮官たちは、その戦闘計画を批判する兵士は誰であっても厳しく罰した。

関連語 severity（名詞）厳格さ、severe（形容詞）厳しい

10 violation（名詞）（法律や協定に）違反する行為／（尊重されるべきものへの）不当な扱い

例文訳 軍隊による新兵器の実験は停戦協定違反だった。
ラシュモア山の彫像は、アメリカ先住民の神聖な土地の侵害と言えるかもしれない。

ヒント 使い方 violation は、しばしば後ろに of 句を伴う。

関連語 violate（動詞）違反する、violator（名詞）違反者

TOEFL プレップ 18－1

左列の各単語に最も近い意味の単語や語句を選び、空欄にそのアルファベットを書きなさい。

＿＿＿＿＿＿	1. severely	(a) 発明する
＿＿＿＿＿＿	2. prevailing	(b) 崩れ落ちる
＿＿＿＿＿＿	3. devise	(c) 付け足す
＿＿＿＿＿＿	4. colapse	(d) 極端に
＿＿＿＿＿＿	5. annex	(e) 最も一般的な

TOEFL プレップ 18－2

各文を完成させるのに最も適した単語を丸で囲みなさい。

1 その裁判官は、ハリーがシートベルト着用に関する法律（違反／征服）で有罪であると裁決した。

2 ダルマチアは高い山々に守られていたので、帝国はその地域を（頂点／併合）できなかった。

3 私たちは、この新しい病気と戦う方法を（征服／考案）しなければならない。

4 いくつかの武装グループが、外国の侵略者に（抵抗する／崩壊する）ため団結した。

5 敵の平和的な動きは心からのものではないというのが、（最も一般的な／侵略的な）意見だった。

TOEFL サクセス 18

文章を読んで学んだ語彙を復習します。後に続く質問に答えなさい。

[例文訳]

古代ローマ帝国の北アフリカ征服は、一般的な見方では、ローマ帝国のヨーロッパでの冒険ほど面白いものではない。実は、ローマ帝国がイタリア半島を越えて最初に併合した土地の１つが、北アフリカのカルタゴ周辺の地域であった。カルタゴとローマは紀元前 264 年から地中海沿岸の交易の支配権をめぐって争っていた（ポエニ戦争と呼ばれている）。第二次ポエニ戦争中の紀元前202年、カルタゴの将軍ハンニバルは、大方の軍事的常識を破り、アルプス山脈を越えて進軍し、ローマの中心地を攻撃するという巧妙な計画を考えだした。寒冷な気候と険しい地形は、その多くが象に乗っていたハンニバル軍に、極端な緊張を与えた。ローマ人はハンニバルの攻撃に抵抗し、彼の大胆な侵略軍は崩壊した。結局、ローマ帝国は第三次ポエニ戦争（紀元前149～146年）でカルタゴにとどめをさした。117年にその頂点に達したローマ帝国は、北アフリカ全域とペルシャ湾からイギリスまでの領土を支配した。

読解のポイント In the end **は、長いプロセスの最終段階を示す。**

1　この文章の重要な情報を最もよく表しているのはどの文か？

a. ローマ人は侵略者に抵抗することに非常に成功していた。

b. ハンニバルはローマを侵略するために象でアルプス越えを試みた。

c. ローマとカルタゴは、ポエニ戦争として知られる3つの戦争を戦った。

d. ローマの最初の海外征服の1つは、北アフリカのカルタゴであった。

2　この文章の筆者は、ハンニバルがアルプスを越えてローマを攻撃したことをどのように考えているか？

a. ほとんどの軍司令官がするようなことではない。

b. まさにローマ軍がかつてしていたことである。

c. 象にとって残酷なことだ。

d. 象は山を越えられないので、非現実的だ。

History

Target Words

1. chronologically	6. diminish
2. coincide	7. longitude
3. consequence	8. milieu
4. core	9. Orwellian
5. deny	10. reconciliation

Definitions and Samples

1. **chronologically** *adv.* In order according to time
Allen's book is arranged **chronologically**, from the First Crusade in 1095 to the fall of Granada in 1492.
Usage tips *Chronologically* is often used with *arranged*, *organized*, *listed*, or some other word for order.
Parts of speech chronology *n*, chronological *adj*

2. **coincide** *v.* Happen or exist at the same time
The Viking attacks on western Europe **coincided** with an abnormally warm period in the Earth's climate.
Usage tips *Coincide* is often followed by a *with* phrase.
Parts of speech coincidence *n*, coincidental *adj*, coincidentally *adv*

3. **consequence** *n.* A result, often one much later in time than the cause
One **consequence** of global warming may be the flooding of low-lying islands.
Usage tips *Consequence* usually implies something negative or serious about the result.
Parts of speech consequent *adj*, consequently *adv*

4. **core** *n.* an area or object at the center
The **core** of India's film industry is in Bombay, where all but a few film studios are located.
Usage tips *Core* is often followed by another noun (e.g., *core principle*) or by an *of* phrase.

5. **deny** *v.* Say that something is not true

Movie star Allen Butcher **denied** that he and the Princess of Denmark were getting married.

Usage tips *Deny* is often followed by the *-ing* form of a verb or by a *that* clause.

Parts of speech denial *n*, deniably *adv*

6. **diminish** *v.* Make something smaller or weaker; become smaller or weaker

The Protestant Reformation **diminished** the power of the Roman Catholic Pope.

Mr. Partridge's influence in the company **diminished** after he relocated to a branch office.

7. **longitude** *n.* A system of imaginary lines running from north to south along the Earth's surface, where each line is numbered from 0° to 180° west or east

The prime meridian, a line running through Greenwich, England, is marked as 0° **longitude**.

Parts of speech longitudinal *adj*, longitudinally *adv*

8. **milieu** *n.* General environment or surroundings

Many Vietnam veterans did not feel comfortable in the antiwar social **milieu** of the 1970s.

9. **Orwellian** *adj.* Frightening and overcontrolled by a government that interferes in nearly every aspect of personal life

Biometric devices like eye-scanners allow an **Orwellian** level of government knowledge about everyone's location.

Usage tips *Orwellian* comes from George Orwell, a British author of the 20th century who wrote a novel called *1984* about a grim future of government control.

10. **reconciliation** *n.* Coming back together peacefully after having been enemies

South Africa avoided a bloodbath after apartheid by setting up a Truth and **Reconciliation** Commission.

Parts of speech reconcile *v*, reconciliatory *adj*

TOEFL Prep 19-1 **Find the word or phrase that is closest in meaning to each word in the left-hand column. Write the letter in the blank.**

______	1. deny	(a) say something isn't true
______	2. chronologically	(b) an end to being enemies
______	3. consequence	(c) middle
______	4. reconciliation	(d) in the order in which events happened
______	5. core	(e) result

TOEFL Prep 19-2 **Circle the word that best completes each sentence.**

1. When a nation becomes unwilling to listen to its allies, its international influence will (deny / diminish).
2. The release of many new movies (coincides / consequences) with the start of the holiday period.
3. The (core / milieu) of Roman power shifted to Constantinople after Rome was attacked repeatedly by armies from the north.
4. As our government becomes better at monitoring us, an (Orwellian / coincidental) future awaits us.
5. As you move directly east from one point on the Earth to another, your (longitude / chronology) changes.

TOEFL Success 19 **Read the passage to review the vocabulary you have learned. Answer the questions that follow.**

Revisionist history promotes a new view of *chronological* events, usually for political purposes. Radical revisionists *diminish* the credibility of a previous view and may even *deny* that certain events happened at all. Some revisionist Asian historians have ignored long-standing conflicts among native

---

TOEFL Prep 19-1 1. a 2. d 3. e 4. b 5. c
TOEFL Prep 19-2 1. diminish 2. coincides 3. core 4. Orwellian 5. longitude

peoples and have explained Asia's conflicts as a *consequence* of colonialism and its class-oriented cultural *milieu*. **Good motives** among the revisionists—to promote *reconciliation* among traditional rivals—**don't excuse bad history**. History is valuable only if its stories *coincide* with verifiable facts. From far away, an observer may see clearly that a given conflict had nothing to do with colonialism and a lot to do with 1,000-year-old rivalries. But this is not likely to matter much to a confirmed revisionist historian. At its *core*, revisionism—by the government in particular—is an *Orwellian* exercise in thought control, not honest science.

Bonus Structure **Good motives don't excuse bad history.** Even though revisionists are trying to achieve a good social goal, they shouldn't distort history to do so.

1. Which sentence best expresses the essential information of this passage?
   a. Historians constantly revise history in the light of new facts.
   b. Revisionist history is less concerned with accuracy than with promoting a point of view.
   c. A new way of studying history, revisionism, has been very successful in Asia.
   d. Revisionist history is the only way to accurately relate events.

2. Why does the author of this reading mention Asia?
   a. because it offers an example of attempts at revisionist history
   b. because a civil war occurred between revisionists and others
   c. because it is the birthplace of revisionist history
   d. because it was colonized by Europeans and needs a revisionist history

TOEFL Success 19 1. b 2. a

社会
レッスン 19

歴史

意味と例文

1 chronologically（副詞） 時系列で見ると

例文訳 アレンの本は、1095年の第一回十字軍から1492年のグラナダ陥落まで年代順に並べられている。

ヒント 使い方 chronologicallyは、arranged、organized、listedなど順序を表す語と一緒に使われることが多い。

関連語 chronology（名詞）年表、年代学、chronological（形容詞）年代順の

---

2 coincide（動詞） 同時に起こる、または存在する

例文訳 バイキングによる西ヨーロッパ攻撃は、地球の気候が異常に温暖だった時期と一致していた。

ヒント 使い方 coincideは後ろにwith句を伴うことが多い。

関連語 coincidence（名詞）偶然の一致、coincidental（形容詞）（偶然に）一致する、coincidentally（副詞）（偶然に）一致して

---

3 consequence（名詞） （多くの場合、原因よりもはるかに後の）結果

例文訳 地球温暖化の結果的影響の1つとして、低地の島々が洪水に見舞われる可能性がある。

ヒント 使い方 consequenceは、通常、その結果についての否定的な、または深刻なことを意味する。

関連語 consequent（形容詞）結果として起こる、consequently（副詞）その結果

---

4 core（名詞） 中心となる範囲や物体

例文訳 インドの映画産業の中心はボンベイにあり、いくつかを除いてほぼすべての映画スタジオがそこにある。

ヒント 使い方 coreの後には、他の名詞（例：core principle）、またはof句が続くことが多い。

---

5 deny（動詞） （あることが）真実ではないと言う

例文訳 映画スターのアレン・ブッチャーは、デンマーク王女と結婚することを否定した。

 使い方　denyの後には、動詞の〜ing形またはthat節が続くことが多い。

関連語　denial（名詞）否定、deniably（副詞）否定的に

6 diminish（動詞）（あるものを）小さくまたは弱くする／小さくまたは弱くなる

例文訳　プロテスタントの宗教改革は、カトリック教会のローマ教皇の力を弱めた。
パートリッジ氏の会社での影響力は、彼が支店に異動した後に弱まった。

7 longitude（名詞）地球の表面に沿って北から南に走る仮想の線のことで、各線には西または東に0°から180°までの数が付けられている（経度）

例文訳　本初子午線はイギリスのグリニッジを通る線で、経度0°と示されている。

関連語　longitudinal（形容詞）経度の、縦の、長期的な、longitudinally（副詞）縦に、長期的に

8 milieu（名詞）一般的な環境や周囲の状況

例文訳　多くのベトナム帰還兵は、1970年代の反戦的な社会状況のなかで居心地がよくなかった。

9 Orwellian（形容詞）個人の生活のほぼすべての局面に干渉してくる政府に過剰に管理されている恐ろしい様子

例文訳　アイ・スキャナーのような生体測定装置によって、政府はすべての人の位置情報をオーウェルの小説並みに知ることができるようになる。

ヒント 使い方　Orwellianという言葉は、20世紀のイギリス人作家、ジョージ・オーウェルに由来する。彼は『1984』という政府による統制がもたらす暗い未来についての小説を書いた。

10 reconciliation（名詞）（敵対していた後で）平和的に関係性が元に戻ること

例文訳　南アフリカは、「真実和解委員会」を設置することでアパルトヘイト後の大殺りくを回避した。

関連語　reconcile（動詞）和解させる、reconciliatory（形容詞）和解的な

TOEFL プレップ 19-1

左列の各単語に最も近い意味の単語や語句を選び、空欄にそのアルファベットを書きなさい。

______	1. deny	(a) あることを真実ではないと言う
______	2. chronologically	(b) 敵であることの終わり
______	3. consequence	(c) 中心
______	4. reconciliation	(d) 出来事が起こった順に
______	5. core	(e) 結果

TOEFL プレップ 19-2

各文を完成させるのに最も適した単語を丸で囲みなさい。

1 ある国が、同盟国の意見を聞こうとしなくなると、その国の国際的な影響力は（否定する／弱まる）だろう。

2 多くの新作映画の公開は、休暇の時期の始まりと（一致する／結果）。

3 ローマが北からの軍隊に何度も攻撃された後、ローマ帝国の権力の（中核／環境）はコンスタンティノープルに移った。

4 政府が私たちを監視することに長けてくると、（オーウェル風の／偶然に一致する）未来が待っている。

5 地球上のある地点から別の地点に向かって東にまっすぐ移動すると、（経度／年表）が変わる。

TOEFL サクセス 19

文章を読んで学んだ語彙を復習します。後に続く質問に答えなさい。

[例文訳]

歴史修正主義は、時系列の出来事に対して新しい見方を促すもので、通常政治的な目的を持つ。急進的な修正主義者は、従来の見方の信頼性を低下させ、ある出来事が起こったこと自体を否定することさえある。アジアの歴史修正主義者の中には、その国の民族間の長年の紛争を無視して、アジアの紛争を、植民地主義とその階級志向の文化的環境の結果であると説明する者がいる。そのような歴史修正主義者には、伝統的な敵対関係の和解を進めるという良い動機があるが、それは悪い歴史を免責するものではない。歴史は、その物語が検証可能な事実と一致するときのみ価値がある。遠くから見れば、特定の紛争は植民地主義とは無関係であり、1,000年前からの対立が大きく関係しているということがはっきりとわかるかもしれない。しかし、このことは確固たる歴史修正主義者にとっては、あまり重要ではないだろう。その核心において歴史修正主義は、特に政府によるものの場合、オーウェル的な思想統制の実践であり、誠実な科学ではない。

読解のポイント **「良い動機は悪い歴史を免責するものではない」これは、たとえ修正主義者が社会的に良い目標を達成しようとしているとしても、彼らは歴史を歪曲すべきではないという意味。**

1　この文章の重要な情報を最もよく表しているのはどの文か？

a. 歴史家は、新しい事実に照らし合わせて、常に歴史を修正する。

b. 歴史修正主義は、正確さよりも、考え方を広めることを重視する。

c. 歴史研究の新しい方法である修正主義は、アジアで大きな成功を収めている。

d. 歴史修正主義は、出来事を正確に関連づける唯一の方法である。

2　この文章の筆者がアジアに言及しているのはなぜか？

a. アジアは歴史修正主義の試みの一例を示しているから。

b. 修正主義者と他の人々の間で内戦が起こったから。

c. アジアは歴史修正主義の発祥の地だから。

d. アジアはヨーロッパ人によって植民地化され、歴史修正主義を必要としているから。

Financial Systems

Target Words

1. allocate
2. commodity
3. decline
4. equity
5. inflation
6. net
7. per capita
8. regulate
9. subsidy
10. tangible

Definitions and Samples

1. **allocate** *v.* To give out different amounts for different purposes

The budget **allocates** $58 billion to the military and only about $2 billion to education.

Usage tips Things that can be *allocated* are things that can be "spent"—money, time, energy, etc.

Parts of speech allocation *n*, allocable *adj*

2. **commodity** *n.* A thing that can be bought and sold, such as grain, oil, or wood

Tulip bulbs were one of the most valuable **commodities** in seventeenth-century Holland.

Usage tips A thing is called a *commodity* only in the context of buying or selling it.

3. **decline** *v.* To decrease in power or amount

America's railroads **declined** because the automobile dominated American life.

Parts of speech decline *n*

4. **equity** *n.* The value of one's share in an investment

Barnard's **equity** in the business was one-third, or about $350,000.

Usage tips In this meaning, *equity* is always singular and usually followed by an *in* phrase.

5. inflation *n.* A situation in which prices for many items rise quite fast

During the rapid **inflation** of the 1970s, prices for food and fuel sometimes rose 20 percent in a single month.

Parts of speech inflate *v*, inflationary *adj*

6. net *adj.* After all costs have been subtracted from an amount

My gross salary is around $46,000, but my **net** pay is closer to $38,000.

Parts of speech net *v*, net *n*

7. per capita *adv.* For each person

Research shows we're likely to sell 15 light bulbs **per capita** per year in medium-sized cities.

Parts of speech per capita *adj*

8. regulate *v.* Control according to a set of rules

Trading on the New York Stock Exchange is **regulated** by officials of the exchange and by federal law.

Parts of speech regulation *n*, regulatory *adj*, regulator *n*

9. subsidy *n.* Money given by a government or other organization to support an activity

Federal **subsidies** to grain farmers have helped them stay in business despite three years of bad weather.

Parts of speech subsidize *v*

10. tangible *adj.* Obviously real because it can be seen, touched, or otherwise observed

One **tangible** benefit of putting electrical cables underground is a clearer view of the sky.

TOEFL Prep 20-1 **Cross out the one word or phrase that doesn't fit into each of the lists.**

1. things that can be allocated
   money　　time　　temperature　　attention
2. kinds of commodities
   oil　　sadness　　corn　　meat
3. tangible things
   fairness　　a road　　trees　　money
4. things you can have equity in
   a company　　a house　　a child　　a racehorse

TOEFL Prep 20-2 **Circle the word that best completes each sentence.**

1. Buy a car now, before (equity / inflation) drives the price up.
2. Most investors make a mistake. During a stock-market (decline / subsidy) they get frightened and sell.
3. The government is giving a (regulation / subsidy) to tobacco farmers so they can compete with foreign producers.
4. Cortecal Inc. estimates that it spends $80 (per capita / net) on its annual picnic and on its New Year party for the company's 1,300 employees.
5. I think that artificial "holidays" like Valentine's Day or Secretary's Day are just an attempt to turn private feelings into a(n) (commodity / equity).

TOEFL Success 20 **Read the passage to review the vocabulary you have learned. Answer the questions that follow.**

The great unsettled question of economics is: "How much should the government *regulate* business?" Conservatives

TOEFL Prep 20-1　1. temperature　2. sadness　3. fairness　4. a child
TOEFL Prep 20-2　1. inflation　2. decline　3. subsidy　4. per capita　5. commodity

generally argue for a *decline* in government involvement, but they favor certain *subsidies* to farmers, steelmakers, or airplane manufacturers. Some conservatives also see no conflict between their small-government views and their eagerness for the government to *allocate* more money for roads into national forests. The *net* result of these incursions into national forests is a *tangible* infrastructure that helps some companies but not the public. Publicly owned trees, land, and oil become *commodities* from which a few private companies (many owned by small-government conservatives) profit. No *per capita* benefit goes to the American people, **aside perhaps from** the brief anti-*inflation* effect that comes with new oil exploration.

Bonus Structure **Aside perhaps from** means "maybe except for."

1. What is the main idea of this reading?
   a. Conservatives have tried to keep others from expanding government regulations.
   b. Even though conservatives say they want to limit government involvement in business, they actually do often favor it.
   c. There are several views about the proper role for government in business.
   d. Small-government conservatives want the government to allocate a certain amount of federal money per capita to help all Americans.

2. Which of the following does the author claim?
   a. Industries will become subsidies.
   b. Oil exploration causes inflation.
   c. Some elements of nature will become commodities.
   d. Infrastructure will be made of trees, oil, and land.

TOEFL Success 20 1. b 2. c

お金
レッスン 20

金融システム

意味と例文

1 allocate（動詞） （目的別に）異なる量を配る

例文訳 その予算では、軍事費に580億ドルが割り当てられ、教育費には約20億ドルしか割り当てられていない。

ヒント 使い方 割り当てられる（allocated）ものとは、お金、時間、エネルギーなど、「費やす」ことができるもの。

関連語 allocation（名詞）割り当て、allocable（形容詞）割り当て可能な

2 commodity（名詞） （穀物や石油、木材など）売買できるもの

例文訳 チューリップの球根は、17世紀のオランダでは最も価値のある商品の1つだった。

ヒント 使い方 あるものがcommodityと呼ばれるのは、それを売買するという文脈においてのみである。

3 decline（動詞） （力や量が）減少する

例文訳 自動車が米国人の生活を支配するようになったため、米国の鉄道は衰退した。

関連語 decline（名詞）減少、衰え

4 equity（名詞） （投資における）取り分の価値

例文訳 そのビジネスにおけるバーナードの持ち分は3分の1、つまり約35万ドルだった。

ヒント 使い方 この意味では、equityは常に単数形で、通常は後ろにin句を伴う。

5 inflation（名詞） 多くの品の価格が急速に上昇する状況（インフレ）

例文訳 1970年代の急激なインフレの際には、食料品や燃料の価格が

たった1カ月で20%上昇したこともあった。

関連語 inflate（動詞）膨らませる、（物価などを）つりあげる、inflationary（形容詞）インフレーションの

6 net（形容詞） （ある金額から）すべての費用を差し引いた後の

例文訳 私の額面給与は約46,000ドルだが、正味の手取り給与は38,000ドルほどだ。

関連語 net（動詞）純益をもたらす、net（名詞）純益、最終結果

7 per capita（副詞） 1人当たり

例文訳 調査によると、中規模都市では年間1人当たり15個の電球が売れる見込みだ。

関連語 per capita（形容詞）1人当たりの

8 regulate（動詞） （一連の規則に従って）管理する

例文訳 ニューヨーク証券取引所での取引は、同取引所の職員と連邦法によって規制されている。

関連語 regulation（名詞）規制、regulatory（形容詞）取り締まる、regulator（名詞）規制者、調節器

9 subsidy（名詞） ある活動を支援するために政府や他の組織から与えられる資金（助成金）

例文訳 穀物農家への連邦補助金は、3年間の悪天候にもかかわらず彼らが経営を維持する助けになった。

関連語 subsidize（動詞）助成金を与える

10 tangible（形容詞） （目で見たり触ったり、それ以外の方法で気づくことができることから）明らかに実在する

例文訳 電線を地中に埋めることの明白な利点は、空が遮られずに見えるということだ。

TOEFL プレップ 20－1

それぞれの定義に当てはまらない単語や語句を１つ選び、線を引いて消しなさい。

1	割り当て可能なもの			
	お金	時間	温度	注意
2	商品の種類			
	石油	悲しみ	トウモロコシ	肉
3	実体のあるもの			
	公平性	道路	木	お金
4	持ち分を手にできるもの			
	会社	家	子ども	競走馬

TOEFL プレップ 20－2

各文を完成させるのに最も適した単語を丸で囲みなさい。

1 （持ち分／インフレ）で価格が上がる前に、今すぐ車を買おう。

2 ほとんどの投資家は間違いを犯す。株式市場の（下落／補助金）の最中に、怖くなって売るのだ。

3 政府はタバコ農家が外国の生産者と競争できるように（規制／補助金）を与えている。

4 コルテカル社では、1,300 人の従業員のための年に一度のピクニックと新年会に、（1 人当たり／純益）80 ドルを費やしていると見積もっている。

5 私は、バレンタインデーやセクレタリーズデーのような人工的な「祝日」は、個人的な感情を（商品／持ち分）に変えようとする試みに過ぎないと思う。

TOEFL サクセス 20

文章を読んで学んだ語彙を復習します。後に続く質問に答えなさい。

[例文訳]

経済学における大きな未解決問題は「政府はビジネスをどの程度規制すべきか」である。保守派の人たちは一般的に政府の関与の減少を主張しているが、農家や鉄鋼会社、航空機製造会社への特定の補助金には賛成している。また、保守派の中には、小さな政府という考え方と、国有林の中に道路を建造するために政府はより多くのお金を割り当ててほしいと思う気持ちになんの矛盾も感じない人もいる。このような国有林への侵入がもたらす最終結果として、有形のインフラが整備されるが、それは一部の企業のためのものであり、一般市民のためのものではない。公的に所有されている木々、土地、石油は、少数の民間企業（その多くは小さな政府主義の保守派が所有）が利益を得るための商品となる。米国民に届く1人当たりの利益は、新たな石油開発に伴う一時的なインフレ防止効果を除いて、おそらく何もない。

読解のポイント Aside perhaps from は「おそらく～を除いて」という意味。

1 この文章の主旨はどれか？

a. 保守派は、他の人々が政府の規制を拡大しないようにしてきた。

b. 保守派は、ビジネスへの政府の関与を制限したいと言っているにもかかわらず、実際にはそれを支持することが多い。

c. ビジネスにおける政府の適切な役割については、いくつかの考え方がある。

d. 小さな政府主義の保守派は、政府が米国民全体を助成するために国民1人当たりに一定額の連邦資金を割り当てることを望んでいる。

2 筆者の主張は次のうちどれか？

a. 産業が補助金制になるだろう。

b. 石油開発はインフレーションを引き起こす。

c. 自然界のいくつかの要素は商品になるだろう。

d. インフラは、木々や石油、土地でつくられるだろう。

Wealth and Social Class

Target Words

1. accumulate
2. affluence
3. elite
4. impoverish
5. luxury
6. nobility
7. prestige
8. privileged
9. prosper
10. working class

Definitions and Samples

1. **accumulate** *v.* To build up a large amount of something
Over several generations, the Hardington family **accumulated** vast wealth by buying and selling land.
Parts of speech accumulation *n*

2. **affluence** *n.* Wealth and the style of life that goes with it
Mohadzir grew up amid **affluence**, which poorly prepared him for his grad student days in crowded apartments with no servants.
Parts of speech affluent *adj*

3. **elite** *adj.* Belonging to a special, honored group
Messner is an **elite** climber who recently ascended an 8,000-meter mountain without extra oxygen.
Parts of speech elite *n*, elitist *adj*

4. **impoverish** *v.* To make a person or group poor
The collapse of the steel industry **impoverished** several counties in eastern Ohio.
Parts of speech impoverishment *n*

5. **luxury** *n.* Extreme comfort, beyond what anyone needs
Automakers try to give their cars an image of **luxury** by including extras like heated seats and sophisticated entertainment systems.
Parts of speech luxuriate *v*, luxurious *adj*

6. nobility *n.* A group of socially prominent people with special titles given by a king or queen, such as "duke" or "countess"

In the Middle Ages, the **nobility** supposedly followed a code that required them to take care of poorer people who lived near their estates.

Usage tips *Nobility* is used as a name for a group of distinguished people; it can also mean "a highly dignified form of behavior."

Parts of speech noble *n*, noble *adj*

7. prestige *n.* Honor and respect for being better than the average

The Grassleys enjoyed the **prestige** of living in the historic town, but they did not feel at home there.

Parts of speech prestigious *adj*

8. privileged *adj.* Able to enjoy special advantages because of one's position (usually because of being born into a wealthy or powerful family)

Despite his **privileged** position in one of America's most powerful families, the politician tried to portray himself as an ordinary person.

Parts of speech privilege *n*

9. prosper *v.* To do very well in one's business or personal life

Vargas **prospered** after finally patenting his new inventions.

Usage tips A person can prosper; so can a group, a company, or an area.

Parts of speech prosperity *n*, prosperous *adj*

10. working class *n.* People with low-paying (often unskilled) jobs who are not poor but who are not securely in the middle class

The Farrelly family, like other members of the **working class**, were proud of their jobs and did not want any handouts from charity or the government.

TOEFL Prep 21-1 Find the word or phrase that is closest in meaning to each word in the left-hand column. Write the letter in the blank. Note: Pay careful attention to small differences in meaning among the words.

______	1. impoverish	(a) enjoying special advantages
______	2. elite	(b) to succeed
______	3. prosper	(c) to make extremely poor
______	4. accumulate	(d) belonging to a small group with excellent achievements
______	5. privileged	(e) build up wealth

TOEFL Prep 21-2 Complete each sentence by filling in the blank with the best word or phrase from the list. Change the form of the word if necessary. Use each word only once.

affluence luxury nobility prestige working class

1. The ______ in the hotel was obvious from such features as solid-gold faucets and stairs made of Italian marble.
2. In a show of his extreme ______, Jim Lavich flew 1,500 people to the Bahamas for his wife's birthday party and ordered 300 casks of wine for them to drink.
3. The oldest and most respected furniture maker in western Michigan, VanEden Inc., earned its ______ by using good materials and listening to its customers.
4. France's ______ was dismantled after the royal family was killed and lesser aristocrats were jailed during the revolution.
5. In the United States, many ______ families do not have health insurance because their employers don't offer it.

TOEFL Success 21 Read the passage to review the vocabulary you have learned. Answer the questions that follow.

The United States may be a land of opportunity, but not truly

---

TOEFL Prep 21-1 1. c 2. d 3. b 4. e 5. a
TOEFL Prep 21-2 1. luxury 2. affluence 3. prestige 4. nobility 5. working class

of equal opportunity. There are no titles of *nobility* as in Europe, but astounding *affluence* is passed on in *privileged* families, and this makes all the difference. **Studies in the 1970s** found that a child of the elite and a child of the *working class* may start out with similar intelligence and drive, but the rich child is about 30 times more likely to *prosper*. The rich child goes to high-*prestige* schools, where his or her education may be only slightly above average, but where the child *accumulates* friendships with future leaders. The privileged child becomes comfortable with *luxury* and is at ease in situations where powerful people meet. The working-class child from a less-prestigious college is not likely to wind up *impoverished*, but neither is he or she likely to attend many parties of Yale or Vassar alumni.

Bonus Structure The reference to **studies in the 1970s** indicates some objective evidence for the author's point.

1. Which sentence best expresses the essential information of this passage?
   a. The American economy is unfair and must be changed.
   b. Rich people have natural advantages in education and social contacts that help them succeed.
   c. Children accept one another as friends; only later in life do differences of wealth drive them apart.
   d. The only way to make money in America is to work and accumulate it yourself.

2. Why does the author of this reading mention Yale and Vassar?
   a. They are elite schools attended by many future leaders.
   b. They are where government officials have secret meetings.
   c. They try to give working-class children a chance they can't get at other schools.
   d. Their high fees impoverish working-class children.

TOEFL Success 21 1. b 2. a

お金
レッスン21

富と社会階級

意味と例文

1 accumulate (動詞) **(何かを大量に) ためる**

例文訳 ハーディントン家は何世代にもわたり、土地を売買することで莫大な富を築いた。

関連語 accumulation (名詞) 蓄積

---

2 affluence (名詞) **富やそれに伴うライフスタイル**

例文訳 モハジールは裕福な環境で育ったため、大学院生時代に使用人のいないぎゅうぎゅう詰めのアパートで暮らすための準備があまりできていなかった。

関連語 affluent (形容詞) 裕福な

---

3 elite (形容詞) **特別な名誉ある集団に所属している**

例文訳 メスナーは、最近8,000メートル級の山を追加の酸素なしで登ったエリート登山家だ。

関連語 elite (名詞) エリート、elitist (形容詞) エリート主義の

---

4 impoverish (動詞) **(人や集団を) 貧しくさせる**

例文訳 鉄鋼業の崩壊が、オハイオ州東部のいくつかの郡を困窮させた。

関連語 impoverishment (名詞) 貧窮

---

5 luxury (名詞) **(必要性を超えた) 極端な快適さ**

例文訳 自動車メーカーは、ヒーター付きシートや洗練された娯楽システム等のオプションを搭載することで、自社の車に高級品のイメージを持たせようとしている。

関連語 luxuriate (動詞) 大いに楽しむ、luxurious (形容詞) 贅沢な

---

6 nobility (名詞) **国王や女王から「公爵」や「伯爵夫人」などの特別な称号を与えられた、社会的に際立った人々の集団 (貴族)**

例文訳 中世では、貴族は自分の領地の近くに住む貧しい人たちの面

倒を見ることを命じる規則に従っていたと考えられている。

使い方 nobility は、高名な人々の集団を指す名称として使われる。「非常に威厳のある行動様式」を意味することもある。

関連語 noble（名詞）貴族、noble（形容詞）高貴な、気高い

---

7 prestige（名詞）（平均より優れていることで得られる）名誉と敬意

例文訳 グラスレイ家は、その歴史的な町に住んでいるということで威信を得ていたが、そこではくつろいだ気持ちにはならなかった。

関連語 prestigious（形容詞）名声のある、一流の

---

8 privileged（形容詞）（通常は、裕福または有力な家に生まれたという立場のおかげで）特別な恩恵を享受できる

例文訳 米国で最も有力な家系の１つに属するという特権的な立場にもかかわらず、その政治家は、自分自身をごく普通の人間と示そうとした。

関連語 privilege（名詞）特権、特典

---

9 prosper（動詞）（仕事や私生活で）非常にうまくいく

例文訳 ヴァーガスは、ついに自分の新しい発明品の特許を取得したのちに成功を収めた。

ヒント 使い方 prosper の主語は、人だけでなく、集団や会社、地域のこともある。

関連語 prosperity（名詞）繁栄、成功、prosperous（形容詞）繁栄している、成功した

---

10 working class（名詞）貧しいわけではないが安定して中流階級にいるわけでもない（多くの場合は熟練を要しない）低賃金の仕事に就いている人

例文訳 ファレリー家は、他の労働者階級者たちと同様、自分たちの仕事に誇りを持っており、慈善事業や政府からのどんな施しも求めなかった。

TOEFL プレップ 21－1

左列の各単語に最も近い意味の単語や語句を選び、空欄にそのアルファベットを書きなさい。注意：それぞれの単語の意味の小さな違いに気をつけること。

________	1. impoverish	(a) 特別なメリットを享受する
________	2. elite	(b) 成功する
________	3. prosper	(c) 極端に貧しくさせる
________	4. accumulate	(d) 優れた功績を持つ小さな集団に属する
________	5. privileged	(e) 富を築く

TOEFL プレップ 21－2

リストの中から空欄に当てはまる適切な単語や語句を選んで、各文を完成させなさい。必要に応じて単語を活用させること。どれも一度しか使用できません。

affluence　luxury　nobility　prestige　working class

1　そのホテルの________は、純金の水栓やイタリア製大理石の階段などから明らかだった。

2　ジム・ラヴィッチは、自分の並外れた________を見せるため、妻の誕生日パーティーに1,500人をバハマまで飛行機で呼び寄せ、彼らが飲むために300樽のワインを注文した。

3　ミシガン州西部で最も古く、最も評判のいい家具メーカーであるヴァンエデン社は、良い材料を使い、顧客の声に耳を傾けることで________を得た。

4　フランスの________は、王族が殺された後に解体され、小貴族たちは革命の間に投獄された。

5　米国では、多くの________の家族が健康保険に加入していない。雇用主が保険を提供していないためである。

TOEFL サクセス 21

文章を読んで学んだ語彙を復習します。後に続く質問に答えなさい。

［例文訳］

米国は機会の多い国かもしれないが、真に平等な機会が与えられるわけではない。ヨーロッパにあるような貴族の称号はないが、特権的な家系では驚くほどの富が受け継がれていて、それが大きな違いを生んでいる。1970年代の研究では、エリートの子どもと労働者階級の子どもは、最初は同程度の知能や意欲を持っている可能性はあるが、金持ちの子どものほうが30倍成功しやすいということがわかった。金持ちの子どもは名高い学校に通い、そこでの教育水準は平均よりわずかに高い程度かもしれないが、将来のリーダーたちとの交友関係を積み重ねることができる。特権階級の子どもは、贅沢を心地よく感じるようになり、有力者が集まる状況でリラックスしていられる。名門でない大学出身の労働者階級の子どもは、貧困に陥ることにはならないだろうが、イェール大学やヴァッサー大学の卒業生が集まるようなパーティーに何度も参加することもないだろう。

読解のポイント　**1970年代の研究を参照することで、筆者の論点を支える客観的根拠を示している。**

1　この文章の重要な情報を最もよく表しているのはどの文か？

a. 米国の経済は不公平であり、変えられなければならない。

b. 裕福な人たちは、成功の助けとなる教育や社会的な交友関係といったメリットを生まれつき持っている。

c. 子どもたちはお互いを友達として受け入れる。のちの人生において初めて、富の差から違いが生まれる。

d. 米国でお金を稼ぐ唯一の方法は、働いて自分で貯めることだ。

2　筆者はなぜイェール大学とヴァッサー大学に言及しているのか？

a. 両方とも、多くの未来のリーダーたちが通うエリート校だから。

b. 両方とも、政府高官が秘密の会議を行う場所だから。

c. 両方とも、他の学校では得られないチャンスを労働者階級の子どもたちに与えようとしているから。

d. 両方とも、高い授業料が労働者階級の子どもたちを困窮させるから。

Personal Property

Target Words

1. acquire
2. assess
3. asset
4. hazardous
5. jointly
6. lease
7. liability
8. proprietor
9. safeguard
10. sole

Definitions and Samples

1. acquire *v.* To get something, usually something with special value or meaning

Bart hoped to **acquire** the 1898 D Indian Head penny, which would make his collection complete.

Usage tips Unlike *get*, *acquire* implies that a possession has special value or meaning.

Parts of speech acquisition *n*, acquisitive *adj*

2. assess *v.* To estimate the value of something

The Barnes building was **assessed** at $1.3 million, but it can probably sell for much more than that.

Parts of speech assessor *n*, assessment *n*

3. asset *n.* A possession that has positive value

For a typical family, their home is their most valuable **asset** and their car is the next most valuable.

Usage tips Some examples of assets are real estate, cash, and stock shares.

4. hazardous *adj.* Dangerous

Parents have to be careful not to buy children's clothes and toys made of **hazardous** materials.

Parts of speech hazard *n*, hazardously *adv*

5. jointly *adv.* Together with one or more other parties

In most states, a husband and wife are assumed to own all their possessions **jointly**.

Parts of speech join *v*, joint *n*

6. **lease** *v.* To rent something for a long time (several months or years)
   Some drivers prefer to **lease** a car rather than buy one.
   Parts of speech lease *n*, lessor *n*, lessee *n*

7. **liability** *n.* Legal responsibility for harming a person or property; a disadvantage
   Before you go river rafting, you sign a document releasing the trip leaders from **liability** in case of injury.
   Henderson is just a **liability** to our work team, because he never finishes anything on time.
   Usage tips In its second meaning, *liability* is often followed by a *to* phrase.
   Parts of speech liable *adj*

8. **proprietor** *n.* Owner, usually of a business or a building
   The **proprietor** of Hekman's Windows is Nels Hekman, grandson of the people who established the factory.
   Usage tips Very often, *proprietor* is followed by an *of* phrase.
   Parts of speech proprietary *adj*

9. **safeguard** *v.* To protect
   A burglar-alarm system **safeguards** our house when we go away on vacation.
   Usage tips *Safeguard* implies continuous protection over a long time.

10. **sole** *adj.* Only
    Many people have wanted to invest in Harry's publishing business, but he remains the **sole** owner.
    Usage tips *Sole* almost always appears before the noun it modifies. It does not come after a linking verb like *be*.
    Parts of speech solely *adv*

TOEFL Prep 22-1 **Find the word that is closest in meaning to each word in the left-hand column. Write the letter in the blank.**

______	1. assess	(a) dangerous
______	2. hazardous	(b) evaluate
______	3. jointly	(c) protect
______	4. liability	(d) responsibility
______	5. safeguard	(e) together

TOEFL Prep 22-2 **Circle the word that best completes each sentence.**

1. The building company is trying to (safeguard / acquire) the whole neighborhood so it can put up a mall.
2. To the average farm family, every child was (an asset / a liability), one more set of hands to gather eggs or plant beans.
3. Gary's Cookie Shop has to move because the owner of the building won't renew the (lease / asset).
4. The (hazardous / sole) adult influence on Sarah as she grew up was her grandmother.
5. Some people are born with the disease, but others (acquire / assess) it later in life.

TOEFL Success 22 **Read the passage to review the vocabulary you have learned. Answer the questions that follow.**

It is not easy to make a living as the *proprietor* of apartment buildings. There is a huge initial expense, not only to *acquire* the properties but to *assess* the buildings and to remove any *hazardous* materials like lead-based paint. A landlord also has to buy the best *liability* insurance available just to *safeguard* the investment. Otherwise, one tragic accident could wipe out

---

TOEFL Prep 22-1 1. b 2. a 3. e 4. d 5. c
TOEFL Prep 22-2 1. acquire 2. an asset 3. lease 4. sole 5. acquire

the value of the entire *asset*. Because of this expense, **it's rare** to find a *sole* individual owning such a property. The risk is more often taken on *jointly* by a group of investors who then split the profits from the *leases*.

Bonus Structure **It's rare** is the opposite of "it's common."

1. What is the main idea of this reading?
   a. Being a landlord is enjoyable.
   b. It costs a lot of money to be a landlord.
   c. Friendships can be destroyed by owning property jointly.
   d. Income from leases is greater than a landlord's expenses.

2. Which of the following is *not* an expense mentioned in the reading?
   a. property taxes
   b. insurance
   c. making the property safe
   d. buying the building you hope to rent

TOEFL Success 22 1. b 2. a

お金
レッスン22

個人資産

意味と例文

1 acquire（動詞） （通常は、特別な価値や意味のあるものを）手に入れる

例文訳 バートは、自分のコレクションを完成させることになる1898年のDインディアンヘッドのペニー硬貨を手に入れたがっていた。

ヒント 使い方 getとは異なり、acquireはその所有物が特別な価値や意味を持つことを暗に意味している。

関連語 acquisition（名詞）獲得、買収、acquisitive（形容詞）欲深い

2 assess（動詞） （あるものの）価値を見積もる

例文訳 バーンズのビルは130万ドルと評価されたが、おそらくそれよりもずっと高い価格で売れるだろう。

関連語 assessor（名詞）査定人、assessment（名詞）評価、査定

3 asset（名詞） プラスの価値を持つ所有物（資産）

例文訳 一般的な家庭にとっては、家が最も価値のある資産であり、車はその次に価値のあるものだ。

ヒント 使い方 資産の例には、不動産、現金、株式などがある。

4 hazardous（形容詞） 危険な

例文訳 親は、危険な素材でつくられた子ども服やおもちゃを買わないように気をつけなければならない。

関連語 hazard（名詞）危険なもの、脅威、hazardously（副詞）危険を伴って

5 jointly（副詞） （1人かそれ以上の仲間と）一緒に

例文訳 ほとんどの州では、夫と妻はすべての財産を共同で所有しているとみなされる。

関連語 join（動詞）参加する、合流する、joint（名詞）関節

6 lease (動詞) 長期間（数カ月または数年）何かを借りる

例文訳 ドライバーの中には、車を購入するのではなくリースすることを好む者もいる。

関連語 lease（名詞）賃貸借契約、lessor（名詞）賃貸人、lessee（名詞）賃借人

7 liability (名詞) （人や所有物に危害を加えたことに対する）法的責任／負債

例文訳 川下りに行く前には、怪我をしたときにその活動のリーダーの責任を免除する書類にサインをする。
ヘンダーソンは何一つ時間通りに終わらせないので、私たちの作業チームにとってただの足手まといになっている。

ヒント 使い方 lability が２つめの意味で使われる場合、その後にはしばしば to 句を伴う。

関連語 liable（形容詞）～しがちである、～しやすい

8 proprietor (名詞) （通常は事業や建物の）所有者

例文訳 ヘクマンズ・ウィンドウズのオーナーは、工場の設立者の孫であるニルス・ヘクマンだ。

ヒント 使い方 proprietor は、後ろに of 句を伴うことが非常に多い。

関連語 proprietary（形容詞）所有者の

9 safeguard (動詞) 守る

例文訳 私たちが休暇で出かけているときには、侵入警報システムが家を守ってくれる。

ヒント 使い方 safeguard は、長期間にわたって継続的に守ることを意味する。

10 sole (形容詞) 唯一の

例文訳 多くの人がハリーの出版事業に投資したいと考えてきたが、彼はただ１人のオーナーであり続けている。

ヒント 使い方 sole はほとんどの場合、それが修飾する名詞の前にくる。be 動詞のような連結動詞の後にはこない。

関連語 solely（副詞）単独で

TOEFL プレップ 22-1

左列の各単語に最も近い意味の単語を選び、空欄にそのアルファベットを書きなさい。

______	1. assess	(a) 危険な
______	2. hazardous	(b) 評価する
______	3. jointly	(c) 保護する
______	4. liability	(d) 責任
______	5. safeguard	(e) 一緒に

TOEFL プレップ 22-2

各文を完成させるのに最も適した単語を丸で囲みなさい。

1 その建築会社は、ショッピングモールを建てるために、近隣全体を（保護／買収）しようとしている。

2 平均的な農家にとって、すべての子どもは（資産／負債）であり、卵を集めたり豆を植えたりするさらなる働き手であった。

3 建物の所有者が（賃貸借契約／資産）を更新しようとしないので、ゲイリーズ・クッキーショップは移転しなければならない。

4 サラが成長していく間に影響を受けた（危険な／唯一の）大人は、祖母だった。

5 その病気を持って生まれる人もいるが、あとになって（手に入れてしまう／査定する）人もいる。

TOEFL サクセス 22

文章を読んで学んだ語彙を復習します。後に続く質問に答えなさい。

[例文訳]

マンションのオーナーとして生計を立てるのは簡単ではない。物件を取得するだけでなく、建物を査定したり鉛系塗料などの危険物質を除去したりするのにも莫大な初期費用がかかる。また、投資した物件を守るためだけに、最適の責任保険にも加入しなければならない。さもないと、一度の不幸な事故で資産全体の価値が失われてしまう可能性があるからだ。このような費用がかかるため、たった1人がこのような物件を所有していることはまれである。投資家のグループが共同でリスクを負い、賃貸借契約の利益を分配しあっていることが多い。

読解のポイント It's rare は It's common（よくある）の反対の意味。

1　この文章の主旨はどれか？

a. 大家でいるのは楽しい。

b. 大家になるためにはたくさんのお金がかかる。

c. 共同で物件を所有することで友情が壊れることがある。

d. 賃貸による収入は、大家の支出よりも大きい。

2　次のうち、文章中で言及されていない費用はどれか？

a. 固定資産税

b. 保険

c. 物件の安全性を高める費用

d. 賃借希望の建物の購入費用

Employment

Target Words

1. compensate
2. dynamic
3. enterprising
4. exploit
5. incentive
6. industrious
7. marginal
8. merit
9. promote
10. resign

Definitions and Samples

1. compensate *v.* To give an employee money or other things in exchange for the work he or she does

My pay doesn't properly **compensate** me for my efforts, but my other benefits, like health insurance, fill in the gap.

Usage tips *Compensate* is often followed by a *for* phrase.

Parts of speech compensation *n*, compensatory *adj*

2. dynamic *adj.* Full of energy

This job requires a **dynamic** person, someone who will look for opportunities instead of just waiting around for them.

Parts of speech dynamism *n*, dynamically *adv*

3. enterprising *adj.* Creative in thinking of ways to make money

Immigrants are often among the most **enterprising** members of society, partly because anyone brave enough to make an overseas move is likely to be a risk-taker.

Parts of speech enterprise *n* (Note: There is no verb "to enterprise.")

4. exploit *v.* To take advantage of; to treat inconsiderately in order to profit

The company tried to **exploit** the low interest rates to expand operations.

The foreign mining company **exploited** our copper resources and then simply left.

Parts of speech exploitation *n*, exploitive *adj*

5. incentive *n.* A possible benefit that motivates a person to do a certain thing

This city's willingness to support its public schools gave us an **incentive** to move here with our two young children.

Usage tips *Incentive* is usually followed by a *to* phrase.

6. industrious *adj.* Willing to work hard

The Dutch settlements in Ottawa County were founded by **industrious** farmers who objected to frivolous behavior such as dancing.

Usage tips Only people can be *industrious*; companies cannot.

Parts of speech industriousness *n*, industriously *adv*

7. marginal *adj.* Not very significant or effective

Our new advertising campaign had only **marginal** success, raising sales by a mere 3 percent.

Parts of speech marginally *adv*

8. merit *n.* Value; success based on one's work, not on luck

Pay raises at our company are based on **merit**, as determined by a committee of managers.

Usage tips *Merit* is uncountable.

Parts of speech merit *v*, meritorious *adj*

9. promote *v.* To move someone to a higher position in a company

Because of his excellent handling of the Vredeman account, Jim Harris was **promoted** to vice president.

Usage tips *Promote* is very often followed by a *to* phrase indicating the position one has been moved up to.

Parts of speech promotion *n*

10. resign *v.* To quit one's job

Because of controversy over his leadership style, Morton **resigned** from his job as president.

Parts of speech resignation *n*

TOEFL Prep 23-1 **Find the word or phrase that is closest in meaning to each word in the left-hand column. Write the letter in the blank.**

______	1. compensate	(a) good at finding business opportunities
______	2. dynamic	(b) hard-working
______	3. enterprising	(c) energetic
______	4. industrious	(d) move up
______	5. promote	(e) pay

TOEFL Prep 23-2 **Circle the word that best completes each sentence.**

1. Some companies move their factories to poor countries in order to (exploit / compensate) the desperation of people who are willing to work for very low wages.
2. For the last five years, we've seen only (dynamic / marginal) improvements in our productivity.
3. Judging by actual money-generating (promotion / merit), Williams is the company's most valuable employee.
4. I had a lot of (compensation / incentive) to move to our new facility in Minnesota, because two of my brothers live there.
5. Unless my employer stops polluting local rivers, I'm going to (resign / exploit).

TOEFL Success 23 **Read the passage to review the vocabulary you have learned. Answer the questions that follow.**

In the 1960s and 1970s, America was reaching the end of its role as a manufacturing power. Old-style systems of *compensation*, **especially** company pension plans, were impoverishing many companies. Much to the disadvantage

---

TOEFL Prep 23-1 1. e 2. c 3. a 4. b 5. d
TOEFL Prep 23-2 1. exploit 2. marginal 3. merit 4. incentive 5. resign

of less-*industrious* workers, companies started demanding *merit*, not just seniority, before someone could be *promoted*. Many managers who were only *marginally* effective were encouraged to *resign*. These changes were painful, but unavoidable, symptoms of a growth spurt in the U.S. economy. Economies grow and change just as people do. A truly *enterprising* businessperson knows how to *exploit* these large changes and become involved in tomorrow's *dynamic* businesses, not yesterday's. There's still plenty of money to be made in America, a very effective *incentive* for workers to adapt to new conditions.

Bonus Structure **Especially** introduces an outstanding example.

1. Which sentence best expresses the essential information of this passage?
   a. Most companies cannot afford to compensate their employees like they used to.
   b. Anyone interested in making a lot of money should move to the United States.
   c. The 1960s and 1970s were times of great change for the American economy.
   d. Just as retailers adapt to economic change, so must manufacturers.

2. The author of this article expresses a negative opinion about______.
   a. businesspersons
   b. workers who depended on seniority for promotion
   c. companies that exploit changes in the economy
   d. the American economy as a whole

TOEFL Success 23 1. c 2. b

お金
レッスン23

雇用

意味と例文

1 compensate (動詞) （仕事の対価として）従業員にお金やその他のものを与える

例文訳 私の給料は、労力に適切に報いるものではないが、健康保険などの他の福利厚生がそのギャップを埋めている。

ヒント 使い方 compensateは後ろにfor句を伴うことが多い。

関連語 compensation (名詞)補償、報酬、compensatory (形容詞)補償の

2 dynamic (形容詞) エネルギーに満ちあふれている

例文訳 この仕事に必要なのは、ただ待っているだけではなく自分からチャンスを探しに行くような、ダイナミックな人物だ。

関連語 dynamism (名詞) 活発さ、活動力、dynamically (副詞) ダイナミックに、活発に

3 enterprising (形容詞) お金を稼ぐ方法の考え方が創造的な

例文訳 移民は、社会の中で最も進取の気性に富んだ人々であることが多く、それは一つには、海外に進出する勇気のある人はリスクを負うことをいとわない傾向があるからだ。

関連語 enterprise (名詞) 企業(注意:"to enterprise"という動詞はない)

4 exploit (動詞) 利用する／（利益を得るために）無分別に扱う

例文訳 その企業は事業を拡大するのに低金利を利用しようとした。外国の鉱山会社は私たちの銅資源を利用すると、あっさりと撤退してしまった。

関連語 exploitation (名詞) 搾取、開発、exploitive (形容詞) 搾取的な

5 incentive (名詞) （人があることをする）動機となり得る利益

例文訳 この街が公立学校を積極的に支援していることが、幼い子ど

も２人を連れてここに引っ越してくる動機になった。

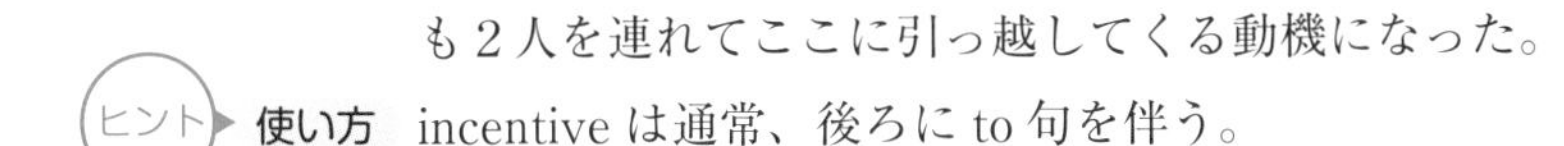

ヒント **使い方** incentive は通常、後ろに to 句を伴う。

---

6 industrious （形容詞） 努力を惜しまない

例文訳 オタワ郡のオランダ人入植地は、ダンスのような軽薄な行為に反対する勤勉な農民たちによって設立された。

ヒント **使い方** industrious を使えるのは人についてだけで、企業には使えない。

関連語 industriousness （名詞） 勤勉さ、industriously （副詞） 勤勉に

---

7 marginal （形容詞） あまり重要でない、またはあまり効果的でない

例文訳 新しい広告キャンペーンの成果はわずかで、売上高はたった３％しか伸びなかった。

関連語 marginally （副詞） わずかに

---

8 merit （名詞） 価値／（運ではなく）自分の働きに基づく成功

例文訳 当社の昇給は、経営委員会によって決定される功績に基づいている。

ヒント **使い方** merit は数えられない名詞。

関連語 merit （動詞） 値する、meritorious （形容詞） 賞賛に値する、価値のある

---

9 promote （動詞） （会社の中である人を）より高い地位に移動させる

例文訳 フレーデマンの件を見事に処理したことで、ジム・ハリスは副社長に昇進した。

ヒント **使い方** promote は非常に多くの場合、後ろに移動先の地位を表す to 句を伴う。

関連語 promotion （名詞） 昇進

---

10 resign （動詞） 仕事を辞める

例文訳 モートンは、彼のリーダーシップスタイルをめぐる論争が原因で、社長を辞任した。

関連語 resignation （名詞） 辞職

TOEFL プレップ 23－1

左列の各単語に最も近い意味の単語や語句を選び、空欄にそのアルファベットを書きなさい。

______	1. compensate	(a) ビジネスチャンスを見つけるのが得意である
______	2. dynamic	(b) よく働く
______	3. enterprising	(c) 精力的な
______	4. industrious	(d) 昇進させる
______	5. promote	(e) 賃金を支払う

TOEFL プレップ 23－2

各文を完成させるのに最も適した単語を丸で囲みなさい。

1 とても低い賃金で働くことをいとわないような人々の必死の思い（を搾取する／に報いる）ために、貧しい国に工場を移す企業もある。

2 この５年間、私たちの生産性は（精力的な／わずかな）向上しか見られていない。

3 現実にお金を生み出しているという（昇進／功績）で判断すると、ウィリアムスはその会社で最も価値のある社員だ。

4 私の２人の兄弟がミネソタ州に住んでいるので、ミネソタの新しい施設に移るには多くの（報酬／動機）があった。

5 雇用主が地元の川を汚染するのを止めない限り、私は（辞職する／搾取する）つもりだ。

TOEFL サクセス 23

文章を読んで学んだ語彙を復習します。後に続く質問に答えなさい。

[例文訳]

1960 年代から 1970 年代にかけて、米国は世界の製造力としての役割の終わりを迎えようとしていた。旧態依然とした報酬制度、特に企業年金制度は、多くの企業を疲弊させていた。勤勉さに欠ける労働者にとっては大いに不都合なことだが、企業は誰かを昇進させる前には、単なる年次ではなく、功績を求めるようになった。わずかな効果しか上げられない管理職の多くは、辞職するよう勧められた。これらの変化は、米国経済の急成長の、痛みを伴うが避けることのできない兆しであった。経済も人間と同じように成長し、変化していくものである。真に進取の気性に富むビジネスパーソンは、この大きな変化を利用して、昨日のビジネスではなく、明日のダイナミックなビジネスに携わる方法を知っている。米国にはまだまだ生み出されるお金があり、それは労働者にとって、新しい環境に適応するための非常に有効な励みとなる。

読解のポイント especially **は、顕著な例を紹介している。**

1 この文章の重要な情報を最もよく表しているのはどの文か？

a. ほとんどの企業は、以前のように従業員に報酬を与える余裕がない。

b. たくさんお金を稼ぐことに興味がある人は誰でも、米国に移住するべきだ。

c. 1960年代と1970年代は、米国経済にとって大きな変化の時代だった。

d. 小売業者が経済の変化に適応するように、製造業者も適応しなければならない。

2 この文章の筆者は、次のうちどれに対して否定的な意見を述べているか。

a. ビジネスパーソン

b. 昇進に関して年功序列を頼っていた労働者

c. 経済の変化を利用する企業

d. 米国経済全体

International Trade

Target Words

1. distill
2. entrepreneurial
3. extract
4. haggle
5. intrepid
6. merchant
7. proportionately
8. prototype
9. reward
10. shuttle

Definitions and Samples

1. distill *v.* To remove one liquid from a mixture of liquids by boiling; to get something valuable from a confusing mix of ideas

The forest peoples of Southeast Asia **distill** an alcoholic drink called arak from a paste of palm berries.

Even though the professor's lectures are long and confusing, Brian can usually **distill** the main ideas from them.

Parts of speech distillation *n*, distillery *n*

2. entrepreneurial *adj.* Able to create business opportunities from a wide variety of circumstances

Many engineers of the 1970s made great computers, but only a few were **entrepreneurial** enough to see the business possibilities in the new machines.

Parts of speech entrepreneur *n*

3. extract *v.* To take out

International mining companies came to the Malay Peninsula to **extract** the region's massive tin deposits.

Parts of speech extraction *n*, extractor *n*

4. haggle *v.* To argue back and forth about a price

The customer and the shopkeeper **haggled** over the silver plate for more than an hour.

Usage tips *Haggle* is often followed by a phrase with *over* or *about*.

Parts of speech haggler *n*

5. **intrepid** *adj.* Fearless
For nearly 200 years, only the most **intrepid** colonists would cross the Appalachian Mountains.

6. **merchant** *n.* A person who makes a living by selling things
The spice **merchants** of the eastern markets charged top prices to the Dutch and British sailors, who had come too far to sail away without buying.
Usage tips The word *merchant* might be preceded by another noun telling what the merchant sells (e.g., *spice merchant* or *wine merchant*).
Parts of speech merchandise *v*, merchandise *n*, mercantile *adj*

7. **proportionately** *adv.* In an amount appropriate to each of several recipients
The food aid was distributed **proportionately** per family, with larger families receiving more.
Parts of speech proportion *n*, proportionate *adj*, proportionally *adv*

8. **prototype** *n.* The first one made of a machine or system
The airplane manufacturer uses robots to test every **prototype**, just in case there is a problem with the design.

9. **reward** *n.* Something one gets for having done well
The greatest **reward** of being a parent is to see your child make a wise decision.
Usage tips *Reward* might be followed by an *of* or *for* phrase naming what one has done well.
Parts of speech reward *v*

10. **shuttle** *v.* To move back and forth often between two places
The small jet **shuttles** between Kuala Lumpur and Singapore nearly every two hours.
Parts of speech shuttle *n*

TOEFL Prep 24-1 **Find the word or phrase that is closest in meaning to each word in the left-hand column. Write the letter in the blank.**

______	1. haggle	(a) brave
______	2. intrepid	(b) in appropriate amounts
______	3. extract	(c) argue about price
______	4. entrepreneurial	(d) take out
______	5. proportionately	(e) business-oriented

TOEFL Prep 24-2 **Circle the word that best completes each sentence.**

1. To avoid disease, many people drink only (distilled / extracted) water, which has been boiled to evaporation and then recondensed on a cold surface.
2. Most business travelers do not find it exciting to (haggle / shuttle) between one location and another.
3. According to the laws in this state, tobacco can be sold only by certain licensed (merchants / entrepreneurs) at special tobacco stores.
4. One early (reward / prototype) of the computer was called ENIAC and was as big as an average-sized laboratory.
5. The children were punished (intrepidly / proportionately), with the leaders getting greater penalties than those who simply followed along.

TOEFL Success 24 **Read the passage to review the vocabulary you have learned. Answer the questions that follow.**

Tomatoes, potatoes, and hot peppers, all originally from South or Central America, are among several plants that have *disproportionately* influenced cooking around the world. This happened only after a few *intrepid* eaters got beyond

---

TOEFL Prep 24-1 1. c 2. a 3. d 4. e 5. b
TOEFL Prep 24-2 1. distilled 2. shuttle 3. merchants 4. prototype 5. proportionately

common fears about potatoes, tomatoes, and other products. *Entrepreneurial* hunters for new food products hardly knew what they were *haggling* for when they tried to *extract* from foreign markets goods that would sell well at home. *Shuttling* between Europe and exotic lands, Italians, Spaniards, and Britons in particular brought back food *prototypes* that were not obviously good things to eat—cinnamon bark, cousins of the dreaded nightshade (tomatoes), and even the pollen from a crocus flower (saffron). **As a glance at** international cookbooks will show, many creative *merchants* were well *rewarded* not just with financial success, but with culture-changing influence.

Bonus Structure **As a glance at** introduces evidence for the author's claim.

1. According to this reading, why did merchants have "culture-changing influence"?
   a. They found new ways to get from one country to another.
   b. Many of the plants they sold were poisonous and killed off some populations.
   c. They made it possible for cultures to develop new dishes.
   d. They spread European cooking habits around the world.

2. Cinnamon, tomatoes, and saffron are mentioned to make the point that_______.
   a. many of the new plants merchants introduced were from Asia
   b. some strange-looking foods from odd sources were eventually accepted
   c. nightshade was unfairly dreaded by Europeans
   d. nearly every part of a plant can be turned into a kind of food

TOEFL Success 24 1. c 2. b

お金
レッスン24

国際貿易

意味と例文

1 distill （動詞） （液体の混合物を沸騰させて）１つの液体を取り除く／（混乱したさまざまな考えから）価値のあるものを得る

例文訳 東南アジアの森林地帯に住む人々は、パームベリーのペーストからアラックと呼ばれるアルコール飲料を蒸留する。
その教授の講義は長くてわかりにくいにもかかわらず、ブライアンはたいてい、主要なアイデアを抽出することができる。

関連語 distillation（名詞）蒸留、distillery（名詞）蒸留所

2 entrepreneurial （形容詞） （さまざまな状況から）ビジネスチャンスを生み出せる

例文訳 1970年代、多くの技術者が優れたコンピュータをつくりだしたが、その新しい装置にビジネスの可能性を見出せるほど起業家精神のある者はごくわずかだった。

関連語 entrepreneur（名詞）起業家

3 extract （動詞） 取り出す

例文訳 マレー半島に大量に埋蔵されているスズを採掘するために、国際的な鉱業会社がやってきた。

関連語 extraction（名詞）抽出、採取、extractor（名詞）抽出者、抽出装置

4 haggle （動詞） （価格をめぐって）口論する

例文訳 客と店主はその銀の皿をめぐって１時間以上も価格交渉した。

ヒント 使い方 haggleの後にはoverやaboutを使った語句が続くことが多い。

関連語 haggler（名詞）価格の交渉人

5 intrepid （形容詞） 恐れを知らない

例文訳 200年近くの間、最も勇猛な入植者だけがアパラチア山脈を越えていた。

---

6 merchant（名詞） 物を売ることで生計を立てている人

例文訳 東の市場の香辛料商人は、オランダ人やイギリス人の船乗りたちに対して、遠くからやって来たのに買わずに帰るはずはないと最も高額の値段をつけた。

ヒント 使い方 merchantという言葉の前には、その商人が売るものを表す別の名詞が付くことがある（例：香辛料商人、ワイン商人）。

関連語 merchandise（動詞）売買する、merchandise（名詞）商品、mercantile（形容詞）商業の、商人の

---

7 proportionately（副詞） 複数の受取人それぞれに適した量で（比例して）

例文訳 食糧援助は家族ごとに人数に比例して分配され、人数の多い家族はより多く受け取った。

関連語 proportion（名詞）割合、proportionate（形容詞）比例した、つり合った、proportionally（副詞）比例して、つり合って

---

8 prototype（名詞） （機械やシステムでつくられた）最初のもの

例文訳 その飛行機メーカーは、設計に問題がある場合に備えて、すべての試作品をテストするのにロボットを使用している。

---

9 reward（名詞） （うまくやったことに対して）得られるもの

例文訳 親としての最大の報酬は、子どもが賢明な決断をするのを見ることだ。

ヒント 使い方 rewardの後には、うまくやった事柄を示すof句やfor句が続くことがある。

関連語 reward（動詞）報酬を与える

---

10 shuttle（動詞） （2つの場所の間を頻繁に）行き来する

例文訳 その小型ジェット機は、クアラルンプールとシンガポール間をほぼ2時間ごとに往復している。

関連語 shuttle（名詞）定期往復便

TOEFL プレップ 24－1

左列の各単語に最も近い意味の単語や語句を選び、空欄にそのアルファベットを書きなさい。

______	1. haggle	(a) 勇敢な
______	2. intrepid	(b) 適切な量で
______	3. extract	(c) 価格について議論する
______	4. entrepreneurial	(d) 取り出す
______	5. proportionately	(e) ビジネス志向の

TOEFL プレップ 24－2

各文を完成させるのに最も適した単語を丸で囲みなさい。

1 多くの人は病気を防ぐために、沸騰させて蒸発させた後、冷たい表面で再凝縮させた、（蒸留された／抽出された）水だけを飲む。

2 ほとんどのビジネス旅行者は、ある場所と別の場所を（交渉／行き来）することを楽しいと感じない。

3 この州の法律によると、タバコは特別なタバコ店で特定の資格を持った（商人／起業家）しか販売できない。

4 コンピュータの初期の（報酬／試作品）の１つはENIACと呼ばれ、平均的な大きさの実験室と同じくらいの大きさだった。

5 子どもたちは（勇猛に／［責任の大きさに］比例して）罰せられ、リーダーたちは単に従っただけの子どもよりも大きな罰を受けた。

TOEFL サクセス 24

文章を読んで学んだ語彙を復習します。後に続く質問に答えなさい。

［例文訳］

トマト、ジャガイモと唐辛子は、いずれも中南米が原産の植物であり、世界中の料理にあまりにも大きな影響を与えてきた。食に対して勇敢な少数の人たちがジャガイモやトマト、その他の産物に対して一般的に持たれていた恐怖心を克服して初めて、そういうことが起きた。新しい食べ物を求める起業家精神あふれる人たちは、自国でよく売れるであろう商品を外国の市場から引き出そうとしているとき、自分が一体何をめぐって交渉しているのかほとんどわかっていなかったのである。ヨーロッパと異国の間を行き来しながら、特にイタリア人、スペイン人、イギリス人は明らかに食べるのに適しているとは言えないような食べ物の見本——シナモンの樹皮、恐ろしいイヌホオズキの親戚（トマト）、さらにはクロッカスの花粉（サフラン）——を持ち帰った。世界中の料理本をちょっと見るだけでもわかるように、多くの創造的な商人は、経済的な成功だけでなく、文化を変えるほどの影響力で十分に報われたのだ。

読解のポイント As a glance at で著者の主張の根拠を紹介している。

1 この文章によれば、なぜ商人は「文化を変えるほどの影響力」を持っていたのか？

a. ある国から別の国へ行くための新しい方法を見つけたから。
b. 販売した植物の多くは毒を持っていて、一部の人々を殺したから。
c. 文化が新しい料理を発展させることを可能にしたから。
d. ヨーロッパの料理の習慣を世界中に広めたから。

2 シナモン、トマト、サフランが挙げられているのは、何を強調するためか？

a. 商人が持ち込んだ新しい植物の多くはアジアからのものだったこと。
b. 素材が変わっていて見た目が風変わりな食べ物でも、最終的には受け入れられたこと。
c. ヨーロッパではイヌホオズキは不当に恐れられていたこと。
d. 植物のほぼすべての部分は食べられるようにすることができること。

Politics

Target Words

1. advocate	6. contest
2. authority	7. election
3. bitterly	8. inaugurate
4. candidate	9. policy
5. coalition	10. poll

Definitions and Samples

1. **advocate** *v.* To speak out in favor of something
Some environmentalists **advocate** removing large dams from the Columbia River.
Usage tips *Advocate* is usually followed by a term for a process or action, very often the-*ing* form of a verb
Parts of speech advocate *n*, advocacy *n*

2. **authority** *n.* The power to make decisions, to tell others what to do.
The governor has the **authority** to call the legislature together for emergency sessions.
Usage tips A *to* phrase often follows *authority*.
Parts of speech authorize *v*, authoritative *adj*

3. **bitterly** *adv.* Strongly and with a lot of bad feelings
Senator Thomas **bitterly** opposed the movement to design a new state flag.
Parts of speech bitterness *n*, bitter *adj*

4. **candidate** *n.* Someone who wants to be chosen, especially in an election, for a position
In most U.S. elections, there are only two major-party **candidates** for president.
Usage tips *Candidate* is often followed by a *for* phrase.
Parts of speech candidacy *n*

5. **coalition** *n.* A group of several different groups or

countries that are working together to achieve a certain goal.
Several local churches, mosques, synagogues, and temples formed a **coalition** to promote understanding among people of different religions.

6. **contest** *v.* To challenge
Dave Roper, who narrowly lost the mayor's race, **contested** the results, demanding a recount of the votes.
Usage tips The noun *contest* can mean a game, especially one played for a prize.
Parts of speech contest *n*

7. **election** *n.* A process in which people choose officials
Because of problems with vote-counting four years ago, international observers monitored this year's **election** to make sure it was fair.
Parts of speech elect *v*, elective *adj*

8. **inaugurate** *v.* To bring into public office; to start formally
The U.S. president is elected in November but is not **inaugurated** until the following January.
An effort to bring electric service to farms and small towns was **inaugurated** with the Rural Electrification Act of 1936.
Usage tips When it means "bring into public office," *inaugurate* is usually in the passive voice.
Parts of speech inauguration *n*, inaugural *adj*

9. **policy** *n.* An approved way for approaching a certain kind of situation
The **policy** said that government money could not be given to any private hospital.

10. **poll** *v.* To find out a small group's opinion so that you can guess what a much larger group thinks
The newspaper **polled** 500 registered voters and found that only 27 percent were in favor of expanding the city zoo.
Parts of speech poll *n*, pollster *n*

TOEFL Prep 25-1 **Find the phrase that best describes each word in the left-hand column. Write the letter in the blank.**

______	1. policy	(a) a process of choosing
______	2. candidate	(b) a kind of power
______	3. authority	(c) a kind of person
______	4. coalition	(d) a way of handling a situation
______	5. election	(e) a kind of group

TOEFL Prep 25-2 **Complete each sentence by filling in each blank with the best word from the list. Change the form of the word if necessary. Use each word only once.**

advocated   *bitterly*   *contest*   *inaugurated*   *polled*

1. In the early twentieth century, politicians fought______ about whether the U.S. dollar should be based on gold.
2. Only one month after he was______, President Harrison fell sick and died.
3. My opponent says that I cheated on my taxes. I______ that charge, and I will prove him wrong.
4. Their predictions about the election results were not very accurate because they______too few people in advance.
5. Last year, the Freedom Party______giving medical treatment even to people who could not pay for it.

TOEFL Success 25 **Read the passage to review the vocabulary you have learned. Answer the questions that follow.**

In the history of U.S. presidential *elections*, the year 1876 stands out as one of the oddest. That year, *polls* suggested that one person had won the popular vote but another had won more official electoral votes—just as happened in the year 2000. In 1876, however, the election was so *bitterly*

TOEFL Prep 25-1　1. d　2. c　3. b　4. e　5. a
TOEFL Prep 25-2　1. bitterly　2. inaugurated　3. contest　4. polled　5. advocated

contested that a special electoral commission was given the *authority* to determine which *candidate*—Republican Rutherford B. Hayes or Democrat Samuel J. Tilden—had won. This commission represented a *coalition* of interests. The Democrats favored this because otherwise the head of the Senate, Republican Thomas Ferry, would probably have been allowed to declare the winner. In the end, the Democrats were disappointed, as the commission *advocated* the Republican cause. The situation was not settled until March 2 of 1877, only three days before the scheduled *inauguration* of a new president—Hayes, **as it turned out**. Only then did America find out who its new leader would be. Americans seem not to have learned many lessons from 1876, however, because in 2000 there was still no official *policy* on how to settle an election that hung on a few contested votes. The problem was settled (by the Supreme Court) much faster in 2000, but still, no real system had been set up to deal with the situation.

Bonus Structure **As it turned out** is an adverbial clause indicating an eventual resolution of a long-standing problem.

1. In what way was the 1876 election even odder than that in 2000?
   a. It happened much earlier.
   b. It involved only two major candidates.
   c. One person won the popular vote and another won the electoral vote.
   d. The uncertainty over who would win the presidency lasted many months.

2. Who decided the outcome of the 1876 election?
   a. a special electoral commission
   b. Thomas Ferry
   c. the Supreme Court
   d. Rutherford B. Hayes

TOEFL Success 25 1. d 2. a

政府と正義
レッスン25

政治

意味と例文

1 advocate（動詞） （あることを）支持して発言する

例文訳 環境保護主義者の中には、コロンビア川から大きなダムを撤去することを提唱している人もいる。

ヒント 使い方 advocateの後ろには通常、過程や行動を表す語が続き、動詞の～ing形であることが非常に多い。

関連語 advocate（名詞）主張者、支持者、advocacy（名詞）支持、弁護

2 authority（名詞） 決定を下したり、他人に何をすべきかを命令したりする力

例文訳 知事には、緊急時に議会を招集する権限がある。

ヒント 使い方 authorityは後ろにto不定詞句を伴うことが多い。

関連語 authorize（動詞）権限を与える、authoritative（形容詞）命令的な、権威のある

3 bitterly（副詞） 強く、悪い感情を大いに持って

例文訳 トーマス上院議員は、新しい州旗をデザインするという動きに激しく反対した。

関連語 bitterness（名詞）激しさ、苦さ、bitter（形容詞）激しい、つらい、苦い

4 candidate（名詞） （特に選挙において、ある地位を求めて）選ばれることを望んでいる人

例文訳 米国のほとんどの大統領選挙では、二大政党からしか候補者が出てこない。

ヒント 使い方 candidateは後ろにfor句を伴うことが多い。

関連語 candidacy（名詞）立候補

5 coalition（名詞） ある目標を達成するために協力し合う複数の異なる集団や国のグループ（連合）

例文訳 地元の教会、モスク、シナゴーグや寺院が、宗教が異なる人々の間での理解を促進するため、連合を結成した。

6 contest (動詞) 挑戦する／異議を申し立てる

例文訳 市長選に僅差で敗れたデイヴ・ローパーは、結果に異議を唱え、票の再集計を要求した。

ヒント 使い方 名詞 contest は、勝負や競技、特に賞を与えられる競争を意味する。

関連語 contest (名詞) 競争、コンテスト

7 election (名詞) 人々が公職者を選ぶプロセス（選挙）

例文訳 4年前の選挙では開票作業に問題があったため、今年の選挙では開票が公正に行われるように国際的なオブザーバーが監視した。

関連語 elect (動詞) 選挙する、elective (形容詞) 選挙の、選挙で選ばれる

8 inaugurate (動詞) 公職に就かせる／正式に開始する

例文訳 米国の大統領は11月に選出されるが、翌年の1月までは就任しない。

1936年の農村電化法により、農場や小さな町に電力を送る取り組みが開始された。

ヒント 使い方 「公職に就かせる」という意味の場合、inaugurate は通常受動態で使用される。

関連語 inauguration (名詞) 就任、就任式、開始、inaugural (形容詞) 就任の、開始の

9 policy (名詞) （ある種の状況に取りかかるための）承認された方法

例文訳 その方針では、政府の資金を私立病院に提供することはできないとされていた。

10 poll (動詞) より大きな集団がどう考えているかを推測するために小さな集団の意見を調査する（世論調査をする）

例文訳 新聞社が500人の登録有権者に世論調査をしたところ、市の動物園の拡張に賛成した人は27%しかいなかった。

関連語 poll (名詞) 世論調査、投票、投票結果、pollster (名詞) 世論調査員

TOEFL プレップ 25−1

左列の各単語の説明として最もふさわしいものを選び、空欄にそのアルファベットを書きなさい。

________	1. policy	(a) 選出のプロセス
________	2. candidate	(b) ある種の権力
________	3. authority	(c) ある種の人
________	4. coalition	(d) ある状況を処理する方法
________	5. election	(e) ある種の集団

TOEFL プレップ 25−2

リストの中から空欄に当てはまる適切な単語を選んで、各文を完成させなさい。必要に応じて単語を活用させること。なお、各単語は一度しか使用できません。

advocated bitterly contest inaugurated polled

1 20世紀初頭、米国のドルは金を基準にすべきかどうか、政治家たちは________争った。

2 ________からわずか1カ月後、ハリソン大統領は病気になり、亡くなった。

3 相手は、私が税金をごまかしたと言っている。私はその告発に________、彼が間違っていることを証明するつもりだ。

4 事前に________した人が少なすぎたため、彼らの選挙結果の予測はあまり正確ではなかった。

5 昨年自由党は、医療費を払えない人にも医療を提供することを________。

TOEFL サクセス 25

文章を読んで学んだ語彙を復習します。後に続く質問に答えなさい。

[例文訳]

米国の大統領選挙の歴史の中で、1876年は最も変わった年の１つとして際だっている。その年の世論調査では、まさしく2000年の大統領選のときに起きたのと同じように、一般投票ではある候補者が勝っていたものの、より公式な選挙人投票では別の候補者が勝つと予想されていた。しかし1876年の選挙はその結果についてあまりに激しい論争が起き、特別選挙委員会に対して、共和党のラザフォード・B・ヘイズ、民主党のサミュエル・J・ティルデンのどちらの候補者が勝ったのかを決定する権限が与えられることとなった。この委員会は、さまざまな利害関係者の連合にあたるものであった。民主党はこれを支持した。さもなければ、上院議長である共和党のトーマス・フェリーがどちらが勝者かを宣言することを許されてしまうかもしれなかったからである。だが結局、民主党は失望することになる。委員会は共和党の主張を支持したからだ。事態がようやく収束したのは1877年３月２日、予定されていた新大統領の就任式のわずか３日前だった。新大統領は、結局のところヘイズであった。そのとき初めて、米国は新しいリーダーが誰になるのかを知った。しかし、米国人は1876年のこの事態から多くの教訓を学んでいないようで、2000年になっても、論争が起きるようなわずかな票にかかった選挙をどう決着させるかについて、公式な方針はないままだった。2000年の選挙においては、問題は（最高裁によって）ずっと速く解決されたが、それでも、こうした状況に対処するための現実的なシステムは確立されていないままだった。

読解のポイント　as it turned out **は、長期にわたる問題が最終的に解決したことを示す副詞節。**

1　1876年の選挙が、2000年のそれよりもさらに奇妙だったのはどのような点か？

a. ずっと昔に起こった点。

b. ２人の主要な候補者だけが関与していた点。

c. １人が一般投票で勝利し、もう１人が選挙人投票で勝利した点。

d. 誰が大統領職に就くのかわからない状態が何カ月も続いた点。

2　1876年の選挙の結果を決めたのは誰か？

a. 特別選挙委員会

b. トーマス・フェリー

c. 最高裁判所

d. ラザフォード・B・ヘイズ

A Reasonable Doubt

Target Words

1. accuse
2. allegedly
3. civil
4. convict
5. guilty
6. offense
7. peer
8. suspect
9. verdict
10. witness

Definitions and Samples

1. accuse *v.* To say that someone did something wrong (e.g., committed a crime)

Jordan was **accused** of using a stolen credit card to buy about $300 worth of electronic equipment.

Usage tips *Accuse* is often in the passive voice; also it is often followed by *of*.

Parts of speech accusation *n*, accuser *n*

2. allegedly *adv.* According to what people say

The chief financial officer of the company **allegedly** took company money for his personal use.

Parts of speech allege *v*, allegation *n*

3. civil *adj.* Involving a dispute between two citizens, not a criminal charge

In a **civil** suit against his neighbor, Barney claimed that the neighbor's dog had bitten him.

Usage tips In a court context, *civil* almost always appears in one of the following phrases: *civil suit*, *civil action*, *civil court*, *civil proceedings*, and *civil penalties*.

4. convict *v.* To decide that someone is guilty of a crime

Dean was **convicted** of assault after the jury saw a video of him striking another man.

Usage tips *Convict* is often in the passive voice; also, it is often followed by *of*.

Parts of speech convict *n*, conviction *n*

5. **guilty** *adj.* Responsible for doing something bad

The jury found that the director was **guilty** of embezzlement.

Usage tips *Guilty* is often followed by an *of* phrase that names a crime or bad deed.

Parts of speech guilt *n*, guiltily *adv*

6. **offense** *n.* A specific act that breaks the law

Convicted twice of reckless driving, Victor will lose his license if he commits another serious traffic **offense**.

Parts of speech offender *n*, offensive *adj*

7. **peer** *n.* A person who is one's social equal

In requiring judgment by "a jury of one's **peers**," U.S. law meant to protect lower-class defendants from the possibly biased judgment of upper-class juries.

8. **suspect** *n.* Someone who, in the opinion of the police, might have committed a certain crime

The police were investigating the activities of five **suspects** in the liquor-store robbery.

Parts of speech suspect *v*, suspicion *n*, suspicious *adj*, suspiciously *adv*

9. **verdict** *n.* A judgment in a court case

It took the jury only 30 minutes to reach a **verdict** of "guilty."

Usage tips *Verdict* is often the object of the verbs *reach* or *arrive at*.

10. **witness** *v.* To see something, especially a crime, happen

After **witnessing** the car theft, Rodney called the police.

Parts of speech witness *n*

TOEFL Prep 26-1 **Find the word or phrase that is closest in meaning to each word in the left-hand column. Write the letter in the blank.**

______	1. accuse	(a) to determine that someone is guilty
______	2. convict	(b) responsible for a crime
______	3. civil	(c) a social equal
______	4. guilty	(d) being related to a personal dispute, not a crime
______	5. peer	(e) to say someone did a bad thing

TOEFL Prep 26-2 **Circle the word that best completes each sentence.**

1. The most likely (suspect / witness) in the murder was the victim's brother, but no one actually saw the crime.
2. The new president (allegedly / guiltily) had his main opponents killed, but he denies it.
3. At one time in the United States, possession of marijuana was a minor (verdict / offense).
4. The (witness / peer) made a poor impression on the jury because he couldn't remember many details about the crime scene.
5. Juries are instructed to arrive at a unanimous (verdict / convict), one agreeable to all members of the jury.

TOEFL Success 26 **Read the passage to review the vocabulary you have learned. Answer the questions that follow.**

One of the most controversial murder cases of the twentieth century was that involving the death of Marilyn Sheppard in 1954. Her husband, Dr. Sam Sheppard, was *accused* of killing her and then injuring himself. An unlikely *suspect*, Sheppard

TOEFL Prep 26-1 1. e 2. a 3. d 4. b 5. c
TOEFL Prep 26-2 1. suspect 2. allegedly 3. offense 4. witness 5. verdict

was highly respected by his *peers* in the medical world. Still, there were odd aspects to the murder that Sheppard could not explain away. Unfortunately for Sheppard, none of his supporters actually *witnessed* the crime, so nobody could back up Sheppard's claim that the real killer was a bushy-haired man whom Sheppard had chased across his lawn and fought with briefly.

Sheppard was eventually *convicted* of the *offense*, **but** many people **doubt**ed the *verdict*. With aggressive help from a lawyer named F. Lee Bailey, Sheppard got a new trial. Bailey suggested many alternatives to Sheppard's guilt, enough that the new jury could not say he was *guilty* beyond a reasonable doubt. Sheppard was released from prison but died soon afterward. His son, Chip, pursued the case through several *civil* and criminal proceedings in an attempt to find out the truth about his mother's murder. Late in the 1990s, new DNA analysis techniques proved that someone other than Sam Sheppard and his family had been in the house that night. Sheppard's story about the bushy-haired man had probably been accurate all along.

Bonus Structure The clause containing **but** and **doubt** signals that arguments against the verdict will be given.

1. Why was the Sheppard case unusual?
   a. A husband was accused of murdering his wife.
   b. The murder occurred in 1954.
   c. Doubt about the guilty verdict led to a second trial.
   d. The accused murderer said he didn't do it.

2. The author of this article implies that Sam Sheppard ______
   a. did not kill his wife
   b. lied about the bushy-haired man
   c. did not love his wife
   d. married again after he got out of prison

TOEFL Success 26 1. c 2. a

合理的な疑い

意味と例文

1 accuse（動詞） ある人が何か悪いことをした（例えば罪を犯した）と言う

例文訳 ジョーダンは、約 300 ドルの電子機器を買うのに、盗んだクレジットカードを使った罪で訴えられていた。

ヒント 使い方 accuse は受動態で使われることが多い。また、後ろに of を伴うことが多い。

関連語 accusation（名詞）告発、非難、accuser（名詞）告発人

---

2 allegedly（副詞） 人が言うところによると

例文訳 その会社の最高財務責任者は、会社の金を個人的な使用のために横領したと言われている。

関連語 allege（動詞）主張する、断言する、allegation（名詞）主張

---

3 civil（形容詞） （刑事告訴ではない）市民同士の争いに関係している

例文訳 バーニーは隣人を相手にした民事訴訟で、隣人の犬に噛まれたと主張した。

ヒント 使い方 法廷の文脈においては、civil はほとんどの場合、次のいずれかの表現で使われる：civil suit（民事訴訟）、civil action（民事訴訟）、civil court（民事裁判所）、civil proceedings（民事訴訟手続き）、civil penalties（民事罰）

---

4 convict（動詞） （ある人がある）犯罪を犯したと結論を下す

例文訳 ディーンは、彼が別の男を殴るビデオを陪審員が見た後、暴行の有罪判決を受けた。

ヒント 使い方 convict は受動態で使われることが多い。また、後ろに of を伴うことが多い。

関連語 convict（名詞）有罪の宣告を受けた人、受刑者、conviction（名詞）有罪判決、確信

---

5 guilty（形容詞）（悪いことをしたと）責められるべきである

例文訳 陪審員は、取締役を横領で有罪とした。

ヒント 使い方 guilty の後には、犯罪や悪い行いを表す of 句が続くことが多い。

関連語 guilt（名詞）罪悪感、有罪、guiltily（副詞）うしろめたい様子で

6 offense（名詞）法を犯す具体的な行為（違反）

例文訳 無謀運転で二度の有罪判決を受けたヴィクターは、再び重大な交通違反を犯すと免許を失うことになる。

関連語 offender（名詞）犯罪者、違反者、offensive（形容詞）無礼な、不快な

7 peer（名詞）（ある人にとって）社会的に対等な人

例文訳 米国の法律は、「自分と同等の地位の陪審員」による判決を要求することで、上流階級の陪審員の偏っている可能性のある判決から下層階級の被告を守ることを目的としていた。

8 suspect（名詞）ある罪を犯した可能性があると警察が判断した人（容疑者）

例文訳 警察は、その酒店強盗の容疑者５人の行動を捜査していた。

関連語 suspect（動詞）嫌疑をかける、怪しいと思う、suspicion（名詞）疑い、suspicious（形容詞）疑っている、疑わしい、suspiciously（副詞）疑い深く

9 verdict（名詞）裁判事件の判決

例文訳 陪審員が「有罪」という評決に至るのに要した時間はわずか 30 分だった。

ヒント 使い方 verdict は動詞 reach や arrival at の目的語になることが多い。

10 witness（動詞）（あること、特に犯罪が起こるのを）目にする

例文訳 ロドニーは車の盗難を目撃すると、警察に通報した。

関連語 witness（名詞）目撃者

TOEFL プレップ 26 － 1

左列の各単語に最も近い意味の単語や語句を選び、空欄にそのアルファベットを書きなさい。

______	1. accuse	(a) ある人を有罪と決定する
______	2. convict	(b) 犯罪に対して責任がある
______	3. civil	(c) 社会的に同等な人
______	4. guilty	(d) 犯罪ではない、個人的な争いに関係している
______	5. peer	(e) ある人が悪いことをしたと言う

TOEFL プレップ 26－2

各文を完成させるのに最も適した単語を丸で囲みなさい。

1 その殺人事件の最も可能性のある（容疑者／目撃者）は被害者の兄だったが、実際に犯行を目撃した人はいなかった。

2 新大統領は主要な敵対者を殺させたと（言われて／うしろめたい様子で）いるが、本人は否定している。

3 米国ではかつて、マリファナの所持は軽微な（評決／罪）だった。

4 その（目撃者／同僚）は犯行現場の詳細をあまり多く思い出せなかったので、陪審員にたいした印象を与えなかった。

5 陪審員は、陪審員全員が合意できる全会一致の（評決／有罪判決）を下すように指示されている。

TOEFL サクセス 26

文章を読んで学んだ語彙を復習します。後に続く質問に答えなさい。

［例文訳］

20世紀で最も物議を醸した殺人事件の1つは、1954年のマリリン・シェパードの死亡に関するものだ。彼女の夫であるサム・シェパード医師は、彼女を殺害し、それから自分自身に傷を負わせたとして告発された。およそ容疑者とは思えないほど、シェパードは医学界の仲間たちから非常に尊敬されていた。それでも、この殺人事件にはシェパードがうまく釈明できない奇妙な点がいくつかあった。シェパードにとって不幸なことに、彼を支持する者は誰ひとり実際に犯行を目撃していなかったので、真犯人は髪のふさふさした男で、自分は自宅の芝生でその男を追いかけてわずかな時間格闘したというシェパードの主張を、誰も裏付けることができなかった。

シェパードは最終的にその罪に対して有罪判決を受けたが、多くの人がその判決を疑っていた。F・リー・ベイリーという弁護士の積極的な支援により、シェパードは再審を勝ち取った。ベイリーはシェパードの罪に代わる多くの可能性を提案してみせた。それは、新しい陪審員が、合理的な疑いを超えて彼が有罪であるとまでは言えなくなるのに十分だった。シェパードは刑務所から釈放されたが、その後すぐに亡くなった。息子のチップは、母の殺害の真相を知ろうとして、いくつかの民事および刑事手続きを通してこの事件を追った。1990年代後半になって、新しいDNA分析技術により、事件の夜、サム・シェパードとその家族以外の誰かが家にいたことが証明された。髪のふさふさした男についてのシェパードの話は、おそらく最初からずっと本当のことだったのだろう。

読解のポイント　butとdoubtを含む節は、判決に対する反論がなされることを意味している。

1　なぜシェパード事件は異例だったのか？
   a.　夫が妻を殺したと訴えられたから。
   b.　その殺人事件は1954年に起きたから。
   c.　有罪判決への疑いが第二審につながったから。
   d.　殺人者として告発されている人が自分はやっていないと言ったから。

2　この文章の筆者は、サム・シェパードについてなんと言っているか？
   a.　妻を殺していなかった。
   b.　髪のふさふさした男について嘘をついた。
   c.　妻を愛していなかった。
   d.　出所後に再婚した。

The Police

Target Words

1. apprehend
2. ascertain
3. bureaucratic
4. condemn
5. evidence
6. implicate
7. inquiry
8. intrusively
9. seize
10. surveillance

Definitions and Samples

1. apprehend *v.* To capture

The police **apprehended** the robbery suspect as he tried to get on a bus to Chicago.

Parts of speech apprehension *n*

2. ascertain *v.* To make sure of

The police failed to **ascertain** that the man they arrested was the Gregory Brown they were really looking for.

Usage tips *Ascertain* is often followed by a *that* clause. Notice that the root of the word is the adjective *certain*, meaning "sure."

3. bureaucratic *adj.* Related to a large organization with a lot of complicated procedures

Before I could speak with the chief, I had to go through a **bureaucratic** runaround of identity checks and written requests unnecessarily complicated.

Parts of speech bureaucracy *n*, bureaucrat *n*

4. condemn *v.* To speak out against something in very strong terms

Religious radicals **condemned** the government for allowing alcohol to be sold in restaurants.

Parts of speech condemnation *n*

5. evidence *n.* Something that makes the truth of a statement seem more likely

The most convincing **evidence** that Garner robbed the store was a videotape from surveillance cameras.

Parts of speech evidence *v*, evident *adj*, evidently *adv*

6. implicate *v.* To suggest that someone was involved in a crime or other wrong behavior

No group claimed responsibility for the bombing, but the type of explosive used **implicates** the Heartland Freedom Militia.

Usage tips *Implicate* is often followed by *in*.

Parts of speech implication *n*

7. inquiry *n.* An investigation

The FBI launched an **inquiry** into the relationship between organized crime and the trucking company.

Parts of speech inquire *v*

8. intrusively *adv.* In a way that brings an unwanted person or thing into someone else's affairs

The new consultant from company headquarters appeared **intrusively** at meetings, staff parties, and other functions where he was not wanted.

Parts of speech intrude *v*, intrusion *n*, intruder *n*, intrusive *adj*

9. seize *v.* To take something against its owner's will

Federal agents can **seize** private homes and other property possibly used in the production or sale of illegal drugs.

Parts of speech seizure *n*

10. surveillance *n.* A process of watching something or someone for a long time, usually because the person is suspected of something

Police **surveillance** of one suspected car thief resulted in the arrest of a whole gang of carjackers.

Usage tips *Surveillance* is often followed by an *of* phrase.

TOEFL Prep 27-1 **Find the word or phrase that is closest in meaning to the opposite of each word in the left-hand column. Write the letter in the blank.**

______	1. ascertain	(a) unnoticeably
______	2. intrusively	(b) simple and straightforward
______	3. seize	(c) give back
______	4. condemn	(d) cause doubt about
______	5. bureaucratic	(e) praise

TOEFL Prep 27-2 **Complete each sentence by filling in the blank with the best word from the list. Change the form of the word if necessary. Use each word only once.**

apprehend evidence implicate inquiry surveillance

1. Officials could not ______ Basil because people in villages and towns throughout the country were willing to hide him.
2. During their ______ of O'Brien's house, detectives took pictures of anyone walking or driving past the house.
3. Until we finish our ______ into the disappearance of the cash, all employees are suspects.
4. Even if there is ______, such as fingerprints, that might ______ someone in a crime, there might be other indications that the person is innocent.

TOEFL Success 27 **Read the passage to review the vocabulary you have learned. Answer the questions that follow.**

The Fourth Amendment to the U.S. Constitution protects citizens from unreasonable search and seizure. Some civil libertarians have *condemned* the federal antidrug *bureaucracy* for threatening this basic right. In a drug case, police need

---

TOEFL Prep 27-1 1. d 2. a 3. c 4. e 5. b
TOEFL Prep 27-2 1. apprehend 2. surveillance 3. inquiry 4. evidence, implicate

no *evidence* to *intrude* on private property, *apprehend* a suspected dealer, and *seize* all the person's property. Property taken under this law may be sold for a profit later by the law-enforcement officials involved in the raid. The target of a raid might be *implicated* only by an unreliable report from an unfriendly neighbor. The police are not required to *ascertain* whether there's any physical evidence of drug activity at the site. **In one case**, *surveillance* of a large California property convinced local authorities to seize it—not because they saw drug activity but because the property was worth a lot of money. The property was taken, and its owner was shot trying to defend himself. A later *inquiry* determined that there were no illegal drugs on the property.

Bonus Structure **In one case** introduces an example.

1. According to this reading, which of these activities does the author oppose?
   a. marijuana possession
   b. surveillance
   c. property seizures
   d. civil libertarians

2. Why does the author of this reading mention the Fourth Amendment?
   a. because drug-related seizures seem to violate it
   b. because it outlaws the use of certain drugs
   c. because it has finally stopped the antidrug forces from seizing property
   d. because he disagrees that Americans should be protected by it

TOEFL Success 27 1. c 2. a

政府と正義
レッスン 27

警察

意味と例文

1 apprehend（動詞） 捕まえる

例文訳 警察は、その強盗の容疑者がシカゴ行きのバスに乗ろうとしたところを逮捕した。

関連語 apprehension（名詞）不安、逮捕

2 ascertain（動詞） 確かめる

例文訳 警察は逮捕した男が、本当に探していたグレゴリー・ブラウンかどうか確認できなかった。

ヒント 使い方 ascertain の後にはしばしば that 節が続く。語根は形容詞の certain で、「確かな、確信している」という意味であることに留意すること。

3 bureaucratic（形容詞） 煩雑な手続きが多い大規模な組織に関連する（官僚的な）

例文訳 長官と話をする前に、私は身分証明書の確認や不必要に複雑な要求書の作成といったお役所的なたらい回しにあわなければならなかった。

関連語 bureaucracy（名詞）官僚主義、bureaucrat（名詞）官僚、官僚主義者

4 condemn（動詞） （非常に強い言葉で何かに）反対を唱える

例文訳 宗教的急進派は、レストランでのアルコール販売を許可したことで政府を激しく非難した。

関連語 condemnation（名詞）激しい非難

5 evidence（名詞） ある発言が真実であることを一層確かにするもの（証拠）

例文訳 ガーナーがその店を襲ったことの最も説得力のある証拠は、監視カメラのビデオテープだった。

関連語 evidence（動詞）明示する、立証する、evident（形容詞）明白な、evidently（副詞）明らかに

6 implicate（動詞） （ある人が犯罪やその他の不正行為に関与していたことを）示唆する

例文訳 その爆破についてはどの集団からも犯行声明は出されていないが、使用された爆弾の種類が、ハートランド・フリーダム・ミリシアの犯行であることを示唆している。

ヒント▶ 使い方 implicate は後ろに in を伴うことが多い。

関連語 implication（名詞）暗示するもの、影響

7 inquiry（名詞） 調査

例文訳 FBI は組織犯罪とそのトラック運送会社の関係について捜査を開始した。

関連語 inquire（動詞）尋ねる、問い合わせる

8 intrusively（副詞） 求められていない人や物を、他人の事情に引き入れるやり方で（でしゃばって）

例文訳 本社から来たその新しいコンサルタントは、会議やスタッフパーティー、その他の望まれていない場に、でしゃばるようにして現れた。

関連語 intrude（動詞）立ち入る、侵入する、intrusion（名詞）侵入、侵害、intruder（名詞）侵入者、intrusive（形容詞）押しつけがましい、でしゃばる

9 seize（動詞） （持ち主の意志に反して何かを）奪う

例文訳 連邦捜査官は、違法薬物の製造や販売に使われている可能性のある個人の家やその他の財産を差し押さえることができる。

関連語 seizure（名詞）押収、差し押さえ、奪取

10 surveillance（名詞） （通常何かの疑いのために物や人を長時間にわたって）監視するプロセス

例文訳 車泥棒の容疑者１人を警察が監視した結果、車泥棒の一団全員の逮捕につながった。

関連語 surveillance は後ろに of 句を伴うことが多い。

TOEFL プレップ 27－1

左列の各単語の反対語に最も近い意味の単語や語句を選び、空欄にそのアルファベットを書きこみなさい。

______	1. ascertain	(a) 人目をひかないように
______	2. intrusively	(b) 簡単でわかりやすい
______	3. seize	(c) 返す
______	4. condemn	(d) 疑問を抱かせる
______	5. bureaucratic	(e) 賞賛する

TOEFL プレップ 27－2

リストの中から空欄に当てはまる適切な単語を選んで、各文を完成させなさい。必要に応じて単語を活用させること。なお、各単語は一度しか使用できません。

apprehend　evidence　implicate　inquiry　surveillance

1 当局者たちがバジルを______できなかったのは、国中の村や町の人々が彼を進んでかくまったからだ。

2 オブライエンの家を______している間、刑事は家の前を歩いている人や車を運転している人全員の写真を撮った。

3 現金が消えたことに関する______が終わるまで、すべての従業員が容疑者だ。

4 指紋など、ある人が犯罪に______と思われる______があったとしても、その人が無実であることを示す他の何かがあるかもしれない。

TOEFL サクセス 27

文章を読んで学んだ語彙を復習します。後に続く質問に答えなさい。

[例文訳]

合衆国憲法修正第４条は、不合理な捜索と押収から市民を守るためのものである。市民的リバタリアン（自由至上主義者）の中には、この基本的な権利を脅かしているとして連邦政府の麻薬対策の官僚主義を非難する人もいる。麻薬事件の場合、警察は私有地に侵入し、売人と思われる人物を逮捕し、その人の財産をすべて押収するのになんの証拠も必要とされない。この法律に基づいて押収された財産は、手入れに関わった取締官によって後日、金儲けのために売り払われるかもしれない。手入れの標的となる人は、敵意のある隣人からの、信頼性に欠ける報告だけをもとにまきこまれるのかもしれない。警察は、現場に薬物使用の物理的証拠があるかどうかを確認することは求められていない。あるケースでは、カリフォルニア州のある広大な土地を監視した結果、地元当局がその土地を差し押さえたが、その理由は麻薬の使用を目撃したからではなく、その土地が多額の価値を持っていたからだった。土地は奪われ、所有者は身を守ろうとして撃たれた。その後の捜査で、敷地内に違法薬物はなかったことが判明した。

読解のポイント In one case **は、一例を紹介している。**

1　この文章によれば、筆者が反対しているのは次のうちどれか？
　a. マリファナの所持
　b. 監視
　c. 財産の差し押さえ
　d. 市民的リバタリアン

2　筆者は、なぜ修正第４条に言及しているのか？
　a. 薬物関連の押収がそれに違反していると考えられるから。
　b. 特定の薬物の使用を禁止しているから。
　c. 麻薬取締官による財産の差し押さえをついに止めたから。
　d. 米国人がこの法律によって守られるべきだということに同意していないから。

Investigating Crimes

Target Words

1. analyze
2. assail
3. contrary
4. hypothesize
5. impair
6. inference
7. objectively
8. suspicious
9. tolerate
10. versus

Definitions and Samples

1. **analyze** *v.* To examine something by looking at its parts
Chemists **analyzed** the white powder and found it to be only a mixture of sugar and salt.
Parts of speech analysis *n*, analyst *n*

2. **assail** *v.* To attack or criticize forcefully
With DNA evidence from the crime scene, the defense lawyer **assailed** the police for falsely arresting his client.
Parts of speech assault *n*, assailant *n*

3. **contrary** *adj.* Opposite
Contrary to most studies, Dr. Ito's work shows the world's climate is not getting warmer.
Usage tips Common phrases are *contrary to* and *on the contrary*.

4. **hypothesize** *v.* To make a guess, the correctness of which will eventually be investigated systematically
Scientists **hypothesize** that planets capable of supporting life exist beyond our solar system, but they have not yet seen any.
Usage tips *Hypothesize* is often followed by a *that* clause.
Parts of speech hypothesis *n*, hypothetical *adj*

5. **impair** *v.* To make something less effective than usual

The snow **impaired** John's ability to hear anyone's footsteps.

Usage tips The object of *impair* is often [*someone's*] *ability to*.

Parts of speech impairment *n*

6. **inference** *n.* A conclusion drawn from evidence

Inspector Dowd's **inference** that Ms. Miller was South African was based on her accent.

Parts of speech infer *v*

7. **objectively** *adv.* Based on unbiased standards, not on personal opinion

I don't like Mr. Rowan, but looking **objectively** at his sales numbers, I saw that he was a very valuable employee.

Parts of speech objective *adj*

8. **suspicious** *adj.* Believing that something is wrong; acting in a way that makes people believe you have done something wrong

The neighbors became **suspicious** of Jim when he bought a big new car and some fancy clothes.

Jim's **suspicious** purchases made his neighbors think he might be getting money illegally.

Parts of speech suspicion *n*, suspiciously *adv*

9. **tolerate** *v.* To avoid getting upset about something

My math teacher **tolerates** a lot of talking in her class, but my history teacher tells us to be quiet.

Parts of speech toleration *n*, tolerance *n*, tolerant *adj*

10. **versus** *prep.* Against

In the debate, it was pro-war senators **versus** antiwar senators.

Usage tips *Versus* is often abbreviated as *vs.* in sports contexts, or simply *v.* in legal contexts.

TOEFL Prep 28-1 **Find the word or phrase that is closest in meaning to each word in the left-hand column. Write the letter in the blank.**

______	1. assail	(a) against
______	2. contrary	(b) guess
______	3. hypothesize	(c) showing differences or opposition
______	4. impair	(d) vigorously attack
______	5. versus	(e) cause problems for

TOEFL Prep 28-2 **Circle the word that best completes each sentence.**

1. Most police departments have laboratories, where scientists (assail / analyze) evidence according to scientific procedures.
2. The new police chief would not (tolerate / impair) any joking around in the police station.
3. Everyone assumed Travis was innocent, despite evidence to the (contrary / suspicious).
4. A judge who feels unable to think (versus / objectively) about a case should withdraw from it.
5. The bomb squad was called after a (suspicious / contrary) package was delivered to the governor's office.

TOEFL Success 28 **Read the passage to review the vocabulary you have learned. Answer the questions that follow.**

In 1979, two British farmers reported that, while sitting on a hill, they suddenly saw the crops below flattened in a perfect circle. They *inferred* that some great force must have come down directly from above to squash the corn and barley. **This** started a public hysteria about so-called crop circles. The patterns pressed into the crops (not all of them were

TOEFL Prep 28-1 1. d 2. c 3. b 4. e 5. a
TOEFL Prep 28-2 1. analyze 2. tolerate 3. contrary 4. objectively 5. suspicious

circles) seemed to have no entry or exit points. Many people *hypothesized* that only alien spaceships could make such bizarre imprints. Others, including Britain's police, *assailed* such wild conclusions. They had a *contrary* theory: Someone was playing a big hoax. Teams of investigators took samples of the plants and the soil, trying to *objectively analyze* the crop circles as if they were a crime scene. Public curiosity often *impaired* the investigators, who had to *tolerate* busloads of tourists flocking to the circles. The farmers in the area, long *suspicious* of the police, approached the case as an instance of police *versus* the people. If the local farmers knew the circles were a hoax, they wouldn't say so.

Bonus Structure **This** refers to the whole situation described in the previous sentence, not to any one noun phrase.

1. According to the article, why did many people think that crop circles were created by alien spaceships?
   a. The circles looked like they had been made from above and had no way in or out.
   b. The observers in 1979 reported seeing a UFO land and make a crop circle.
   c. The plants and soil inside a crop circle contained chemicals not naturally found on Earth.
   d. They were in unusual shapes and contained alien symbols.

2. Why does the author mention "a hoax"?
   a. because one of the locals admitted playing a trick on his neighbors
   b. because most people think that crop circles are evil
   c. because police investigators thought crop circles were made by humans as a joke
   d. because crop circles are probably made by secret government aircraft

TOEFL Success 28 1. a 2. c

政府と正義
レッスン 28

犯罪捜査

意味と例文

1 analyze（動詞）（あちこちを見て何かを）調べる

例文訳 化学者がその白い粉を分析したところ、それはただの砂糖と塩の混合物であることがわかった。

関連語 analysis（名詞）分析、analyst（名詞）分析者、評論家

---

2 assail（動詞） 強烈に攻撃または批判する

例文訳 弁護人は犯行現場のDNAの証拠を使って、彼の依頼人を誤って逮捕した警察を強く糾弾した。

関連語 assault（名詞）暴行、襲撃、assailant（名詞）襲撃者

---

3 contrary（形容詞） 反対の

例文訳 多くの研究に反して、伊藤博士の研究は世界の気候は温暖化していないことを示している。

ヒント 使い方 一般的な言い回しは、contrary to と on the contrary である。

---

4 hypothesize（動詞） （その正しさがいずれ体系的に調査されるような）推測をする

例文訳 科学者たちは、生命を維持できる惑星が太陽系外に存在するという仮説を立てているが、まだそれを見たことはない。

ヒント 使い方 hypothesize の後には、that 節が続くことが多い。

関連語 hypothesis（名詞）仮説、hypothetical（形容詞）仮定の

---

5 impair（動詞） （あるものの効果を通常よりも）低下させる

例文訳 雪は、ジョンが人の足音を聞き取る力を弱めてしまった。

ヒント 使い方 impair の目的語は多くの場合、(someone's) ability to である。

関連語 impairment（名詞）損傷、悪化

---

6 inference （名詞） （証拠から導き出された）結論

例文訳 ミラーさんは南アフリカ人だというダウド警部の推理は、彼女の訛りに基づいていた。

関連語 infer（動詞）推測する、暗示する

7 objectively （副詞） （個人の意見ではなく）公平な基準に基づいて

例文訳 私はローワン氏が好きではないが、彼の販売数を客観的に見ると、彼が非常に有益な社員であることがわかった。

関連語 objective（形容詞）客観的な

8 suspicious （形容詞） あるものが間違っていると信じている（疑い深い）／何か悪いことをしたと人々に思わせるような行動をとっている

例文訳 ジムが大きな新車や高級な服を買うと、近所の人たちはジムを怪しむようになった。
ジムが不審な買い物をしたので、近所の人たちは彼が不法にお金を稼いでいるのではないかと考えた。

関連語 suspicion（名詞）疑い、suspiciously（副詞）疑い深く

9 tolerate （動詞） （何かについて）動揺しない

例文訳 私の数学の先生はクラスでのたくさんのおしゃべりを大目に見てくれるが、歴史の先生は私たちに静かにするように言う。

関連語 toleration（名詞）寛大さ、許容すること、tolerance（名詞）寛容、忍耐、tolerant（形容詞）寛容な、耐性がある

10 versus （前置詞） 対して

例文訳 その討論会では、戦争賛成派の議員対反戦派の議員が議論した。

ヒント 使い方 versusは、スポーツの文脈ではvs.と略され、法律の文脈では単にv.と略されることが多い。

TOEFL プレップ 28－1

左列の各単語に最も近い意味の単語や語句を選び、空欄にそのアルファベットを書きなさい。

________	1. assail	(a) 対して
________	2. contrary	(b) 推測する
________	3. hypothesize	(c) 差異や反対を示している
________	4. impair	(d) 猛烈に攻撃する
________	5. versus	(e) 問題を引き起こす

TOEFL プレップ 28－2

各文を完成させるのに最も適した単語を丸で囲みなさい。

1 ほとんどの警察署には研究所があり、科学者が科学的な手順に従って証拠を（攻撃する／分析する）。

2 その新しい警察署長は署内で冗談を言うのを一切（許さ／損なわ）ないだろう。

3 （反対の／疑わしい）証拠があるにもかかわらず、誰もがトラヴィスは無実だと思った。

4 ある事件に（対して／客観的に）考えることができないと感じているような裁判官は、その件から手を引くべきだ。

5 知事の執務室に（不審な／反対の）小包が届けられると、爆弾処理班が呼ばれた。

TOEFL サクセス 28

文章を読んで学んだ語彙を復習します。後に続く質問に答えなさい。

[例文訳]

1979年、イギリスの2人の農民が、丘の上に座っていたら、突然、下にある作物が完全な円形に倒されているのを見つけたと報告した。彼らは、何か大きな力が上から直接かかって、トウモロコシや大麦が潰されたに違いないと推測した。これをきっかけに、いわゆる「クロップ・サークル」と呼ばれるものをめぐって世間で大騒ぎになった。作物が押されてできた模様（すべてが円というわけではない）は、入口も出口もないように見えた。このような奇妙な刻印は、エイリアンが乗った宇宙船でなければつくれないと、多くの人が仮定した。他方、イギリスの警察などは、このような荒唐無稽な結論を強く非難した。彼らには反対の説があった。誰かが大がかりないたずらをしているというのだ。捜査チームは、現場の植物や土壌のサンプルを採取し、あたかも犯罪現場であるかのようにクロップ・サークルを客観的に分析しようとした。世間の人たちの好奇心が捜査官を苦しめることも多く、捜査官たちは、バスに乗って大勢でクロップ・サークルに押し寄せる観光客を甘んじて受け入れなければならなかった。地元の農民たちは、長い間警察に不信感を持っていたため、この事件を警察と住民の対立の事例としてとらえた。農民たちは、もしサークルがいたずらだと知っていても、それを口にすることはないだろう。

読解のポイント　**ここでのThisは、何か１つの名詞句ではなく、直前の文に書かれている状況全体を指している。**

1　この文章によれば、なぜ多くの人々はクロップ・サークルがエイリアンの宇宙船によってつくられたと考えたのか？

a. 円は上からつくられたように見えて、入口も出口もなかったから。

b. 1979年の発見者が、UFOが着陸してクロップ・サークルをつくっているのを見たと報告しているから。

c. クロップ・サークル内の植物や土壌には、地球上では自然には見られないはずの化学物質が含まれていたから。

d. クロップ・サークルは珍しい形をしていて、エイリアンのシンボルが入っていたから。

2　なぜ筆者は「いたずら」に言及しているのか？

a. 地元住人の１人が、近所の人々にいたずらをしたと認めたから。

b. ほとんどの人がクロップ・サークルは邪悪なものだと思っているから。

c. 警察の捜査官が、クロップ・サークルは人間がジョークとしてつくったものだと思っていたから。

d. クロップ・サークルはおそらく政府の秘密の航空機によってつくられているから。

Government Corruption

Target Words

1. bribery
2. cynically
3. erode
4. evade
5. grotesque
6. integrity
7. prevalent
8. reform
9. scandal
10. unmask

Definitions and Samples

1. bribery *n.* Giving money or other gifts to a government official or other person in authority in order to get special privileges

Bribery of police officers is common in countries where police salaries are very low.

Parts of speech bribe *v*, bribe *n*

2. cynically *adv.* Disrespectfully; emphasizing the weaknesses of otherwise respected things

Employees of the Roadways Department **cynically** referred to their boss as "the banker" because he took so many bribes.

Parts of speech cynic *n*, cynicism *n*, cynical *adj*

3. erode *v.* To wear away and become smaller

People's respect for the government **eroded** as more officials were arrested for corruption.

Usage tips *Erode* can be intransitive (*the beach eroded*) or transitive (*the waves eroded the beach*).

Parts of speech erosion *n*, erosive *adj*

4. evade *v.* To get away from something that tries to catch you

The robbery suspects tried to **evade** the police by fleeing to Canada.

Parts of speech evasion *n*, evasive *adj*

5. **grotesque** *adj.* Extremely unattractive, in a way that catches a lot of attention
Spending $3.5 million to redecorate the governor's house is a **grotesque** misuse of public money.

6. **integrity** *n.* Personal honesty and good character
We don't have a problem with our employees stealing from the store because we hire only people with a lot of **integrity**.

7. **prevalent** *adj.* Common; easy to find because it exists in great amounts
Distrust of elected officials was **prevalent** in our county because many of them were friends with certain candidates.
Parts of speech prevail *v*, prevalence *n*

8. **reform** *v.* To make big improvements
The new law was an attempt to **reform** the system of giving money to political candidates.
Parts of speech reform *n*, reformer *n*

9. **scandal** *n.* A case of wrongdoing that hurts someone's reputation
In the Watergate **scandal**, some of the president's top advisors were revealed to be criminals.
Parts of speech scandalize *v*, scandalous *adj*

10. **unmask** *v.* Reveal; expose something that is hidden
The Forge Trucking Company was eventually **unmasked** as a front for organized crime.

TOEFL Prep 29-1 **Find the word or phrase that is closest in meaning to the opposite of each word in the left-hand column. Write the letter in the blank.**

________	1. cynically	(a) respectfully
________	2. evade	(b) corruption
________	3. integrity	(c) cover up
________	4. prevalent	(d) uncommon
________	5. unmask	(e) get caught

TOEFL Prep 29-2 **Circle the word that best completes each sentence.**

1. The president resigned because a (scandal / bribery) made it impossible for him to lead.
2. Laws that let the police monitor criminals can (erode / evade) the privacy of innocent citizens too.
3. After Downforth Castle was bought by apartment developers, it became a (prevalent / grotesque) jumble of poorly built additions.
4. In some places, people who are pulled over for traffic offenses use (scandal / bribery) to avoid getting a ticket.
5. President Carazza came to office promising (reform / integrity) of the prison system.

TOEFL Success 29 **Read the passage to review the vocabulary you have learned. Answer the questions that follow.**

In many countries, few politicians have enough *integrity* to resist corruption and *bribery*. Because such practices are so *prevalent*, officials often *evade* any personal sense of guilt by pretending that everyone is just as corrupt as they are. Even in cases of really *grotesque* corruption, the kind that might cause a *scandal* in a less-corrupt government, the

TOEFL Prep 29-1 1. a 2. e 3. b 4. d 5. c
TOEFL Prep 29-2 1. scandal 2. erode 3. grotesque 4. bribery 5. reform

general population may not be shocked. Instead, they may *cynically* conclude that government corruption is natural and unavoidable. **In this environment**, the efforts of an honest politician to *unmask* corruption may be *eroded* by the public's lack of interest, causing any efforts at *reform* to fail.

Bonus Structure **In this environment** means "under these conditions."

1. Why do people in some countries not react negatively to corruption?
   a. because they feel it cannot be avoided
   b. because they want reform
   c. because almost everyone in the government is corrupt
   d. because they have paid money to gain influence

2. What effect might a small scandal have in a country where government corruption is not typical?
   a. It could make someone very popular.
   b. It could cause a politician to become cynical.
   c. It could cost a lot of money.
   d. It could cause a government official to lose his or her position.

TOEFL Success 29 1. c 2. d

政府と正義
レッスン29

政府の腐敗

意味と例文

1 bribery（名詞） （特別な恩恵を得るために政府高官やその他の権力者に）金品を渡すこと

例文訳 警察官の贈収賄は、警察官の給料が非常に低い国ではよく見られる。

関連語 bribe（動詞）賄賂を贈る、bribe（名詞）賄賂

---

2 cynically（副詞） 無礼に／（他の点では尊敬されているものの）弱点を強調して

例文訳 道路局の従業員たちは、上司があまりにたくさんの賄賂を受け取っていたので、彼のことを皮肉を込めて「銀行家」と呼んだ。

関連語 cynic（名詞）皮肉屋、cynicism（名詞）冷笑、皮肉な言動、cynical（形容詞）皮肉な、冷笑的な

---

3 erode（動詞） 消耗して小さくなる

例文訳 汚職で逮捕される役人が増えるにつれ、人々の政府への敬意は薄れていった。

ヒント 使い方 erodeは、自動詞（例:the beach eroded　砂浜は侵食された）としても、他動詞（例：the waves eroded the beach　波が砂浜を侵食した）としても使える。

関連語 erosion（名詞）浸食、低下、erosive（形容詞）浸食的な

---

4 evade（動詞） （捕まえようとしてくるものから）逃れる

例文訳 その強盗事件の容疑者たちは、カナダに逃亡して警察から逃れようとした。

関連語 evasion（名詞）回避、言い逃れ、evasive（形容詞）回避的な、言い逃れの

---

5 grotesque（形容詞） （多くの注目を集めるほどに）極めて魅力的でない

例文訳 知事の家の改装に350万ドルも使うのは、公金のとんでもない悪用だ。

6 integrity（名詞） （個人の）誠実さ、優れた人格

例文訳 我々は非常に誠実な人しか採用しないので、従業員が店から盗みを働くといった問題は起きない。

7 prevalent（形容詞） 一般的な／（大量に存在するため）見つけやすい

例文訳 私たちの郡では、選挙で選ばれた公職者の多くが特定の候補者の友人だったため、彼らに対する不信感が蔓延していた。

関連語 prevail（動詞）普及する、打ち勝つ、prevalence（名詞）普及、流布

8 reform（動詞） 大きな改善をする

例文訳 その新法は、政治家の候補者に資金を提供するシステムを改革するための試みだった。

関連語 reform（名詞）改革、改善、reformer（名詞）改革者

9 scandal（名詞） （ある人の評判を落とすような）悪事

例文訳 ウォーターゲート・スキャンダルでは、大統領の上級顧問の何人かが犯罪者であることが明らかになった。

関連語 scandalize（動詞）憤慨させる、あきれさせる、scandalous（形容詞）中傷的な、恥ずべき

10 unmask（動詞） 明らかにする／（隠されているものを）あらわにする

例文訳 フォージュ運送会社は、最終的に組織犯罪の隠れ蓑であると暴かれた。

TOEFL プレップ 29－1

左列の各単語の反対語に最も近い意味の単語や語句を選び、空欄にそのアルファベットを書きなさい。

________	1. cynically	(a) うやうやしく
________	2. evade	(b) 不正
________	3. integrity	(c) 隠蔽する
________	4. prevalent	(d) めったにない
________	5. unmask	(e) 捕まる

TOEFL プレップ 29－2

各文を完成させるのに最も適した単語を丸で囲みなさい。

1　大統領が辞任したのは（スキャンダル／贈収賄）によって国を率いていくことができなくなったからだ。

2　警察が犯罪者を監視できるようにする法律は、無実の市民のプライバシーをも（侵食する／回避する）可能性がある。

3　ダウンフォース城は、マンション開発業者に買収された後、粗末な増築物の（普及している／グロテスクな）寄せ集めになってしまった。

4　交通違反で車を道のわきに止めさせられた人が、切符を切られないように（スキャンダル／賄賂）を使う地域もある。

5　カラッツア大統領は刑務所制度の（改革／誠実）を約束して就任した。

TOEFL サクセス 29

文章を読んで学んだ語彙を復習します。後に続く質問に答えなさい。

［例文訳］

多くの国では、汚職や賄賂に抵抗できるほど誠実な政治家はほとんどいない。このような行為があまりにも蔓延しているため、政治家たちはしばしば、自分と同じように誰もが堕落していると思い込むことで、どんな個人的な罪悪感からも免れる。そこまで堕落していない政府でスキャンダルになるような本当にグロテスクな汚職であったとしても、一般の人々はショックを受けないかもしれない。それどころか、政府の腐敗は自然なことであり、避けることはできないのだと冷笑的に結論づけるかもしれない。このような環境では、誠実な政治家が汚職を明らかにしようと努力しても、国民の関心の低さに侵食され、改革の努力が失敗に終わる可能性がある。

読解のポイント In this environment は、「この状況では」の意味。

1　なぜ一部の国の人々は、汚職に否定的な反応を示さないのか？
　a. 彼らは、汚職を避けることができないと感じているから。
　b. 彼らは、改革を望んでいるから。
　c. 政府のほとんど全員が堕落しているから。
　d. 彼らは影響力を得るためにお金を払ってしまっているから。

2　政府の腐敗が普通ではない国では、小さなスキャンダルはどのような影響を与える可能性があるか？
　a. 人気者を生み出すかもしれない。
　b. 政治家が皮肉屋になるかもしれない。
　c. 多額の費用がかかるかもしれない。
　d. 政府関係者がその地位を失う原因になるかもしれない。

Crimes at Sea

Target Words

1. abduction
2. coerce
3. detain
4. deviant
5. distort
6. intentionally
7. piracy
8. predicament
9. smuggle
10. villainy

Definitions and Samples

1. abduction *n.* Kidnapping

Pirates got many crew members by **abduction**, snatching unlucky citizens from seaport towns.

Parts of speech abduct *v*, abductor *n*

2. coerce *v.* To force; to put pressure on someone to do something

A criminal's confession is not usable in court if the police **coerce** him or her into giving it.

Parts of speech coercion *n*, coercive *adj*

3. detain *v.* To prevent someone, for a relatively short time, from going on their way

The police **detained** at least 20 men for questioning, but charged none of them with a crime.

Parts of speech detention *n*, detainee *n*

4. deviant *adj.* In a style that is not normal and is offensive to many

The artist based his reputation on creating **deviant** works of art that disgusted most of the public.

Usage tips *Deviant* always implies a bad opinion of someone or something.

Parts of speech deviant *n*, deviation *n*, deviate *v*

5. **distort** *v.* To twist or misrepresent; to make something seem different from what it really is

If you hold a pencil in a glass of water, the water **distorts** the appearance of the pencil.

Parts of speech distortion *n*

6. **intentionally** *adv.* On purpose, not by accident

Danny **intentionally** lost his last golf ball because he was tired of playing.

Parts of speech intent *n*, intention *n*, intend *v*, intentional *adj*

7. **piracy** *n.* Stealing a ship or taking its cargo; the unlawful copying of books, music, film, etc.

Modern-day **piracy** occurs mostly near groups of small, uninhabited islands where pirates can hide.

The software company constantly battled **piracy**.

Parts of speech pirate *n*, pirate *v*

8. **predicament** *n.* A difficult situation, one that is hard to get out of

College basketball stars face the **predicament** of wanting to graduate but being tempted by high professional salaries.

9. **smuggle** *v.* To illegally bring things into a country

The pirate Ben Dewar **smuggled** guns to British and Indian fighters in North America.

Parts of speech smuggler *n*, smuggling *n*

10. **villainy** *n.* Exceptional badness, as demonstrated by many serious evil deeds

Fred was not a natural criminal, but he learned all kinds of **villainy** while being jailed for a minor crime.

Parts of speech villain *n*, villainous *adj*

TOEFL Prep 30-1 **Find the word or phrase that is closest in meaning to the opposite of each word in the left-hand column. Write the letter in the blank.**

______	1. detain	(a) clarify
______	2. distort	(b) by accident
______	3. villainy	(c) let go
______	4. intentionally	(d) normal
______	5. deviant	(e) good deeds

TOEFL Prep 30-2 **Choose the word from the list that is closest in meaning to the underlined part of each sentence. Write it in the blank.**

abducted *coerced* *piracy* *predicament* *smuggled*

______ 1. The police force's difficult situation involved a bank robber who threatened to shoot a bank employee if any police approached.

______ 2. Despite laws restricting animal imports, thousands of monkeys and lemurs and other wild animals are brought illegally into the United States.

______ 3. The enemy captured and took away the general's son.

______ 4. Two men were convicted of stealing a boat near the Riau Islands.

______ 5. By threatening to set fire to their ship, the governor of Bermuda pressured the pirate crew to give themselves up.

TOEFL Success 30 **Read the passage to review the vocabulary you have learned. Answer the question that follows.**

The Spanish explorer Pizarro's *abduction* of the Inca King Atahualpa came in 1529. His men *detained* the king, *coerced* the Incas into paying a large ransom in gold and silver, and then *intentionally* killed the king anyway. Their conquest of Peru established the legendary Spanish Main—Spanish holdings on the mainland of Central and South America. The *predicament* for Spain's kings was how to get the riches of the

---

TOEFL Prep 30-1 1. c 2. a 3. e 4. b 5. d
TOEFL Prep 30-2 1. predicament 2. smuggled 3. abducted 4. piracy 5. coerced

New World to Spain. Pirates and privateers ruled the waves. To *distort* what was actually just robbery, the king of England issued "letters of marque," licenses that turned certain pirates into agents of the British government. Their *piracy* against Spanish ships and Spanish gold was considered service to the king or queen of England.

Most pirates with such letters were social *deviants* anyway, and **predictably**, they became embarrassments to the British crown. In 1603, Britain's King James I canceled all his government's letters of marque. The many dangerous, unemployed pirates became buccaneers, a terrifying mix of tough characters that operated from the island of Hispaniola. They conducted merciless raids on Spanish settlements and formed a brotherhood known for theft, torture, *smuggling*, and *villainy* of all sorts.

Bonus Structure **Predictably** means that the information that follows is no surprise.

An introductory sentence for a brief summary of the passage is provided below. Complete the summary by selecting three answer choices that express the most important ideas in the passage. In each blank, write the letter of one of your choices.

The establishment of the Spanish Main provided rich targets for pirates and privateers, often with government encouragement.
•
•
•

a. Pizarro's men abducted King Atahualpa in 1529.
b. By issuing letters of marque, the kings of England gave their approval of raids on Spanish ships.
c. Piracy in the South China Sea was also a problem at this time.
d. Pirates who worked for the English crown were known as buccaneers.
e. Sailing under a letter of marque, a privateer could steal property in the king's name.
f. Eventually, the English crown was embarrassed by the behavior of its privateers and canceled the letters of marque.

TOEFL Success 30 b, e, f

政府と正義
レッスン30

海上の犯罪

意味と例文

1 abduction（名詞） 誘拐

例文訳 海賊は多くの乗組員を、港町から不運な住民を連れ去ること、つまり誘拐することで手に入れた。

関連語 abduct（動詞）誘拐する、abductor（名詞）誘拐犯

---

2 coerce（動詞） 強制する／（誰かに何かをするよう）圧力をかける

例文訳 犯罪者の自白は、それを警察が強要した場合、法廷では有効ではない。

関連語 coercion（名詞）強制、威圧、coercive（形容詞）強制的な、威圧的な

---

3 detain（動詞） （比較的短い時間）ある人が立ち去るのを阻む

例文訳 警察は、少なくとも20人の男性を尋問のために勾留したが、誰も起訴しなかった。

関連語 detention（名詞）勾留、監禁、detainee（名詞）拘留者

---

4 deviant（形容詞） 普通ではなく多くの人に不快感を与えるスタイルで（逸脱した）

例文訳 そのアーティストは、多くの人を不快にさせるような常軌を逸した芸術作品を制作することで評判を築いた。

ヒント 使い方 deviantは常に人やものに対する悪い評価を意味する。

関連語 deviant（名詞）逸脱者、変わった人、deviation（名詞）逸脱、deviate（動詞）逸脱する

---

5 distort（動詞） ねじ曲げる／誤って伝える／（あるものを実際とは）違うように見せる

例文訳 水の入ったグラスの中に鉛筆を入れると、水が鉛筆の見え方をゆがめる。

関連語 distortion（名詞）ゆがめること、ゆがみ、曲解

6 intentionally （副詞） （偶然ではなく）故意に

例文訳 ダニーはゴルフに飽きたので、最後のゴルフボールをわざとなくした。

関連語 intent（名詞）意図、故意、intention（名詞）意図、意志、intend（動詞）～するつもりである、intentional（形容詞）故意の

7 piracy （名詞） 船を盗むこと、船の積み荷を奪うこと／本・音楽・映画などを違法にコピーすること

例文訳 現代の海賊行為は、海賊たちが隠れることのできる小さな無人島群の近くで多く発生している。
そのソフトウェア会社は、常に著作権侵害行為と戦っていた。

関連語 pirate（名詞）海賊、著作権侵害者、pirate（動詞）略奪する、著作権を侵害する

8 predicament （名詞） （抜け出すのが難しいような）困難な状況

例文訳 大学バスケットボールのスター選手は、卒業したくてもその前にプロの高額な給料に誘惑されてしまうという苦境に立たされる。

9 smuggle （動詞） （ある国に）不法にものを持ち込む

例文訳 海賊のベン・デュワーは、北米にいるイギリス人や先住民の戦士たちに銃を密輸していた。

関連語 smuggler（名詞）密輸業者、密輸船、smuggling（名詞）密輸

10 villainy （名詞） （多くの重大な悪行によって示される）並外れた悪さ

例文訳 フレッドは生来の犯罪者ではなかったが、軽罪で投獄されている間にあらゆる悪事を覚えた。

関連語 villain（名詞）悪人、悪役、villainous（形容詞）極悪の

TOEFL プレップ 30－1

左列の各単語の反対語に最も近い意味の単語や語句を選び、空欄にそのアルファベットを書きなさい。

______	1. detain	(a) 明らかにする
______	2. distort	(b) 偶然に
______	3. villainy	(c) 解放する
______	4. intentionally	(d) 通常の
______	5. deviant	(e) よい行い

TOEFL プレップ 30－2

各文の下線部に最も近い意味を持つ単語をリストから選び、空欄に記入しなさい。

abducted　coerced　piracy　predicament　smuggled

______ 1. 警察が近づいたら行員を撃つと銀行強盗が脅迫したために、警察は困難な状況に陥った。

______ 2. 動物の輸入を制限する法律があるにもかかわらず、何千頭もの猿やキツネザルなどの野生動物が米国に違法に持ち込まれている。

______ 3. 敵は将軍の息子を捕らえて連れ去った。

______ 4. リアウ諸島の近くで船を盗んだことで２人の男が有罪になった。

______ 5. バミューダ諸島の総督は、船に火をつけると脅して、海賊船の乗組員に降伏するよう圧力をかけた。

TOEFL サクセス 30

文章を読んで学んだ語彙を復習します。後に続く質問に答えなさい。

［例文訳］

スペインの探検家ピサロがインカ帝国のアタワルパ王を誘拐したのは、1529年のことだった。ピサロの部下は王を監禁し、インカ人に多額の金銀の身代金を無理やり払わせ、その後、故意に王を殺害した。ペルーを征服したことで、伝説的なスパニッシュ・メイン（中南米大陸のスペインの領有地）がつくりだされた。スペインの王たちを困らせていたのは、どうやって新世界の富をスペインに運ぶかということであった。海は、海賊と私掠船の支配下にあった。イギリスの王は、実際には単なる略奪行為であるという実態を歪めるために、特定の海賊をイギリス政府の代理人とする許可証「私掠免許状」を発行した。スペインの船や金を狙う海賊行為は、イギリスの王や女王への奉仕とみなされたのだ。

このような免許状を持つ海賊のほとんどは社会的に逸脱した存在であり、予想通り、彼らはイギリス王室にとって恥ずべき存在となってしまった。1603年、イギリスの王ジェームズ1世は、政府が発行していた私掠免許状をすべて取り消した。職を失った多くの危険な海賊たちは、バッカニアになった。バッカニアとは、粗暴な連中の恐ろしい寄せ集めのようなもので、ヒスパニオラ島を拠点として活動した。彼らはスペイン人居住地を容赦なく襲撃し、窃盗、拷問、密輸など、あらゆる種類の悪事で知られる集団を形成した。

読解のポイント predictablyは、そのあとに続く情報が驚くべきものではないことを意味している。

以下は、この文章の要約の導入である。選択肢の中から最も重要な考えを表している3つを選び、要約文を完成させなさい。それぞれの空欄に、選択したアルファベットを書くこと。

スパニッシュ・メインの成立は、しばしば政府が後押ししたこともあり、海賊や私掠船に格好の標的を与えることとなった。
・
・
・

a. ピサロの部下が1529年にアタワルパ王を拉致した。
b. イギリス王は私掠免許状を発行することで、スペイン船への襲撃を承認した。
c. 南シナ海での海賊行為も当時、問題になっていた。
d. イギリス王室のために働く海賊は、バッカニアとして知られていた。
e. 私掠船は、私掠免許状に基づいて航海することで、王の名において財産を盗むことができた。
f. 結局、イギリス王室は私掠船の行動を恥として、私掠免許状を取り消した。

The War on Drugs

Target Words

1. addictive
2. cartel
3. concentrated
4. interdict
5. juxtapose
6. misconception
7. modify
8. potent
9. residual
10. subtly

Definitions and Samples

1. addictive *adj.* Making someone want it so much that the person feels ill without it

Some drugs, like heroin or methamphetamines, are **addictive** to almost everyone who tries them.

Parts of speech addict *v*, addict *n*, addiction *n*

2. cartel *n.* A small group controlling a certain area of business

The world's major oil producers formed a **cartel** to control the price and supply of petroleum.

3. concentrated *adj.* Strong because large amounts are in a certain space

Concentrated lemon juice is very sour, so I mix it with water when I make lemonade.

Parts of speech concentrate *v*, concentration *n*, concentrate *n*

4. interdict *v.* To keep something from reaching a certain place

With faster patrol boats, the Coast Guard can more easily **interdict** drugs being smuggled by sea.

Parts of speech interdiction *n*

5. juxtapose *v.* Place next to one another

If you **juxtapose** these two similar flowers, you can see

clear differences between them.

Parts of speech juxtaposition *n*

6. **misconception** *n.* A mistaken belief

A common **misconception** about rabbits is that they are a kind of rodent.

Parts of speech misconceive *v*

7. **modify** *v.* Make small changes in order to get a certain result

People who live in high mountains often **modify** their car engines to run well in the thinner air.

Parts of speech modification *n*, modifier *n*

8. **potent** *adj.* Powerful

A very **potent** type of marijuana with surprisingly strong effects became available in Burrytown.

Parts of speech potency *n*

9. **residual** *adj.* Left behind after most of a thing has gone

In the airplane, agents found **residual** traces of heroin.

Usage tips *Residual* is often followed by *trace*, *amount*, or some other word referring to "quantity."

Parts of speech residue *n*

10. **subtly** *adv.* In a quiet, hard-to-notice way

By **subtly** changing the soft drink's formula, we improved its taste and made production cheaper.

Parts of speech subtlety *n*, subtle *adj*

TOEFL Prep 31-1 **Find the word or phrase that is closest in meaning to each word in the left-hand column. Write the letter in the blank.**

______	1. cartel	(a) stop
______	2. interdict	(b) remaining
______	3. juxtaposed	(c) next to
______	4. residual	(d) without drawing attention
______	5. subtle	(e) a kind of group

TOEFL Prep 31-2 **Circle the word that best completes each sentence.**

1. With a (subtle / residual) nod of his head, the inspector signaled his agents.
2. Sunlight is a (concentrated / potent) source of energy for electricity generation, but it can be expensive to collect and store.
3. Things other than drugs can be (addictive / subtle), such as gambling or even television.
4. A security official tries to (modify / interdict) foreign terrorists before they can enter the country.
5. Your advertisement created the (misconception / cartel) that everything was on sale for 50 percent off.

TOEFL Success 31 **Read the passage to review the vocabulary you have learned. Answer the questions that follow.**

Illegal *addictive* drugs, like heroin or cocaine, come from plants grown and harvested mostly by poor farmers. Their small farmhouses *juxtaposed* with the mansions of billionaire drug lords illustrate the unequal payouts to various players in the drug trade. The farmers sell their product cheaply to a drug-distribution *cartel* that is owned by the drug lords.

TOEFL Prep 31-1 1. e 2. a 3. c 4. b 5. d
TOEFL Prep 31-2 1. subtle 2. potent 3. addictive 4. interdict 5. misconception

People working for the cartel **then** refine the drugs into a *concentrated* form, or even *modify* them chemically to make them more *potent* and therefore more valuable. Other cartel members **then** transport the drugs to distributors for sale, smuggling them over huge distances, including international borders. Governments try to *interdict* smugglers, using both new technology and old (like sniffer dogs) to find *residual* traces of drugs. Their occasional successes have led to a popular *misconception* that antidrug campaigns are close to stopping the flow of illegal drugs. On the contrary, as long as drug lords can make vast fortunes in their illegal trade, smugglers will come up with ever-more-*subtle* ways of concealing their goods, and the War on Drugs goes on.

Bonus Structure Because this reading describes a system of operations, the word **then** appears very often.

1. Who makes the most money from the drug trade?
   a. rural farmers
   b. people who refine drugs
   c. drug lords
   d. antidrug officers

2. Schematic table: Write the letter of each phrase in either column A or column B, based on which one it relates to according to the reading.

A. Drug producers and dealers	B. Antidrug forces

   a. subtle ways of hiding drugs
   b. sniffer dogs
   c. high-tech detection
   d. concentrate drugs to make them potent
   e. pay farmers to grow plants that yield drugs

TOEFL Success 31 1. c 2. Column A: a, d, e Column B: b, c

政府と正義
レッスン31

麻薬戦争

意味と例文

1 addictive（形容詞） それがないと気分が悪くなるほど、あるものが欲しくてたまらなくさせる（習慣性の）

例文訳 ヘロインやメタンフェタミンのように、試した人のほとんどが中毒になってしまう薬物がある。

関連語 addict（動詞）中毒にさせる、熱中させる、addict（名詞）常用者、熱狂的愛好者、addiction（名詞）中毒、依存、熱中

---

2 cartel（名詞） （特定のビジネス分野を支配する）小集団

例文訳 世界の主要な石油生産者は、石油の価格と供給をコントロールするためにカルテルを結成した。

---

3 concentrated（形容詞） ある空間に大量に存在するために強い様子（集中した）

例文訳 濃縮されたレモン果汁はとても酸っぱいので、レモネードをつくるときには水と混ぜる。

関連語 concentrate（動詞）集中する、濃縮する、concentration（名詞）集中、濃度、concentrate（名詞）濃縮物

---

4 interdict（動詞） （あるものが特定の場所に）及ばないようにする

例文訳 巡視船がもっと速くなれば、沿岸警備隊は海上経由の麻薬密輸をより簡単に阻止できる。

関連語 interdiction（名詞）禁止、阻止

---

5 juxtapose（動詞） 隣同士に並べる

例文訳 この2種類の似ている花を並べてみると、その違いがよくわかるだろう。

関連語 juxtaposition（名詞）並列

6 misconception（名詞） 間違った信念

例文訳 ウサギに関するよくある誤解は、ウサギはげっ歯類に属しているというものだ。

関連語 misconceive（動詞）誤解する

7 modify（動詞） （ある結果を得るために）小さな変更を加える

例文訳 高山地域に住んでいる人は、空気の薄いところでも走れるように車のエンジンを改造することが多い。

関連語 modification（名詞）（部分的な）変更、修正、modifier（名詞）変更する人、修飾語

8 potent（形容詞） 強い

例文訳 驚くほど強い効果を持つ、非常に強力なタイプのマリファナが、バリータウンで購入できるようになった。

関連語 potency（名詞）効能、潜在力

9 residual（形容詞） （あるものの大半がなくなった後に）残された

例文訳 その飛行機の中で、捜査官たちはヘロインの残留痕跡を発見した。

ヒント 使い方 residualの後にはtraceやamountなどの「量」を表す単語が続くことが多い。

関連語 residue（名詞）残り、残留物

10 subtly（副詞） 静かに気づかれにくいように（微妙に）

例文訳 私たちはその清涼飲料水の製法を微妙に変えることで、味をよくし、生産コストを下げた。

関連語 subtlety（名詞）微妙さ、巧妙さ、subtle（形容詞）微妙な、かすかな、巧妙な

TOEFL プレップ 31－1

左列の各単語に最も近い意味の単語や語句を選び、空欄にそのアルファベットを書きなさい。

________	1. cartel	(a) 止める
________	2. interdict	(b) 残っている
________	3. juxtaposed	(c) 隣の
________	4. residual	(d) 注意をひかない
________	5. subtle	(e) グループの一種

TOEFL プレップ 31－2

各文を完成させるのに最も適した単語を丸で囲みなさい。

1 （かすかな／残りの）頭の動きで、警視は捜査官たちに合図を送った。

2 太陽光は発電のための（凝縮された／強力な）エネルギー源だが、集めたり蓄えたりするためのコストが高くなる可能性がある。

3 薬物以外のものも、例えばギャンブル、あるいはテレビでさえ、（中毒性を持つ／微妙な）ことがある。

4 安全保障担当官は外国人テロリストが入国する前にそれを（修正／阻止）しようとする。

5 あなたの広告は、すべてのものが50パーセント割引で売られているという（誤解／カルテル）を生み出した。

TOEFL サクセス 31

文章を読んで学んだ語彙を復習します。後に続く質問に答えなさい。

[例文訳]

ヘロインやコカインといった中毒性のある違法薬物は、主に貧しい農家で栽培や収穫がなされた植物からつくられる。億万長者の麻薬王の大邸宅と隣り合う農家の小さな家屋は、麻薬取引におけるさまざまなプレーヤーへの配当が不平等であることを示している。農家は、自分たちの作物を、麻薬王が所有する麻薬流通カルテルに安く売る。そしてカルテルで働く人々は、麻薬を精製して濃縮された形にしたり、時には化学的な改変までしたりして、より強力でより価値のあるものにする。それから、カルテルの他のメンバーが、国境を含む膨大な距離を密輸して、密売組織の販売用に麻薬を運ぶ。政府は、薬物の残留痕跡を見つけるための新しい技術と古い技術（麻薬探知犬など）の両方を使って、密輸業者を阻止しようとする。彼らもときに成功することがあるため、麻薬撲滅キャンペーンによって違法薬物の流れがせき止められようとしているという誤解が世間に広がってしまっている。だが実際には、それどころか、麻薬王が違法な取引で巨万の富を得ることができる限り、密輸業者は商品を隠すためのますます巧妙な方法を編み出し、麻薬戦争は続いていくのである。

読解のポイント　**この文章は運営システムについて説明しているので、then が頻繁に使われている。**

1　麻薬取引で最も儲かっているのは誰か？

a. 田舎の農家

b. 麻薬を精製する人

c. 麻薬王

d. 麻薬取締官

2　概略表：文章の内容から、以下のａ～ｂをＡ列またはＢ列のどちらか当てはまるほうに記入しなさい。

A. 麻薬の生産者や密売組織	B. 麻薬取締当局

a. 薬物を隠す巧妙な方法

b. 探知犬

c. ハイテクな探知

d. 薬物を強力にするため濃縮する

e. 農家にお金を払い麻薬の原料となる植物を栽培させる

Family Relationships

Target Words

1. ancestral
2. cohesion
3. descendant
4. inheritance
5. kin
6. legitimate
7. paternal
8. proximity
9. sentiment
10. sibling

Definitions and Samples

1. ancestral *adj.* Relating to family members from earlier generations

Sweden is my **ancestral** homeland, from which my great-grandfather emigrated in 1922.

Parts of speech ancestor *n*, ancestry *n*

2. cohesion *n.* Ability to stay together as a unit

Family **cohesion** is difficult if young people have to go far away to find work.

Usage tips *Cohesion* can also be used to describe forces that keep materials or structures together.

Parts of speech cohere *v*, cohesiveness *n*

3. descendant *n.* A direct relative in a later generation (such as one's son, daughter, or grandchild)

Billy Sobieski claimed to be a **descendant** of Jan Sobieski, a former king of Poland.

Usage tips *Descendant* is often followed by an *of* phrase.

Parts of speech descend *v*, descent *n*

4. inheritance *n.* Things passed down to you from your ancestors

My **inheritance** from my grandmother included her favorite necklace.

Parts of speech inherit *v*, inheritor *n*

5. kin *n.* Relatives

Even though my uncle didn't really like me, he was kind to

me because we were **kin**.

Usage tips A common phrase is *next of kin*, meaning "closest relative."

Parts of speech kinship *n*

6. legitimate *adj.* True and respectable; in the context of family, born of a mother and father who were married to each other

You can skip the meeting if you have a **legitimate** reason. Harcourt had two legitimate children with his wife Hannah and one **illegitimate** son with a woman whom he met while traveling.

Usage tips The opposite of *legitimate* is *illegitimate*.

Parts of speech legitimize *v*, legitimacy *n*

7. paternal *adj.* Relating to a father

My mother's parents have both died, but my **paternal** grandparents are still alive.

Usage tips *Paternal* may appear with *maternal*, meaning "relating to a mother."

8. proximity *n.* Nearness

The house was comfortable, except for its **proximity** to a busy road.

Usage tips *Proximity* can be followed by an *of* phrase or a *to* phrase.

Parts of speech proximate *adj*

9. sentiment *n.* Feelings; opinion based on feelings

I share your **sentiments** about air travel, but I disagree that cars are safer.

Usage tips *Sentiments* (the plural) is more common than *sentiment*.

Parts of speech sentimentality *n*, sentimental *adj*

10. sibling *n.* Brother or sister

My **siblings** and I got together to buy our parents a gift for their anniversary.

Usage tips *Sibling* is often preceded by a possessive noun or pronoun.

TOEFL Prep 32-1 Find the word or phrase that is closest in meaning to each word in the left-hand column. Write the letter in the blank.

______	1. ancestral	(a) fatherly
______	2. descendants	(b) children, grandchildren, etc.
______	3. legitimate	(c) what one thinks or feels
______	4. paternal	(d) acceptable and right
______	5. sentiments	(e) related to earlier generations

TOEFL Prep 32-2 Complete each sentence by filling in the blank with the best word from the list. Change the form of the word if necessary. Use each word only once.

cohesion *inheritance* *kin* *proximity* *siblings*

1. You can't expect to have family ______ if the members don't respect each other.
2. In our family, the ______ who are closest in age get along the best.
3. If someone dies without a will, the possessions usually go to the next of ______.
4. Medical bills in his last year greatly reduced the ______ going to Tom's wife.
5. Legally, parents have the same ______ of relationship to an adopted child as to their biological children.

TOEFL Success 32 Read the passage to review the vocabulary you have learned. Answer the questions that follow.

The nature of the family varies widely from culture to culture. In some societies, family members tend to stay in close *proximity* to their *kin*, never moving more than a few miles away from the *ancestral* home. In other places, while the

---

TOEFL Prep 32-1 1. e 2. b 3. d 4. a 5. c
TOEFL Prep 32-2 1. cohesion 2. siblings 3. kin 4. inheritance 5. proximity

members of one generation may all live near one another, their *descendants* in the next generation scatter widely. In such a case, it's difficult to maintain the same family *cohesion* enjoyed by those who live close together. Sometimes marriage can govern family structure; for example, there may be strict traditions requiring a new bride to leave her *paternal* home and *siblings* to move in with her new husband's family. Such traditions are followed, even by young couples who don't like them, because going against them is likely to result in the loss of *inheritance*. Whatever one's own *sentiments* about family structure, it is important to recognize that one culture's family system is as *legitimate* as another's.

1. Which of the following best states the main idea of this passage?
   a. Different family systems can be found worldwide, but each one deserves respect.
   b. Societies in which children move far away from their parents are not very cohesive.
   c. Although some societies still require a wife to move in with her husband's family, this tradition is dying out.
   d. The most important factor in family happiness is close proximity to your relatives.

2. According to this reading, which family system is most common?
   a. Members of a family living in the same community.
   b. Family members spreading out and living in various cities.
   c. Young couples living with the man's parents.
   d. It is impossible to tell from this reading.

TOEFL Success 32 1. a 2. d

人間関係
レッスン 32

家族関係

意味と例文

1 ancestral （形容詞） **先代からの親族に関する**

例文訳 スウェーデンは私の先祖代々の故国であり、曽祖父は1922年にその国から移民してきた。

関連語 ancestor（名詞）先祖、ancestry（名詞）家系、先祖（全体）

---

2 cohesion （名詞） **1つの集団としてともにいられること（団結）**

例文訳 若者が仕事を見つけるために遠くに行かなければならないと、家族の結束は難しい。

ヒント 使い方 cohesionは、物質や構造物をまとめておく力を表す言葉としても使われる。

関連語 cohere（動詞）結合する、筋が通る、cohesiveness（名詞）結合力があること

---

3 descendant （名詞） **後の世代の直系親族（息子、娘、孫など）**

例文訳 ビリー・ソビェスキは、自分はかつてのポーランド王、ヤン・ソビェスキの子孫であると主張した。

ヒント 使い方 descendantは後ろにof句を伴うことが多い。

関連語 descend（動詞）降りる、遺伝する、descent（名詞）降下、家系、遺伝

---

4 inheritance （名詞） **先祖から受け継がれたもの（遺産）**

例文訳 私が祖母から受け継いだもののなかに、祖母が気に入っていたネックレスがあった。

関連語 inherit（動詞）相続する、受け継いでいる、inheritor（名詞）相続人、継承者

---

5 kin （名詞） **親族**

例文訳 叔父は私のことをあまり好きではなかったが、親戚なので親切にしてくれた。

ヒント 使い方 「近親者」を意味するnext of kinという言い回しがよく使われる。

関連語 kinship（名詞）親類関係

6 legitimate（形容詞） 真実でありきちんとしている／（家庭についての文脈では）結婚している母親と父親の間に生まれた（合法の）

例文訳 正当な理由があれば、あなたは会議を欠席することができる。ハーコートには、妻ハンナとの間に嫡出子が2人と、旅行中に出会った女性との間に非嫡出子の息子が1人いた。

ヒント 使い方 legitimate の反対語は illegitimate（非合法の）。

関連語 legitimize（動詞）合法化する、正当だと示す、legitimacy（名詞）合法性、正当性

7 paternal（形容詞） 父親に関連した

例文訳 母の両親はどちらも亡くなったが、父方の祖父母はまだ生きている。

ヒント 使い方 paternal は「母親に関連した」を意味する maternal と一緒に使われることがある。

8 proximity（名詞） 近さ

例文訳 交通量の多い道路に近いことを除けば、その家は快適だった。

ヒント 使い方 proximity は後ろに of 句や to 句を伴うことがある。

関連語 proximate（形容詞）直接の、直近の

9 sentiment（名詞） 感情／感情に基づく意見

例文訳 飛行機の旅についてのあなたの感想には同意するが、車のほうが安全だという意見には同意できない。

ヒント 使い方 sentiment は単数形よりも複数形で使われることが多い。

関連語 sentimentality（名詞）感情的なこと、感傷、sentimental（形容詞）感情的な

10 sibling（名詞） 兄弟または姉妹

例文訳 私たち兄弟（姉妹）は、両親の結婚記念日にプレゼントを買うために集まった。

ヒント 使い方 sibling の前には、所有名詞や所有代名詞が来ることが多い。

TOEFL プレップ 32−1

左列の各単語に最も近い意味の単語や語句を選び、空欄にそのアルファベットを書きなさい。

________	1. ancestral	(a) 父親らしい
________	2. descendants	(b) 子ども、孫など
________	3. legitimate	(c) 人が考えたり感じたりすること
________	4. paternal	(d) 受け入れ可能で正しい
________	5. sentiments	(e) 前の世代に関連する

TOEFL プレップ 32−2

リストの中から空欄に当てはまる適切な単語を選んで、各文を完成させなさい。必要に応じて単語を活用させること。なお、各単語は一度しか使用できません。

cohesion　inheritance　kin　proximity　siblings

1 メンバーがお互いを尊重していなければ、家族の________を期待することはできない。

2 私たちの家族では、年齢が最も近い________同士が一番仲がいい。

3 遺言書を残さずに死んだ場合、その人の財産は通常、最も近い________に行く。

4 トムの晩年にかかった医療費により、彼の妻に渡る________が大幅に減ってしまった。

5 法的には、親は養子に対しても、実子と同じ________の関係がある。

TOEFL サクセス 32

文章を読んで学んだ語彙を復習します。後に続く質問に答えなさい。

［例文訳］

家族の性質は、文化によって大きく異なる。社会によっては、家族のメンバーは親族の近くにいることが多く、先祖代々の家から数マイル以上離れることは決してない。また別の社会では、ある世代のメンバーは全員近くに住んでいても、次の世代の子どもたちは広く散らばっている。このような場合、近くに住んでいる人たちと同じような家族の結束を保つことは難しい。結婚が家族のあり方を左右することもある。例えば、新婦は父方の家や兄弟姉妹から離れ、新しい夫の家族のもとに移らなければならない、という厳しい伝統があるかもしれない。このような伝統は、それを好まない若い夫婦の場合でも、反すれば、結果的に遺産が手に入らない可能性があるため、きちんと守られているのである。家族のあり方について抱く感情がどのようなものだとしても、ある文化の家族制度は他の文化のそれと同様に正当であると認識することが重要である。

1　この文章の主旨を最もよく表しているのはどれか？

a. 世界にはさまざまな家族制度があるが、それぞれが尊重されるべきである。

b. 子どもが親から遠く離れていく社会は、結束があまり強くない。

c. いまだに妻が夫の家族と同居しなければならない社会もあるが、この伝統は失われつつある。

d. 家族の幸せにとって最も重要なのは、親戚との距離が近いことだ。

2　この文章によると、どのような家族制度が最も一般的か？

a. 家族のメンバーが同じコミュニティに住んでいる家族制度。

b. 家族のメンバーが分散してさまざまな都市に住んでいる家族制度。

c. 若い夫婦が男性の両親と一緒に住む家族制度。

d. この文章からはわからない。

Friendship

Target Words

1. affection
2. associate
3. bond
4. clique
5. confide
6. exclusive
7. fluctuate
8. in common
9. solidarity
10. willing

Definitions and Samples

1. **affection** *n.* An emotional closeness or warmth
I show **affection** for my girlfriend by spending time with her, not by spending money on her.
Usage tips *Affection* is often followed by a *for* phrase.
Parts of speech affectionate *adj*

2. **associate** *v.* To regularly spend time together
Carol doesn't **associate** with people who smoke.
Usage tips *Associate* is often followed by a *with* phrase.
Parts of speech association *n*, associate *n*

3. **bond** *n.* A close connection
Some researchers say that there is an especially strong emotional **bond** between twins.
Usage tips A *between* or *among* phrase—indicating the people or things that are connected—often follows *bond*.
Parts of speech bond *v*

4. **clique** *n.* A small group of friends who are unfriendly to people outside the group
High-schoolers form **cliques** to gain security and acceptance.
Usage tips *Clique* indicates a negative feeling toward a group.
Parts of speech cliquish *adj*

5. **confide** *v.* To tell very personal things
Teenagers are more willing to **confide** in a friend than in a parent.

Usage tips *Confide* is almost always followed by an *in* phrase.

Parts of speech confidence *n*, confidant *n*, confidential *adj*

6. **exclusive** *adj.* Keeping out all but a few people
The most **exclusive** universities accept only a small percentage of people who want to attend.
Usage tips In advertisements, *exclusive* has a positive tone ("so good that only a few people can have it"); in describing relationships ("attached to only one person") the tone is neutral.
Parts of speech exclude *v*, exclusion *n*, exclusively *adv*

7. **fluctuate** *v.* To change often, from one condition to another
Earth's climate **fluctuates** between warm periods and cold periods.
Usage tips *Fluctuate* is usually followed by a *between* phrase (or by a *from . . . to* structure).
Parts of speech fluctuation *n*

8. **in common** *adv.* As a shared characteristic
Billy and Heather have a lot **in common**—basketball, a love of pizza, and an interest in snakes.
Usage tips *In common* very often appears with the verb *to have*.

9. **solidarity** *n.* Standing together despite pressure to move apart
Many student groups declared **solidarity** with the Latino Student Association in their effort to get a Spanish-speaking principal.
Usage tips *Solidarity* is usually used in political contexts.

10. **willing** *adj.* Agreeable and ready to do something
Because of their long friendship, Professor Gardner was **willing** to say a few words at Jones's birthday celebration.
Usage tips *Willing* is almost always followed by a *to* + verb structure.
Parts of speech will *v*, will *n*, willingness *n*

TOEFL Prep 33-1 **Find the word or phrase that is closest in meaning to each word in the left-hand column. Use each letter only once.**

________	1. affection	(a) liking someone or something
________	2. bond	(b) to move back and forth
________	3. clique	(c) standing together in a political cause
________	4. fluctuate	(d) a connection
________	5. solidarity	(e) an exclusive group

TOEFL Prep 33-2 **Circle the word or phrase that best completes each sentence.**

1. Charles is (exclusive / willing) to be friends with Dory, but he is already dating another girl.
2. If I (associate / confide) in you, do you promise to keep what I say a secret?
3. When it comes to weather, Minnesota and North Dakota have a lot (in common / in a bond).
4. One of the main reasons to go to an exclusive college is that you get to (associate / fluctuate) with some of the country's future leaders.
5. The court said that the club's membership rules were unjustly (willing / exclusive) because they kept out people of certain ethnic groups.

TOEFL Success 33 **Read the passage to review the vocabulary you have learned. Answer the questions that follow.**

You can walk into any high school and spot the *cliques*: the jocks hang out here, the geeks there, the Goths and preppies in their areas. Teenagers feel a strong need to belong to a group, to *associate* with people with whom they share

TOEFL Prep 33-1 1. a 2. d 3. e 4. b 5. c
TOEFL Prep 33-2 1. willing 2. confide 3. in common 4. associate 5. exclusive

common interests or goals. Since adolescence is often a time when teens feel turmoil in their home lives, they seek *affection* and friendship outside the home. They look for other young people to *bond* with when their parents don't seem to "understand." Teens going through the various crises of adolescence can more easily *confide* in others their own age, with whom they have more *in common*. Teen cliques are by no means *exclusive*; membership can *fluctuate* on an almost daily basis, but the important thing is that group members feel a sense of *solidarity* and are *willing* to stick together.

1. According to the reading, why do adolescents search for friendship outside the home?
   a. They want to be accepted by the jocks and Goths.
   b. They think their parents don't understand the problems they face.
   c. They want to be in a different clique every day.
   d. They want to talk about their parents with other teenagers.

2. According to the reading, do teens stay in the same groups all the time?
   a. Yes, because their parents want them to.
   b. Yes, because they share common interests.
   c. No, they may move from group to group quite frequently.
   d. No, most groups don't accept new members.

TOEFL Success 33 1. b 2. c

人間関係
レッスン33

友情

意味と例文

1 affection（名詞） 感情的な近さや温かさ

例文訳 私は、恋人のためにお金を使うことではなく、一緒に過ごすことによって彼女への愛情を示す。

ヒント 使い方 affection は後ろに for 句を伴うことが多い。

関連語 affectionate（形容詞）愛情のこもった

2 associate（動詞） 頻繁に一緒に過ごす

例文訳 キャロルはタバコを吸う人とは付き合わない。

ヒント 使い方 associate は後ろに with 句を伴うことが多い。

関連語 association（名詞）協会、関係、associate（名詞）同僚、仲間

3 bond（名詞） 密接なつながり

例文訳 双子の間には特に強い感情的な絆があると言う研究者もいる。

ヒント 使い方 bond の後には、人や物のつながりを表す between 句や among 句が続くことが多い。

関連語 bond（動詞）つながる、くっつける

4 clique（名詞） （外部の人には友好的でない）少人数の友人同士の集まり

例文訳 高校生は、安心感や受容を得るために徒党を組む。

ヒント 使い方 clique は、あるグループに対する否定的な感情を表す。

関連語 cliquish（形容詞）徒党の、排他的な

5 confide（動詞） 非常に個人的なことを話す

例文訳 ティーンエイジャーは親よりも友人に秘密を打ち明けようとするものだ。

ヒント 使い方 confide の後には、ほとんどの場合、in 句が続く。

関連語 confidence（名詞）信頼、自信、confidant（名詞）腹心の友、confidential（形容詞）秘密の

6 exclusive （形容詞） （ごく一部の人以外を）排除する

例文訳 最上位の名門の大学には、希望者のごく一部しか入学できない。

ヒント▶ 使い方 広告においてはexclusiveは肯定的なニュアンス（「少数の人しか持てないほど優れている」）を、人間関係の文脈においては（「１人の人とだけ深く付き合う」）中立的なニュアンスを持っている。

関連語 exclude（動詞）排除する、締め出す、exclusion（名詞）除外、排除、exclusively（副詞）もっぱら、排他的に

7 fluctuate （動詞） （ある状態から別の状態へと）頻繁に変化する

例文訳 地球の気候は、温暖な時期と寒冷な時期の間で変動している。

ヒント▶ 使い方 fluctuateの後には、通常between句または「from ～ to」が続く。

関連語 fluctuation（名詞）変動、動揺

8 in common （副詞） 共通の特徴として

例文訳 ビリーとヘザーには、バスケットボール、ピザ好き、ヘビに興味があることなど、多くの共通点がある。

ヒント▶ 使い方 in commonは、動詞「to have」と一緒に使われることが非常に多い。

9 solidarity （名詞） （ばらばらにさせようとする圧力にもかかわらず）結束すること

例文訳 多くの学生団体が、スペイン語を話す校長を擁立しようとしているラテン系学生協会との連帯を宣言した。

ヒント▶ 使い方 solidarityは通常、政治的な文脈で使われる。

10 willing （形容詞） （あることをするのに）乗り気で準備もできている姿勢

例文訳 ガードナー教授はジョーンズと長年友人関係にあったので、彼の誕生日会でスピーチすることを快く引き受けた。

ヒント▶ 使い方 willingの後にはほとんどの場合、「to ＋動詞」が続く。

関連語 will（動詞）（意志の力で）成し遂げようとする、will（名詞）意志、遺書、willingness（名詞）快く何かを行うこと

TOEFL プレップ 33－1

左列の各単語に最も近い意味の単語や語句を選び、空欄にそのアルファベットを書きなさい。

________	1. affection	(a) 誰かや何かを好きであること
________	2. bond	(b) 行ったり来たりして動くこと
________	3. clique	(c) 政治的な目的のために結束すること
________	4. fluctuate	(d) 結びつき
________	5. solidarity	(e) 排他的なグループ

TOEFL プレップ 33－2

各文を完成させるのに最も適した単語や語句を丸で囲みなさい。

1 チャールズはドリーと友達になることを（排除して／自ら望んで）いるが、すでに他の女の子と付き合っている。

2 もし私があなた（と付き合った／に打ち明けた）ら、私の話を秘密にするって約束する？

3 天気に関しては、ミネソタとノースダコタには（共通した／結びついた）点がたくさんある。

4 名門大学に進学する主な理由の１つは、その国の将来のリーダーたちと（付き合う／変動する）ことができるからだ。

5 裁判官は、そのクラブの会員規則は特定の民族集団の人々を排除するものであるから、不当に（進んでする／排他的である）と言った。

TOEFL サクセス 33

文章を読んで学んだ語彙を復習します。後に続く質問に答えなさい。

［例文訳］

どんな高校に足を踏み入れてみても、徒党を組んでいる学生たちがいるだろう。ここにはジョック（運動ばかりしてるやつ）が、あそこにはギーク（IT 系オタク）が、お決まりのエリアにはゴス（ゴスロックやファッションの愛好家）やプレッピー（お金持ち）がたむろしている。10 代の若者は、グループに属したい、共通の興味や目標を持った人たちと付き合いたいという強い欲求を持っている。思春期は、家庭生活の中で混乱を覚える時期であることが多いため、家庭の外に愛情や友情を求める。親に「理解」されていないと思うときに、親密な絆を結べる他の若者を探すのである。思春期のさまざまな危機を今まさに経験している10代は、共通点の多い同年代の若者に対してのほうが自分について打ち明けやすい。10代の若者がつくるグループは決して排他的ではない。メンバーは毎日のように変動するが、重要なのはグループのメンバーが連帯意識を感じ、一緒にいようとすることである。

1　この文章によれば、なぜ思春期の子どもたちは家の外に友情を求めるのか？

a. ジョックやゴスに受け入れられたいから。

b. 親が自分の直面している問題を理解していないと思っているから。

c. 毎日違うグループの中にいたいと思っているから。

d. 他のティーンエイジャーと自分の両親について話したいから。

2　この文章によれば、10代の若者はずっと同じグループにとどまるか？

a. はい。親がそうさせたがっているから。

b. はい。彼らは共通の趣味を持っているから。

c. いいえ。彼らはかなり頻繁にグループからグループへ移ることもある。

d. いいえ。ほとんどのグループは新しいメンバーを受け入れない。

Passion

Target Words

1. complex
2. despondent
3. devotion
4. dilemma
5. engender
6. loyal
7. passion
8. proliferation
9. reciprocity
10. vanish

Definitions and Samples

1. complex *adj.* Not simple; involving many parts that work together

A modern car engine is too **complex** for most car owners to repair by themselves.

Parts of speech complexity *n*

2. despondent *adj.* Extremely sad and without hope for the future

After his girlfriend left him, Johnson was **despondent** and wouldn't talk to anyone.

3. devotion *n.* A willingness to keep supporting someone you admire

Grant showed great **devotion** to his wife, supporting her during her long illness.

Usage tips *Devotion* is often followed by a *to* phrase.

Parts of speech devote *v*, devotee *n*

4. dilemma *n.* A difficult choice between two things

I was caught in a **dilemma** between traveling by airplane and taking a train, which is slower but more comfortable.

5. engender *v.* To bring into being; to cause to exist

The government's warnings about terrorism **engendered** fear throughout the nation.

Usage tips *Engender* is often followed by a noun for an emotion.

6. **loyal** *adj.* Faithful
Carter was **loyal** to his girlfriend and would not date anyone else.
Usage tips *Loyal* is often followed by a *to* phrase.
Parts of speech loyalty *n*, loyally *adv*

7. **passion** *n.* An extremely strong emotion, like love or anger
Debbie complained that there was no **passion** in her marriage.
Parts of speech passionate *adj*, passionately *adv*

8. **proliferation** *n.* An increase in the number of something and in the number of places it can be found
The **proliferation** of fast-food restaurants has made it harder for Americans to eat healthy lunches.
Usage tips *Proliferation* is very often followed by an *of* phrase.
Parts of speech proliferate *v*

9. **reciprocity** *n.* Doing as much for another as he or she has done for you
Dan was giving a lot of attention to Kelly, but he felt no **reciprocity** in their relationship.
Parts of speech reciprocate *v*, reciprocal *adj*

10. **vanish** *v.* To disappear suddenly
When the sun came out, last night's light snowfall **vanished**.

TOEFL Prep 34-1 **Find the word or phrase that is closest in meaning to the opposite of each word in the left-hand column. Write the letter in the blank.**

______	1. complex	(a) an easy choice
______	2. dilemma	(b) simple
______	3. loyal	(c) a decrease
______	4. proliferation	(d) appear
______	5. vanish	(e) unfaithful

TOEFL Prep 34-2 **Choose the word from the list that is closest in meaning to the underlined part of each sentence. Write it in the blank.**

despondent *devotion to* *engender* *passion* *reciprocity*

________ 1. In a good relationship, there is a lot of give and take.

________ 2. Mr. Foster's strong love for teaching makes him successful.

________ 3. Rhonda was extremely sad after the death of her cat.

________ 4. Sometimes, a small characteristic, like a nice smile, can cause love.

________ 5. My continuing support for the candidate is based on my admiration for her.

TOEFL Success 34 **Read the passage to review the new vocabulary you have learned. Answer the questions that follow.**

Perhaps no emotion is more complex than *passion*. Passion can show itself in a negative way as a burst of anger, or in a more pleasant way, as love. Passion can *engender* blind *devotion* for a lover or plunge a person into *despondent*

TOEFL Prep 34-1 1. b 2. a 3. e 4. c 5. d
TOEFL Prep 34-2 1. reciprocity 2. passion 3. despondent 4. engender 5. devotion to

misery if he or she feels a lack of *reciprocity* in the relationship. Passion and love cause innumerable *dilemmas*, and people constantly seek out ways to understand these emotions, as evidenced by the *proliferation* of articles, books, talk shows, and Web pages devoted to relationships. Many of these forums have *loyal* followings and have become cultural fixtures. The endless flow of information and opinions about the *complex* situations aroused by passion will probably not *vanish* anytime soon.

1. According to this article, which statement about passion is true?
   a. It can have good or bad effects.
   b. It can be easily explained.
   c. It helps people decide what to do.
   d. It is irrational.

2. According to the reading, why are there so many books and other works about passion?
   a. because people want a lot of advice about love
   b. because many people want to write about their own passion
   c. because reading about passion is relaxing
   d. because passion can also show itself as a burst of anger

Relationships

TOEFL Success 34 1. a 2. a

人間関係
レッスン 34

情熱

意味と例文

1 complex (形容詞) 単純でない／(一緒に動く)多くの部分が関わっている

例文訳 現代の車のエンジンは複雑すぎて、車の所有者の大半は自分で修理することができない。

関連語 complexity (名詞) 複雑さ

---

2 despondent (形容詞) 非常に悲しく将来への希望がない

例文訳 恋人に去られた後、ジョンソンは落胆し、誰とも話そうとしなかった。

---

3 devotion (名詞) (自分が賞賛する人を) 支え続けようという気持ち

例文訳 グラントは、妻の長い闘病生活を支え、多大な献身を示した。

ヒント 使い方 devotion は後ろに to 句を伴うことが多い。

関連語 devote (動詞) 捧げる、devotee (名詞) 愛好者、信奉者

---

4 dilemma (名詞) 二者択一の難しい選択

例文訳 私は飛行機で移動するか、時間はかかるがより快適な列車に乗るか、というジレンマに陥った。

---

5 engender (動詞) 生み出す／存在の原因となる

例文訳 政府のテロに対する警告は、国中に恐怖を引き起こした。

ヒント 使い方 engender の後には、感情を表す名詞が続くことが多い。

---

6 loyal (形容詞) 忠実である

例文訳 カーターは恋人に誠実で、他の誰ともデートしなかった。

ヒント 使い方 loyal は後ろに to 句を伴うことが多い。

関連語 loyalty（名詞）忠誠、loyally（副詞）忠実に

---

7 passion（名詞）（愛や怒りのような）非常に強い感情

例文訳 デビーは、自分の結婚生活には情熱がないとこぼした。

関連語 passionate（形容詞）情熱的な、passionately（副詞）情熱的に

---

8 proliferation（名詞）（あるものの数とそれを見つけられる場所が）増えること

例文訳 ファストフード店の急増により、米国人は健康的なランチを食べることがより難しくなった。

ヒント 使い方 proliferation は後ろに of 句を伴うことが非常に多い。

関連語 proliferate（動詞）急増する

---

9 reciprocity（名詞）（相手が自分にしてくれたように）自分も相手にしてあげること

例文訳 ダンはケリーのことをとても気にかけていたが、2人の間に相互関係があるとは感じていなかった。

関連語 reciprocate（動詞）報いる、交換する、reciprocal（形容詞）相互の、互恵的な

---

10 vanish（動詞）突然消える

例文訳 太陽が出てくると、昨夜のわずかな積雪はあっという間に消えてしまった。

TOEFL プレップ 34－1

左列の各単語の反対語に最も近い意味の単語や語句を選び、空欄にそのアルファベットを書きこみなさい。

______ 1. complex (a) 簡単な選択
______ 2. dilemma (b) 単純な
______ 3. loyal (c) 減少
______ 4. proliferation (d) 現れる
______ 5. vanish (e) 不誠実な

TOEFL プレップ 34－2

各文の下線部に最も近い意味を持つ単語をリストから選び、空欄に記入しなさい。

despondent devotion to engender passion reciprocity

______ 1. 良好な関係においては、ギブアンドテイクが多いものだ。
______ 2. 教育に対する強い愛が、フォスター氏を成功に導いている。
______ 3. ロンダは、飼っている猫が死んでとても悲しかった。
______ 4. 素敵な笑顔といった小さな特徴が、ときに愛を引き起こすこともある。
______ 5. 私がこの候補者を支持し続けるのは、彼女に憧れているからだ。

TOEFL サクセス 34

文章を読んで学んだ語彙を復習します。後に続く質問に答えなさい。

[例文訳]

おそらく、情熱ほど複雑な感情はないだろう。情熱は、怒りの爆発のようなネガティブな形で現れることもあれば、愛情のように好ましい形で現れることもある。情熱は、恋人に対する盲目的な献身をもたらすこともあれば、２人の関係に相互性がないと感じたときには、その人を失意のどん底に突き落とすこともある。情熱と愛情は数え切れないほどのジレンマを引き起こし、人々はこれらの感情を理解する方法を常に模索している。このことは、人間関係を扱っている記事や本、トークショー、ウェブページなどが急増していることからも明らかである。こういったフォーラムの多くは、忠実なファンを持ち、文化的に定着している。情熱がもたらす複雑な状況についての情報や意見がとめどなく流れ続けることは、今後もすぐになくなりはしないだろう。

1　この文章によれば、情熱に関するどの説明が正しいか？

a. よい効果も悪い効果もある。

b. 簡単に説明できる。

c. 人々が何をすべきかを決定するのに役立つ。

d. 非合理的である。

2　この文章によれば、なぜ情熱についての本やその他の作品がたくさんあるのか？

a. 人々は愛情についてたくさんのアドバイスを求めているから。

b. 多くの人が自分の情熱について書きたいと思っているから。

c. 情熱について読むとリラックスできるから。

d. 情熱は怒りの爆発として現れることもあるから。

Negative Emotions

Target Words

1. antipathy
2. arrogantly
3. berate
4. contemptuous
5. despise
6. humiliation
7. obnoxious
8. shame
9. stigmatize
10. vitriolic

Definitions and Samples

1. antipathy *n.* A strong, long-lasting negative feeling
My **antipathy** toward telemarketers is so strong that I am often rude to them.
Usage tips *Antipathy* is often followed by a *toward* phrase.

2. arrogantly *adv.* In a way that shows a high opinion of oneself and a low opinion of others
Jenny told us about her party only one day in advance, **arrogantly** thinking we had nothing else to do.
Parts of speech arrogance *n*, arrogant *adj*

3. berate *v.* To say insulting and disrespectful things
The teacher lost his job because he cruelly **berated** students who made mistakes.
Usage tips You can only *berate* someone directly—only when he or she can hear you.

4. contemptuous *adj.* Having no respect
Most scientists are **contemptuous** of reports that aliens from outer space have landed on the Earth.
Usage tips A very common structure is *be contemptuous of*.
Parts of speech contempt *n*, contemptible *adj*, contemptuously *adv*

5. despise *v.* Hate very much

Tom grew to **despise** his greedy and unfriendly boss.

6. **humiliation** *n.* An event that causes someone to feel that she or he has lost the respect of others
Losing the chess tournament was a great **humiliation** for Marie, and she never played chess again.
Parts of speech humiliate *v*

7. **obnoxious** *adj.* Bothersome; doing small things that others don't like
My **obnoxious** neighbor keeps talking to me while I'm trying to read in my backyard.
Parts of speech obnoxiously *adv*

8. **shame** *n.* Dishonor because of being associated with a mistake or bad behavior
Feeling deep **shame** because of their son's crimes, the Ford family moved to a different town.
Usage tips *Shame* is often followed by an *of* or *about* phrase.
Parts of speech shame *v*, shameful *adj*, ashamed *adj*, shamefully *adv*

9. **stigmatize** *v.* To mark with a visible feature that makes other people think, perhaps incorrectly, that someone or something is wrong
Cadbury's beard and tattoos **stigmatized** him as a bad match for Wall Street, so he couldn't find work as a financial analyst.
Parts of speech stigma *n*

10. **vitriolic** *adj.* Showing an extreme, hateful anger
The mayor's **vitriolic** attacks against the city council only made him sound unreasonable.
Usage tips The origin of *vitriolic* is "vitriol," a strong chemical that could cause painful burns.

TOEFL Prep 35-1 **Find the word or phrase that is closest in meaning to each word in the left-hand column. Write the letter in the blank.**

_______	1. arrogantly	(a) very bitter and hurtful
_______	2. berate	(b) to criticize and insult
_______	3. humiliation	(c) annoying
_______	4. obnoxious	(d) too proudly
_______	5. vitriolic	(e) embarrassment

TOEFL Prep 35-2 **Circle the word that best completes each sentence. Be careful: Many words in this chapter are very close in meaning to each other. Pay attention to small details in order to choose the best.**

1. As a teenager, Dean did a lot of stupid things that he now feels (humiliation / shame) about.
2. Many foreigners feel that their appearance (stigmatizes / despises) them in this country.
3. I won't cooperate with Walter now because I remember that he was (obnoxious / contemptuous) of me in the days before my company's success.
4. Mark (despises / berates) Henry and refuses to see him at all.
5. Turkey's historic (antipathy / shame) toward Greece may be softening with the new generation.

TOEFL Success 35 **Read the passage to review the vocabulary you have learned. Answer the questions that follow.**

Some radio talk show hosts are masters of *obnoxious* insults. Callers to such shows should be prepared for *humiliation* if they dare to disagree with the host's views. The host controls whether the caller can speak, so he can *arrogantly berate* the

---

TOEFL Prep 35-1 1. d 2. b 3. e 4. c 5. a
TOEFL Prep 35-2 1. shame 2. stigmatizes 3. contemptuous 4. despises 5. antipathy

caller without allowing the caller to respond. Some shows, especially on AM radio, have hosts who are *contemptuous* of nearly everyone. They regularly use *vitriolic* language to *stigmatize* whole groups of people, such as foreigners, liberals, gays, or women. Some hosts don't actually *despise* the groups they insult. They simply use *antipathy* as a form of entertainment, and they seem to feel no *shame* about the damage they do.

1. Which phrase best describes the author's point of view?
   a. The author enjoys listening to radio talk shows.
   b. The author believes talk shows can cause damage.
   c. The author thinks talk show hosts are disturbing but honest.
   d. The author argues that hosts are ordinary people just doing their jobs.

2. Which people are often berated on radio talk shows, according to the author?
   a. hosts
   b. callers
   c. listeners
   d. advertisers

TOEFL Success 35 1. b 2. b

人間関係
レッスン 35

否定的な感情

意味と例文

1 antipathy (名詞) 長く続く強い否定的な感情

例文訳 私は電話販売員に対する反感が強いため、しばしば彼らに失礼な態度をとってしまう。

ヒント 使い方 antipathy は後ろに toward 句を伴うことが多い。

2 arrogantly (副詞) 自分への評価が高く他人への評価が低いことを示すようにして

例文訳 ジェニーは傲慢にも、私たちには他に何もすることがないと思っていたので、自分のパーティーのことを前日になるまで知らせてこなかった。

関連語 arrogance (名詞) 横柄さ、傲慢さ、arrogant (形容詞) 横柄な、無礼な

3 berate (動詞) 侮辱的で無礼なことを言う

例文訳 その先生は、間違いを犯した生徒をひどく叱責したために、職を失った。

ヒント 使い方 berate は誰かを直接がみがみ叱りつける場合にのみ使われる。

4 contemptuous (形容詞) 敬意を払わない

例文訳 宇宙から来たエイリアンが地球に着陸したという報告を、ほとんどの科学者たちは軽視している。

ヒント 使い方 非常によく使われる構文は be contemptuous of である。

関連語 contempt (名詞) 軽蔑、軽視、contemptible (形容詞) 軽蔑すべき、contemptuously (副詞) 軽蔑して

5 despise (動詞) ひどく嫌う

例文訳 トムは、貪欲で愛想のない上司を軽蔑するようになった。

6 humiliation （名詞） 他者からの敬意を失ったと感じさせる出来事

例文訳 そのチェス大会で負けたことはマリーにとって大きな屈辱で、彼女は二度とチェスをしなかった。

関連語 humiliate （動詞） 恥をかかせる

7 obnoxious （形容詞） 煩わしい／他の人が嫌がるようなちょっとしたことをしている

例文訳 私が裏庭で本を読もうとしていると、はた迷惑な隣人がずっと話しかけてくる。

関連語 obnoxiously （副詞） 気に障るように

8 shame （名詞） （過ちや悪行に関わり合うことによる）不名誉

例文訳 息子の罪を深く恥じて、フォード家は別の町に引っ越した。

ヒント 使い方 shame は of 句や about 句を後ろに伴うことが多い。

関連語 shame （動詞） 恥をかかせる、shameful （形容詞） 恥ずべき、ashamed （形容詞）恥じている、shamefully （副詞）恥ずかしくも

9 stigmatize （動詞） ある人やあるものが間違っていると他の人に思わせる（多くの場合それは真実ではないが）ような目に見える印をつける／汚名を着せる

例文訳 キャドバリーはあごひげとタトゥーのせいで、ウォール街には似合わないという烙印を押されてしまい、金融アナリストとしての仕事が見つからなかった。

関連語 stigma （名詞） 汚名、恥辱、烙印

10 vitriolic （形容詞） 激しく憎悪に満ちた怒りを示している

例文訳 市長の市議会に対する辛辣な攻撃は、彼を理不尽に見せるだけだった。

ヒント 使い方 vitriolic の由来は、痛ましい火傷を引き起こす可能性のある強い化学物質「vitriol（硫酸）」である。

TOEFL プレップ 35－1

左列の各単語に最も近い意味の単語や語句を選び、空欄にそのアルファベットを書きなさい。

________	1. arrogantly	(a) 非常に痛烈で感情を傷つける
________	2. berate	(b) 批判して侮辱する
________	3. humiliation	(c) うっとうしい
________	4. obnoxious	(d) あまりにも誇らしげに
________	5. vitriolic	(e) 恥

TOEFL プレップ 35－2

各文を完成させるのに最も適した単語を丸で囲みなさい。

注意：ここで扱う多くの単語は、互いに非常に近い意味を持っています。最適なものを選ぶため、細かいところにも気を配りましょう。

1 10代の頃、ディーンはたくさんの愚かなことをしたが、今ではそれを（屈辱／恥ずかしいこと）だと思っている。

2 多くの外国人は、この国では自分たちは外見によって（汚名を着せられている／軽蔑されている）と感じている。

3 私はいまやウォルターに協力するつもりはない。なぜなら、私の会社が成功するまで彼は私（に不愉快な態度で／を軽視して）いたことを覚えているからだ。

4 マークはヘンリーを（軽蔑している／叱責している）ので、彼に会うことを完全に拒否している。

5 トルコのギリシャに対する歴史的な（反感／恥）は、新しい世代とともに和らいでいるかもしれない。

TOEFL サクセス 35

文章を読んで学んだ語彙を復習します。後に続く質問に答えなさい。

［例文訳］

ラジオのトークショーの司会者の中には、不快な侮辱の達人がいる。そういった番組の出演者たちは、あえて司会者の意見に反対するならば、屈辱を受けることを覚悟しなければならない。司会者は出演者が発言できるかどうかをコントロールできるので、出演者の答弁を許すことなく、傲慢に出演者を非難することができるのだ。特にAMラジオでは、司会者がほとんどすべての人を馬鹿にするような番組がある。彼らは、外国人、リベラル派、同性愛者、女性といった人々の集団全体に汚名を着せるために、辛辣な言葉を繰り返し投げかける。司会者の中には、自分が侮辱している集団を実際には軽蔑していない人もいる。彼らは嫌悪感を娯楽の1つとして利用しているだけで、自分が与えているダメージについてまったく恥ずかしいとは感じていないように見える。

1　筆者の視点を最もよく表している文はどれか？

a. 筆者はラジオのトークショーを聞くことを楽しんでいる。

b. トークショーは、ダメージを与える可能性があると筆者は考えている。

c. トークショーの司会者は厄介な存在だが正直だと筆者は思っている。

d. 司会者は自分の仕事をしているだけの普通の人だと筆者は主張している。

2　筆者によれば、ラジオのトークショーでしばしば非難される人は誰か？

a. 司会者

b. 出演者

c. 視聴者

d. 広告主

人間関係

Parenting

Target Words

1. autonomy
2. cascading
3. cloak
4. demographic
5. dire
6. embrace
7. hover
8. novice
9. overwhelming
10. plummet

Definitions and Samples

1. **autonomy** *n.* Freedom to make one's own decisions
Parents have to give their children some degree of **autonomy** by the time they reach their teens, especially in areas like choosing their own clothes and hairstyles.
Parts of speech autonomous *adj*

2. **cascading** *adj.* Falling or moving onward through several stages from one point to another, like a series of waterfalls
Power company officials are worried about **cascading** outages, where the failure of one plant could cause a series of failures down the line.
Usage tips In its original meaning, a *cascade* is a waterfall.
Parts of speech cascade *v*, cascade *n*

3. **cloak** *v.* To hide; make something difficult to see
The two athletes smile and shake hands when they meet, but these gestures **cloak** a deep dislike for one another.
Usage tips A *cloak* is a large coat.
Parts of speech cloak *n*

4. **demographic** *adj.* Related to the characteristics of a society or other group of people
One big **demographic** change is that now more than 30 percent of the population is under the age of 20.
Parts of speech demographics *n*, demographer *n*

5. dire *adj.* Extremely bad
Because the father lost his job and the mother had serious health problems, the family was in **dire** economic circumstances.
Usage tips Common phrases include *dire circumstances* and *dire straits*.

6. embrace *v.* To eagerly take hold of something; to hug
After being chosen class president, Annie **embraced** the position as an opportunity to make positive changes.
Usage tips In its original meaning, *embrace* means to put one's arms around something.
Parts of speech embrace *n*

7. hover *v.* To stay near a person or place, like a bird or a helicopter constantly staying overhead
The teacher **hovered** near the group of students, trying to hear what they were talking about.
Parts of speech hover *n*

8. novice *n.* Someone without much earlier experience at a task
In the 1970s, George Lucas was a **novice** and often asked for advice from more experienced filmmakers.
Parts of speech novitiate *n*

9. overwhelming *adj.* So large or intense that someone has difficulty understanding or controlling it.
Suddenly getting hundreds of thousands of visitors, the website found its popularity **overwhelming**—far more than its server could handle.
Parts of speech overwhelm *v*

10. plummet *v.* To fall a long way in a short time
The price of stocks **plummeted** yesterday after the government announced some negative data about the economy.
Parts of speech plummet *n*

TOEFL Prep 36-1 **Choose the word from the list that is closest in meaning to the underlined part of each sentence. Write it in the blank.**

autonomy hover demographic novices overwhelming

__________ 1. The school gives its students a lot of freedom in choosing their classes.

__________ 2. Students who had been at the school for several years liked to play tricks on the newcomers.

__________ 3. Most of the information the government collected was about the population, including average family size, income level, and the ages of respondents.

__________ 4. In big cities, TV news stations use helicopters to stay in one place in the air over busy roads to monitor the traffic.

__________ 5. When I got back from vacation, the number of e-mails in my mailbox was more than I was able to deal with.

TOEFL Prep 36-2 **Circle the word that best completes each sentence.**

1. I believe that wealth gently (cascades / plummets) from the richest classes of society down to the poorest.
2. After he got a terrible disease while traveling through the jungle, Barton's health was in (demographic / dire) condition.
3. After learning the new technique, I (cloaked / embraced) it as a great way to keep children interested in class.
4. People in their early 20s still seek occasional help from their parents, but they need a high degree of (novice / autonomy) in order to develop normal adult skills.
5. Donald was big, loud, and outspoken in his criticism of his coworkers. However, this behavior (cloaked / hovered) a deep lack of confidence in his own abilities.

TOEFL Success 36 **Read the passage to review the**

TOEFL Prep 36-1 1. autonomy 2. novices 3. demographic 4. hover 5. overwhelming
TOEFL Prep 36-2 1. cascades 2. dire 3. embraced 4. autonomy 5. cloaked

vocabulary you have learned. Answer the questions that follow.

The popularity of books and TV series about proper parenting *cloaks* an ugly reality: The quality of parenting in American households is falling. Given the *overwhelming* importance of parenting—not just to the family but to society as a whole—Americans are underprepared for it. *Demographic* changes have had a *cascading* effect, so that parenting competence is much harder for Americans to develop. For example, as the number of children per American household has *plummeted*, fewer Americans have grown up witnessing their own siblings being cared for at home. This creates an experience gap early in life that is hard to overcome later, especially since fewer and fewer parental *novices* live near Grandma and Grandpa, who might otherwise offer on-the-spot advice. Experts disagree about the overall social effects of our lack of parenting skill. Families still carry on, so how *dire* can things be? Most researchers see not collapse but a change in quality, with underskilled parents producing a generation poorly prepared to *embrace* their own adulthood in their early 20s. It doesn't help that modern parents tend to *hover* over their 20-something children, taking care of most of their needs long after the point when those young adults should have achieved *autonomy*. These are the famous "helicopter parents"—always there, always watchful, and always interfering.

1. Which sentence best expresses the essential information of this passage?
   a. Americans are having fewer children than ever before.
   b. Parents in the United States don't have enough training to do the job.
   c. Too many Americans move away from their parents before having their own children.
   d. You can't be a bad parent if you hover over your kids.

2. The author of this passage thinks it's a good idea to ______.
   a. not have children unless you go to parenting classes
   b. let children be raised by their grandparents
   c. observe how your parents raise your brothers or sisters
   d. take jobs that provide free child care for employees

TOEFL Success 36 1. b 2. c

人間関係
レッスン 36

子育て

意味と例文

1 autonomy（名詞） 自分で決断する自由

例文訳 親は子どもが 10 代になるまでに、特に服や髪型を選ぶ場面などで、ある程度の自主性を持たせるべきである。

関連語 autonomous（形容詞）自立した、自治権のある

---

2 cascading（形容詞） 連続する滝のように、ある地点から別の地点へといくつかの段階を経て落ちていったり進んでいったりする

例文訳 電力会社の職員は、1つの工場の故障が連続して故障を引き起こす可能性のあるカスケード停電を心配している。

ヒント 使い方 cascade の元々の意味は「滝」。

関連語 cascade（動詞）滝のように落ちる、cascade（名詞）小さな滝

---

3 cloak（動詞） 隠す／（何かを）見えにくくする

例文訳 その2人のアスリートは会うと笑顔で握手をするが、その仕草には互いに対する深い嫌悪感が隠されている。

ヒント 使い方 cloak とは大きなコートのことである。

関連語 cloak（名詞）マント、覆い隠すもの

---

4 demographic（形容詞） ある社会や人々の他の集団の特徴に関する（人は統計上の）

例文訳 人口動態の大きな変化の一つは、今では人口の 30％以上が 20 歳未満であることだ。

関連語 demographics（名詞）人口統計、demographer（名詞）人口統計学者

---

5 dire（形容詞） 非常に悪い

例文訳 父親は失業し、母親は深刻な健康問題を抱えていたため、その家族は悲惨な経済状況にあった。

 使い方　一般的な表現としては、dire circumstances（悲惨な状況）や dire straits（絶体絶命の危機）などがある。

---

6 embrace （動詞）　何かを熱心につかむ／抱きしめる

例文訳　学級委員長に選ばれると、アニーは前向きな変化をもたらす機会としてこの役職を受け入れた。

ヒント 使い方　embrace の元々の意味は「何かに腕をまわす」。

関連語　embrace（名詞）抱擁、容認

---

7 hover （動詞）　常に上空にとどまっている鳥やヘリコプターのように人や場所の近くにい続ける（ホバリングする）

例文訳　その先生は何を話しているのかを聞き取ろうとして、生徒たちの近くをうろうろしていた。

関連語　hover（名詞）空中にとどまっていること、うろうろしていること

---

8 novice （名詞）　（ある仕事に）あまり経験がない人

例文訳　1970 年代、ジョージ・ルーカスはかけ出しだったので、経験豊富な映画監督たちによくアドバイスを求めていた。

関連語　novitiate（名詞）見習い期間

---

9 overwhelming （形容詞）　理解したりコントロールしたりするのが困難なほど大きいまたは激しい（圧倒的な）

例文訳　そのインターネットサイトは、突然何十万人もの訪問者を受け、サーバーの処理能力をはるかに超えるほどの圧倒的な人気サイトになった。

関連語　overwhelm（動詞）圧倒する、困惑させる

---

10 plummet （動詞）　（短時間で）長い距離を落ちる

例文訳　政府が経済に関するネガティブなデータを発表したことで、昨日、株価が急落した。

関連語　plummet（名詞）おもり、急落

TOEFL プレップ 36－1

各文の下線部に最も近い意味を持つ単語をリストから選び、空欄に記入しなさい。

autonomy　hover　demographic　novices　overwhelming

__________ 1. この学校では、授業を選ぶにあたり、生徒たちに多くの自由が与えられている。

__________ 2. この学校に何年も在籍している生徒たちは、新顔にいたずらをするのが好きだった。

__________ 3. 政府が収集した情報のほとんどは、平均的な家族の人数、所得水準、回答者の年齢などを含む住民に関するものだった。

__________ 4. 大都市ではテレビの報道機関が、交通量の多い道路の上空一カ所にとどまって交通状況を観察するのにヘリコプターを使っている。

__________ 5. 休暇から戻ってくると、私のメールボックス内の電子メールの数は、対応しきれないほどになっていた。

TOEFL プレップ 36－2

各文を完成させるのに最も適した単語を丸で囲みなさい。

1　私は、富とは社会の最も裕福な層から最も貧しい層へと緩やかに（流れ落ちる／急降下する）ものだと思っている。

2　ジャングルを旅しているときにひどい病気にかかってから、バートンは（人口統計上の／悲惨な）健康状態になった。

3　私は新しい技術を学んだ後、子どもたちが授業に興味を持ち続けるための素晴らしい方法として、それを（覆い隠し／喜んで取り入れ）た。

4　20代前半の人々はまだときどき親に助けを求めるが、普通の大人としての能力を伸ばすためには高度な（見習い期間／自主性）が必要だ。

5　ドナルドは大柄で声が大きく、同僚を遠慮なく批判していた。しかし、この行動は彼自身の能力に対する自信の深い欠如を（覆い隠して／空中浮遊して）いた。

TOEFL サクセス 36

文章を読んで学んだ語彙を復習します。後に続く質問に答えなさい。

［例文訳］

きちんとした子育てをテーマにした本や連続テレビ番組の人気は、醜い現実を覆い隠している。米国の家庭における子育ての質が低下している、という現実だ。家族にとってだけでなく社会全体にとっても子育ては非常に重要であるにもかかわらず、米国人にはその準備が十分にできていない。人口動態の変化が連鎖的に影響して、米国人にとって子育ての能力を伸ばすことがずっと難しくなっている。例えば、米国の一世帯当たりの子どもの数が一気に減少したことで、自分の兄弟姉妹が家庭で世話をされている様子を見て育つ人は少なくなった。このことは人生の早い段階で経験のギャップを生み、後になってからこれを克服するのは難しい。特に、子育ての初心者が、近くに住んでいればすぐに助言をくれるであろう「おじいちゃん、おばあちゃん」の近くに住むことがますます少なくなっているからだ。子育てスキルの不足による社会への全体的な影響については、専門家の間でも意見が分かれている。家族は依然として続いていくが、状況はどれほど深刻になりうるのだろうか？　研究者のほとんどは、20 代前半になっても大人になる準備ができていない世代を生み出す未熟な親たちによって、崩壊ではなく、質の変化が起きていると見ている。現代の親が 20 代の子どものそばでうろうろし、自主性を確立すべき時期を過ぎても長く、必要なもののほとんどを満たしてあげるという傾向は、なんの役にも立たない。これこそが有名な「ヘリコプターペアレント」と呼ばれるもので、そういう親はいつもそこにいて、いつも見張っていて、そしていつも干渉するのである。

1　この文章の重要な情報を最もよく表しているのはどの文か？

a. 米国人の子どもの数はかつてないほど減っている。

b. 米国の親は役割を果たすのに十分な訓練を受けていない。

c. 自分の子どもを持つ前に親元を離れてしまう米国人が多すぎる。

d. 子どものそばをうろうろしているとしても、悪い親にはなりえない。

2　筆者が良いアイデアだと考えているのは、次のうちどれか？

a. 育児教室に通わない限り、子どもを持たないこと。

b. 祖父母が子どもを育てるようにすること。

c. 親が自分の兄弟姉妹をどのように育てているか観察すること。

d. 従業員に無料の託児サービスを提供している仕事に就くこと。

LESSON 37 Culture

Social Rebels

Target Words

1. adolescent
2. cause
3. conflict
4. delinquency
5. fringe
6. hedonistic
7. hypocritically
8. manipulation
9. rebel
10. status quo

Definitions and Samples

1. adolescent *adj.* Characteristic of a teenager; not fully grown up

In policy meetings, George refuses to reason with anyone and just scowls in an **adolescent** way.

Parts of speech adolescent *n*, adolescence *n*

2. cause *n.* A political or social goal that one believes is right and works to achieve

Our river cleanup effort would be more effective if someone famous spoke out for the **cause**.

3. conflict *v.* To fit so poorly together that the differences cause a problem

A teenager's need for security can **conflict** with his desire for independence from his family.

Parts of speech conflict *n*

4. delinquency *n.* Serious misbehavior; not doing what one should do

Because of his laziness and **delinquency**, Lefty was an unreliable friend.

Usage tips A common combination is *juvenile delinquency*, meaning "criminal behavior by a teenager."

Parts of speech delinquent *n*, delinquent *adj*

5. fringe *n.* Edge; in social contexts, parts of society that look or act very different from most people

Punk music got its start at the **fringe** of London's rock music culture.

Usage tips *Fringe* implies an edge that is uneven and not very solid.

Parts of speech fringy *adj*

6. hedonistic *adj.* Excessively interested in seeking pleasure

Suddenly wealthy, Allen fell into a **hedonistic** life of parties, expensive dinners, and heavy drinking.

Usage tips *Hedonistic* usually implies that the pleasures are wrong.

Parts of speech hedonist *n*, hedonism *n*, hedonistically *adv*

7. hypocritically *adv.* In a way that accuses other people of weaknesses that the speaker also possesses

Henry spent $2,500 on a new suit and then **hypocritically** accused me of spending too much on clothes.

Parts of speech hypocrite *n*, hypocrisy *n*, hypocritical *adj*

8. manipulation *n.* Quietly moving or influencing people or things in order to get what you want

Bob's **manipulation** of the boss's feelings led to his promotion.

Parts of speech manipulate *v*, manipulator *n*, manipulative *adj*

9. rebel *v.* To go against an established system or authority

The people of Ghurdia **rebelled** against the dictator and set up a new government.

Usage tips *Rebel* works well in political contexts and in contexts of personal relationships.

Parts of speech rebel *n*, rebellion *n*

10. status quo *n.* The systems and conditions that exist now

Let's just maintain the **status quo** until we can think of a better way.

TOEFL Prep 37-1 Find the word or phrase that is closest in meaning to each word in the left-hand column. Write the letter in the blank.

______	1. adolescent	(a) not doing what you're supposed to
______	2. conflict	(b) clash; not fit together
______	3. delinquency	(c) edge
______	4. fringe	(d) like a teenager
______	5. status quo	(e) current conditions

TOEFL Prep 37-2 Complete each sentence by filling in the blank with the best word from the list. Change the form of the word if necessary. Use each word only once.

cause hedonistic hypocritically manipulation rebel

1. Senator Bond, who often lied to Congress, ______ called the president a liar.
2. Some monks criticized the well-fed, art-loving people of fifteenth-century Florence for being ______.
3. During the 1970s, college students fought for one______ after another, from saving the whales to changing the government.
4. Even though it's illegal, ______ of lawmakers by rich companies is common.
5. It's natural for young people to ______ against society, but not with violence.

TOEFL Success 37 Read the passage to review the vocabulary you have learned. Answer the questions that follow.

Many *adolescents* and young adults go through a period when they *rebel* against what they perceive as an insincere world. Teens may take up *causes* such as radical environmentalism,

---

TOEFL Prep 37-1 1. d 2. b 3. a 4. c 5. e
TOEFL Prep 37-2 1. hypocritically 2. hedonistic 3. cause 4. manipulation 5. rebel

protesting against the *status quo.* They may choose clothes that annoy their parents and associate with people from the *fringes* of society. This is a delicate period in a person's life, full of chances to make bad decisions that could lead to juvenile *delinquency* and even jail. **Conversely**, it can be a time of personal discovery that strengthens teens in a moral rejection of *hedonistic* lifestyles. At this age they may fearlessly speak up against *hypocritically* self-righteous authorities and against *manipulation* by the news media. These adolescent protests can lead to *conflicts* within families and communities, but stirring things up can also lead to serious reflection and positive change.

Bonus Structure **Conversely** means "on the other hand."

1. Which sentence best expresses the essential information of this passage?
   a. Teens are hedonistic and self-serving.
   b. Many teenagers are radical environmentalists.
   c. Adolescents often create conflicts in their communities.
   d. Teenage rebellion can cause problems, but it can be positive too.

2. According to the reading, what is one possible positive effect of teen rebellion?
   a. Adults might try to make positive changes.
   b. Teens may get in trouble with the police.
   c. Teens may become responsible adults later in life.
   d. Adults might imitate teens and also rebel.

TOEFL Success 37 1. d 2. a

文化
レッスン37

社会的反乱

意味と例文

1 adolescent（形容詞） ティーンエイジャーに特有の／完全には成長しきっていない

例文訳 政策会議では、ジョージは誰とも論じ合おうとせず、思春期の若者のようにただ顔をしかめている。

関連語 adolescent（名詞）若者、青年、adolescence（名詞）思春期

---

2 cause（名詞） （正しいと信じてそれを達成しようと努力する）政治的または社会的目標

例文訳 川の清掃活動は、著名な人がその目的について賛意を示してくれればもっと効果的になるだろう。

---

3 conflict（動詞） （まとまらないあまり相違点が）問題を引き起こす

例文訳 10代の若者の安心感を求める気持ちは、家族から自立したいという気持ちと対立することがある。

関連語 conflict（名詞）衝突、対立

---

4 delinquency（名詞） 深刻な不正行為／やるべきことをやらないこと

例文訳 レフティは怠惰と非行のために、信頼できない友人だった。

ヒント 使い方 よく使われる組み合わせは juvenile delinquency で、「10代の若者による犯罪行為」という意味。

関連語 delinquent（名詞）（未成年の）非行者、delinquent（形容詞）非行の

---

5 fringe（名詞） 縁、周辺／（社会的文脈において）大半の人とは見た目や行動が大きく異なる一部の人々

例文訳 パンクミュージックは、ロンドンのロックミュージック文化の周辺で始まった。

ヒント 使い方 fringeとは、不均一であまりしっかりしていない縁の部分を意味している。

関連語 fringy（形容詞）周辺の、房飾りのついた

6 hedonistic（形容詞） 過剰なまでに快楽を追求したいと思っている

例文訳 突然裕福になったアレンは、パーティーや高価なディナー、大酒を楽しむ快楽主義的な生活に陥った。

ヒント▶ 使い方 hedonistic は通常、その快楽が悪いことであると暗示している。

関連語 hedonist（名詞）快楽主義者、hedonism（名詞）快楽主義、hedonistically（副詞）快楽主義的に

7 hypocritically（副詞） 話し手自身も持っている弱点について他の人を非難するようなやり方で

例文訳 ヘンリーは新しいスーツに 2,500 ドルも使ったのに、私のことを服にお金をかけすぎだと偽善的に非難した。

関連語 hypocrite（名詞）偽善者、hypocrisy（名詞）偽善、hypocritical（形容詞）偽善的な、見せかけの

8 manipulation（名詞） （欲しいものを手に入れるために）人や物をひそかに動かしたり、影響を与えたりすること

例文訳 ボブは上司の気持ちを操ることで昇進した。

関連語 manipulate（動詞）巧みに扱う、操る、manipulator（名詞）巧みに操る人、操作する人、manipulative（形容詞）巧みに扱う、ごまかしの

9 rebel（動詞） 既成のシステムや権威に逆らう

例文訳 グルディアの人々は独裁者に反抗し、新政府を樹立した。

ヒント▶ 使い方 rebel は、政治的な文脈や個人的な人間関係の文脈でよく使われる。

関連語 rebel（名詞）反逆者、rebellion（名詞）反乱

10 status quo（名詞） 現在あるシステムや状態

例文訳 もっとよい方法を思いつくまで、現状を維持しよう。

TOEFL プレップ 37－1

左列の各単語に最も近い意味の単語や語句を選び、空欄にそのアルファベットを書きなさい。

______	1. adolescent	(a) やるべきことをやらない
______	2. conflict	(b) ぶつかり合う、うまくまとまらない
______	3. delinquency	(c) 縁
______	4. fringe	(d) ティーンエイジャーのような
______	5. status quo	(e) 現在の状況

TOEFL プレップ 37－2

リストの中から空欄に当てはまる適切な単語を選んで、各文を完成させなさい。必要に応じて単語を活用させること。なお、各単語は一度しか使用できません。

cause　hedonistic　hypocritically　manipulation　rebel

1　議会でよく嘘をついていたボンド上院議員は、______大統領を嘘つきと呼んだ。

2　一部の修道士は、15 世紀のフィレンツェの太って芸術を愛する人々を______と批判した。

3　1970 年代、大学生はクジラの保護から政府の変革まで、次々と______を掲げて戦った。

4　違法であるにもかかわらず、資産の豊富な企業による議員の______はよくあることだ。

5　若者が社会に対して______のは自然なことだが、暴力によるものであってはいけない。

TOEFL サクセス 37

文章を読んで学んだ語彙を復習します。後に続く質問に答えなさい。

［例文訳］

多くの思春期の若者や青年は、不誠実だと感じる世界に対して反抗する時期を過ごすものである。ティーンエイジャーは、過激な環境保護のような目標に賛同して、現状に抗議することもある。親が嫌がるような服を選んだり、社会の周辺で生きる人たちと付き合ったりすることもあるだろう。この時期は人生の中でもデリケートな時期であり、若者の非行や刑務所にさえつながりかねない誤った判断をする機会がたくさんある。一方で、快楽主義的なライフスタイルを倫理的に拒絶できるように10代の若者を鍛える、自己発見の時期にもなりうる。この年代は、偽善的で独善的な権力者や、ニュースメディアによる情報操作に対して、恐れずに声を上げることもある。このような青年期の抗議行動は、家族や地域社会内での対立につながることもあるが、騒動を引き起こすことが、真剣な反応や前向きな変化をもたらすこともある。

読解のポイント Conversely は「一方で」を意味する。

1 この文章の重要な情報を最もよく表しているのはどの文か？

a. ティーンエイジャーは、快楽主義的で利己的だ。

b. 多くのティーンエイジャーは、過激な環境保護主義者だ。

c. 青年期の若者はしばしば地域社会で対立を引き起こす。

d. ティーンエイジャーの反抗は問題を引き起こすこともあるが、ポジティブなこともある。

2 この文章によると、ティーンエイジャーの反抗がもたらす可能性のあるポジティブな効果とはどれか？

a. 大人が前向きな変化を起こそうとするかもしれない。

b. ティーンエイジャーが警察とトラブルになるかもしれない。

c. ティーンエイジャーが、のちのち責任ある大人になるかもしれない。

d. 大人がティーンエイジャーの真似をして、反抗するかもしれない。

Painting and Sculpture

Target Words

1. abstract
2. context
3. depict
4. dimension
5. esthetically
6. intrinsic
7. perspective
8. portrayal
9. realism
10. spectrum

Definitions and Samples

1. abstract *adj.* Not concrete and realistic; not obviously related to everyday experience

Abstract painting became popular partly because early photography was very realistic.

Parts of speech abstraction *n*

2. context *n.* A larger environment that something fits into

In the **context** of Soviet Russia, public art had to be about the triumph of communism and its leaders.

Usage tips The preposition *in* often comes before *context*, and an *of* phrase often comes after it.

Parts of speech contextualize *v*, contextual *adj*

3. depict *v.* To show in pictures

Michelangelo's painting on the ceiling of the Sistine Chapel **depicts** nine scenes from the Bible.

Parts of speech depiction *n*

4. dimension *n.* A direction or surface along which something can be measured; an aspect

The three **dimensions** of physical objects are length, width, and depth.

One **dimension** of the bad relationship between the two countries is their long history of economic competition.

Parts of speech dimensional *adj*

5. esthetically *adv.* In a way that relates to beauty or

appearance
The outside of the office building is **esthetically** pleasing, but the inside is dark and unpleasant.

Usage tips *Esthetically* is often spelled with an "a" at the beginning: *aesthetically*.

Parts of speech esthetic *n*, esthete *n*, esthetic *adj*

6. **intrinsic** *adj.* Being part of the basic nature of something
Frequent elections are **intrinsic** to a democratic system.

Parts of speech intrinsically *adv*

7. **perspective** *n.* A way of seeing from a particular location; a way of thinking about something
From my **perspective**, the entire town can be seen through a set of large windows.
They held different **perspectives** on how to care for their aging parents.

8. **portrayal** *n.* A description or drawing that reflects a certain point of view
Most **portrayals** of Abraham Lincoln emphasize his sense of humor and his honesty.

Usage tips *Portrayal* is often followed by an *of* phrase to indicate what is being described.

Parts of speech portray *v*, portrait *n*

9. **realism** *n.* A technique that tries to picture something as it really looks
Realism was popular among seventeenth-century Flemish painters like Rembrandt van Rijn.

Parts of speech realist *n*, realistic *adj*, realistically *adj*

10. **spectrum** *n.* A range of different things, usually colors
Bart's colorful designs include every color of the **spectrum**, from deep blue to vibrant red.

Usage tips The phrase *the spectrum* frequently means "the colors that the human eye can see."

TOEFL Prep 38-1 Find the word or phrase that is closest in meaning to each word in the left-hand column. Write the letter in the blank.

______	1. abstract	(a) to show
______	2. depict	(b) depiction
______	3. esthetically	(c) presenting an idea, not a realistic picture
______	4. perspective	(d) in a way that relates to beauty
______	5. portrayal	(e) way of seeing things from a certain place

TOEFL Prep 38-2 Circle the word that best completes each sentence.

1. The materials that go into a work of art usually have little (abstract / intrinsic) value.
2. In the 1970s, artists known as "the Boston School" revived (realism / context) by rejecting abstract techniques and trying to capture the actual appearance of their subjects.
3. The colors of light that we can see are known as the visible (spectrum/ perspective).
4. Medieval artists did not try to use (context / perspective) to give a sense of depth to their paintings.
5. The small, separate strokes of impressionist paintings give the works a dreamlike (portrayal / dimension).

TOEFL Success 38 Read the passage to review the vocabulary you have learned. Answer the questions that follow.

Whether something is "art" is largely a matter of opinion. Art that most people consider to have no *intrinsic* value can contain a great treasure of ideas and invention to someone who sees something special in it. Styles in all the arts

TOEFL Prep 38-1 1. c 2. a 3. d 4. e 5. b
TOEFL Prep 38-2 1. intrinsic 2. realism 3. spectrum 4. perspective 5. dimension

range over a wide *spectrum*. Some good art is *esthetically* unchallenging and easy to understand. Other works are strange forms, **totally** out of *context* to everyone but the artist. One artist's *portrayal* of an everyday object, such as a bouquet of flowers, may be grounded in *realism* and easily recognizable. Another painter's *depiction* of the same bouquet may be very *abstract*, resembling flowers only in the artist's mind. Regardless of the artist's approach, the best art reveals new *dimensions* of experience and looks at the world from a fresh *perspective*.

Bonus Structure **Totally** means "completely" or "in every way."

1. Which sentence best expresses the essential information of this passage?
   a. Styles of art have changed throughout history.
   b. Realistic art has more meaning than abstract art.
   c. Esthetically pleasing art is too simple to contain much meaning.
   d. Works of art can mean different things, depending on one's perspective.

2. According to this reading, what is one big difference between abstract art and realistic art?
   a. Abstract art is harder to sell.
   b. Abstract art is harder to understand.
   c. Abstract art is harder to produce.
   d. Abstract art is harder to look at.

TOEFL Success 38 1. d 2. b

文化
レッスン38

絵画と彫刻

意味と例文

1 abstract（形容詞） 具体的でも現実的でもない／明らかに日常の経験とは関連がない

例文訳 抽象絵画が人気になった理由の一部は、初期の写真がとても写実的だったからだ。

関連語 abstraction（名詞）抽象概念、抽象化

---

2 context（名詞） （あるものを内包している）大きな環境

例文訳 ソ連の文脈では、パブリックアートは共産主義とその指導者たちの勝利を描いたものでなければならなかった。

ヒント 使い方 context の前には前置詞 in が来ることが多く、後ろには of 句が来ることが多い。

関連語 contextualize（動詞）文脈を述べる、関連づける、contextual（形容詞）文脈上の、前後関係の

---

3 depict（動詞） 絵で示す

例文訳 システィーナ礼拝堂の天井に描かれたミケランジェロの絵には、聖書の９つの場面が描かれている。

関連語 depiction（名詞）描写

---

4 dimension（名詞） （何かを測ることができる）方向や面／側面

例文訳 物理的な物体の３つの次元は、長さ、幅、深さである。
その２国間の悪い関係の１つの側面は、長年にわたる経済競争の歴史である。

関連語 dimensional（形容詞）次元の

---

5 esthetically（副詞） 美しさや外見に関するやり方で

例文訳 そのオフィスビルの外観は、美的に楽しめるものだが、建物の中は暗くて居心地が悪い。

ヒント 使い方 estheticallyは頭に“a”を付けてつづることが多い（aesthetically）。

関連語 esthetic（名詞）美学、美意識、esthete（名詞）審美眼のある人、esthetic（形容詞）美学の

---

6 intrinsic（形容詞） あるものの基本的な性質の一部である（本質的な）

例文訳 頻繁な選挙は、民主主義システムにとって本質的なものである。

関連語 intrinsically（副詞）本質的に

---

7 perspective（名詞） （特定の場所からの）見方／（あることについての）考え方

例文訳 私のいるここからは、大きな窓を通して街全体が見渡せる。
高齢の両親をどう世話するかについて、彼らは異なる考えを抱いていた。

---

8 portrayal（名詞） （ある視点を反映した）記述や線画

例文訳 エイブラハム・リンカーンに関するほとんどの描写は、彼のユーモアのセンスと誠実さを強調している。

ヒント 使い方 portrayal の後には、描写されている内容を示すための of 句が続くことが多い。

関連語 portray（動詞）描く、表現する、portrait（名詞）肖像画、人物描写

---

9 realism（名詞） 実際に見えるとおりに描こうとする手法

例文訳 写実主義は、レンブラント・ファン・レインなど17世紀のフランドル地方の画家たちの間で流行した。

関連語 realist（名詞）写実主義者、現実主義者、realistic（形容詞）写実主義の、写実的な、現実的な、realistically（副詞）写実的に、現実的に

---

10 spectrum（名詞） さまざまなものの範囲（通常は色に使われる）

例文訳 バートのカラフルなデザインには、深い青から鮮やかな赤まで、色彩スペクトルのあらゆる色が含まれている。

ヒント 使い方 the spectrum は、しばしば「人間の目に見える色」を意味する。

TOEFL プレップ 38－1

左列の各単語に最も近い意味の単語や語句を選び、空欄にそのアルファベットを書きなさい。

______	1. abstract	(a)	見せる
______	2. depict	(b)	描写
______	3. esthetically	(c)	写実的な絵ではなく、着想を示すこと
______	4. perspective	(d)	美しさに関連したやり方
______	5. portrayal	(e)	ある場所からの物事の見方

TOEFL プレップ 38－2

各文を完成させるのに最も適した単語を丸で囲みなさい。

1 芸術作品に使われる材料には、通常（抽象的な／本質的な）価値はほとんどない。

2 1970年代、「ボストンスクール」と呼ばれる芸術家たちは、抽象的な手法を否定し、被写体の実際の姿をとらえようとすることで、（写実主義／文脈）を復活させた。

3 私たちが見ることのできる光の色を可視（スペクトル／視点）という。

4 中世の画家は、絵に奥行きを感じさせるために（文脈／遠近法）を使おうとはしなかった。

5 印象派の絵画では、小さく分かれた筆触が作品に夢のような（描写／次元）を与えている。

TOEFL サクセス 38

文章を読んで学んだ語彙を復習します。後に続く質問に答えなさい。

［例文訳］

あるものが「芸術」であるかどうかは、大いに意見の分かれるところだ。大半の人にとっては本質的な価値がないとみなされる芸術でも、その中に特別なものを見出す人にとっては、アイデアや発明の偉大な宝庫になりうる。すべての芸術のスタイルは、幅広い範囲にわたっている。優れた芸術の中には美学的に挑戦的ではないが、理解しやすいものもある。また、奇妙な形で、その作品の作者以外の人にとってはまったく脈絡がない作品もある。ある画家による花束のような日常的なものの描写は、写実主義に基づいていて、わかりやすいかもしれない。別の画家が同じ花束を描くと、その画家の頭の中でだけ花に似ているという非常に抽象的なものになるかもしれない。どのようなアプローチであっても、最高の芸術は経験の新しい次元を示すとともに新たな視点から世界を見ている。

読解のポイント Totally は「完全に、あらゆる面で」を意味している。

1　この文章の重要な情報を最もよく表しているのはどの文か。

a. 芸術のスタイルは歴史の中で変化してきた。
b. 写実的な芸術は、抽象的な芸術よりも意義がある。
c. 美的に楽しませてくれる芸術作品は、単純すぎてあまり意味を持たない。
d. 芸術作品は、人の視点によって異なるものを意味しうる。

2　この文章によれば、抽象画と写実画の大きな違いは何か？

a. 抽象画のほうが売るのが難しい。
b. 抽象画のほうが理解するのが難しい。
c. 抽象画のほうがつくるのが難しい。
d. 抽象画のほうが眺めるのが難しい。

LESSON 39 Culture

The Written Word

Target Words

1. advent
2. ambiguous
3. connotation
4. decipher
5. denote
6. illiterate
7. ingenious
8. inscription
9. phonetic
10. symbolic

Definitions and Samples

1. advent *n.* Coming; arrival

The **advent** of the automobile greatly increased the demand for petroleum.

Usage tips *Advent* is usually followed by an *of* phrase.

2. ambiguous *adj.* Having more than one possible meaning

The sentence *It's hard to say* is **ambiguous**, with different meanings in different contexts.

Parts of speech ambiguity *n*, ambiguously *adv*

3. connotation *n.* A meaning implied, not stated directly

When my boss says, "Thank you," the **connotation** is that she's done talking and I should leave.

Parts of speech connote *v*

4. decipher *v.* To figure out the meaning, even though it is written in a code or an unknown language

The Rosetta Stone helped archaeologists **decipher** ancient Egyptian writing.

Usage tips A cipher is a code or puzzle; *decipher* means "solve a puzzle written in code."

5. denote *v.* To mean something clearly and directly

An "X" next to a name on this list **denotes** a person who has been chosen for the soccer team.

Parts of speech denotation *n*

6. illiterate *adj.* Unable to read

In many villages nearly everyone was **illiterate** and unschooled, and the few who could read held great power.

Parts of speech illiterate *n*, illiteracy *n*

7. ingenious *adj.* Very clever and imaginative

Ann thought up an **ingenious** way to keep other people from accidentally taking her pens.

Parts of speech ingenuity *n*, ingeniously *adv*

8. inscription *n.* Something written into a piece of rock or metal

The **inscription** on my ring says "August 1," because that was the day of our wedding.

Parts of speech inscribe *v*

9. phonetic *adj.* Related to the sounds in a language

Children learning to write often make up **phonetic** spellings, based on the way a word sounds.

Parts of speech phonetics *n*, phonetically *adv*

10. symbolic *adj.* Acting as a sign for some other thing or idea

Since the 1970s, yellow ribbons have been **symbolic** of hope that someone will return from a dangerous situation.

Usage tips *Symbolic* is often followed by an *of* phrase indicating the meaning of a symbol.

Parts of speech symbolize *v*, symbol *n*, symbolically *adv*

TOEFL Prep 39-1 Find the word or phrase that is closest in meaning to each word in the left-hand column. Write the letter in the blank.

______	1. advent	(a) approach or arrival
______	2. decipher	(b) newly invented in a clever way
______	3. ingenious	(c) to figure out the meaning
______	4. inscription	(d) related to spoken sounds
______	5. phonetic	(e) something written into a hard surface

TOEFL Prep 39-2 Complete each sentence by filling in the blank with the best word from the list. Change the form of the word if necessary. Use each word only once.

ambiguous connotation denote illiterate symbolic

1. If my father told me to be quiet, the ______ was "I have a headache."
2. The president's response, "Wait and see," was ______, meaning that perhaps he would take action, perhaps not.
3. In English writing, a mark called an apostrophe usually ______ a missing letter, as in *isn't* for is not.
4. A circle with a plus attached (♀) is ______ of "woman" and of the planet Venus.
5. Farley was a poor, ______ boy from a remote area who later taught himself to read and write.

TOEFL Success 39 Read the passage to review the vocabulary you have learned. Answer the questions that follow.

Johannes Gutenberg's *ingenious* use of movable type in his printing press had a wide range of effects on European societies. **Most obviously**, readers no longer had to *decipher* odd handwriting, with *ambiguous* lettering, in order to read

---

TOEFL Prep 39-1 1. a 2. c 3. b 4. e 5. d
TOEFL Prep 39-2 1. connotation 2. ambiguous 3. denotes 4. symbolic 5. illiterate

a written work. Gutenberg gave each letter standard forms, a move that had *connotations* far beyond the printing business. The *inscriptions* on tombstones and roadside mileposts, for example, could now be standardized. The cost of books decreased. Even *illiterate* people benefited indirectly from the *advent* of this invention, as the general level of information in society increased. However, Gutenberg's press was of limited use for languages that used picture-like symbols for writing instead of a *phonetic* system. Systems of *symbolic* pictographs, each of which *denotes* a word, require many thousands of characters to be cast into lead type by the printer. Phonetic systems, like the Latin alphabet, use the same few characters, recombined in thousands of ways to make different words.

Bonus Structure **Most obviously** introduces an easy-to-see effect and implies that less clear effects will come later.

1. According to this reading, how did the invention of the printing press benefit illiterate people?
   a. It helped them learn to read.
   b. It raised the level of information in a society.
   c. It lowered the cost of books.
   d. It saved them from having to read ambiguous handwriting.

2. Why was Gutenberg's press not very practical for languages that use picture-like symbols?
   a. because character-based languages are made of pictographs
   b. because phonetic alphabets are clearer
   c. because there are too many characters to make movable type for each one
   d. because Gutenberg was European, so he didn't know any character-based languages

TOEFL Success 39 1. b 2. c

文化
レッスン 39

書き言葉

意味と例文

1 advent（名詞） 到来／到着

例文訳 自動車の登場により、石油の需要が大幅に増加した。

ヒント 使い方 advent は通常後ろに of 句を伴う。

---

2 ambiguous（形容詞） 2つ以上の意味を持ちうる

例文訳 "It's hard to say" は、文脈によって異なる意味を持つ曖昧な文だ。

関連語 ambiguity（名詞）多義性、曖昧さ、ambiguously（副詞）曖昧に

---

3 connotation（名詞） （直接言われるのではなく）暗に示されている意味

例文訳 私の上司が「ありがとう」と言った場合、その意味するところは話が終わったから帰ってくれということだ。

関連語 connote（動詞）言外の意味を含む

---

4 decipher（動詞） （暗号や未知の言語で書かれているにもかかわらず）その意味を理解する

例文訳 ロゼッタストーンは、考古学者が古代エジプトの文字を解読するのに役立った。

ヒント 使い方 cipher とは暗号やパズルのことで、decipher は「暗号で書かれたパズルを解く」という意味。

---

5 denote（動詞） 明確かつ直接的な意味を持つ

例文訳 このリストの名前の横にある「X」は、そのサッカーチームに選ばれた人であることを示している。

関連語 denotation（名詞）明示的意味、表示

---

6 illiterate （形容詞） 文字が読めない

例文訳 多くの村ではほとんどの人が文字を読めず、学校教育も受けていないので、文字を読める少数の人が大きな力を持っていた。

関連語 illiterate（名詞）読み書きのできない人、あることにうとい人、illiteracy（名詞）読み書きできないこと、無学

7 ingenious （形容詞） 非常に賢く想像力に富む

例文訳 アンは、他の人が誤って自分のペンを持っていかないようにするための独創的な方法を考え出した。

関連語 ingenuity（名詞）発明の才、巧妙さ、ingeniously（副詞）独創的に、巧妙に

8 inscription （名詞） （岩石や金属片に）書かれたもの

例文訳 私の指輪には「８月１日」という銘刻があるが、これは私たちが結婚式を挙げた日だからだ。

関連語 inscribe（動詞）（石、金属などに）記す

9 phonetic （形容詞） 言語の音に関連する

例文訳 文字の書き方を学んでいる子どもたちは、単語の音に基づいて表音的なつづりをつくりだすことがよくある。

関連語 phonetics（名詞）音声学、phonetically（副詞）音声学的に、発音通りに

10 symbolic （形容詞） 他のものや考えを示すしるしとして機能する（象徴的な）

例文訳 1970年代以降、黄色いリボンは、危険な状況から誰かが戻ってくるという希望を象徴するものになった。

ヒント 使い方 symbolic の後には、象徴の意味を示している of 句が続くことが多い。

関連語 symbolize（動詞）象徴する、symbol（名詞）象徴、symbolically（副詞）象徴的に

TOEFL プレップ 39－1

左列の各単語に最も近い意味の単語や語句を選び、空欄にそのアルファベットを書きなさい。

＿＿＿＿＿＿	1. advent	(a) 近づくまたは到着すること
＿＿＿＿＿＿	2. decipher	(b) 賢明な方法で新たに考案された
＿＿＿＿＿＿	3. ingenious	(c) 意味を理解すること
＿＿＿＿＿＿	4. inscription	(d) 口頭での音声に関連する
＿＿＿＿＿＿	5. phonetic	(e) 硬い表面に書かれたもの

TOEFL プレップ 39－2

リストの中から空欄に当てはまる適切な単語を選んで、各文を完成させなさい。必要に応じて単語を活用させること。なお、各単語は一度しか使用できません。

ambiguous　connotation　denote　illiterate　symbolic

1 父が私に静かにしろと言うとき、その＿＿＿＿＿＿は「私は頭が痛いんだ」だった。
2 大統領の「様子を見よう」という答えは、行動を起こすかもしれないし、起こさないかもしれないという＿＿＿＿＿＿なものだった。
3 英語の文章では、“isn't”が“is not”を表すように、通常アポストロフィーと呼ばれる記号が欠けている文字を＿＿＿＿＿＿。
4 円にプラスをつけたもの（♀）は、「女性」と金星の＿＿＿＿＿＿。
5 ファーリーは、人里離れた地域出身の貧しく＿＿＿＿＿＿少年で、後に独学で読み書きを覚えた。

TOEFL サクセス 39

文章を読んで学んだ語彙を復習します。後に続く質問に答えなさい。

［例文訳］

ヨハネス・グーテンベルクが印刷機に活版（可動活字）を巧みに取り入

れたことは、ヨーロッパの社会に幅広い影響を与えた。最も明らかなのは、文書を読む際に、曖昧な書き方をされた癖のある手書きの文字を解読する必要がなくなったということだ。グーテンベルクはそれぞれの文字に標準となる形を与えたが、これは印刷業の域をはるかに超える意味を持っていた。例えば、墓石や里程標に刻まれる文字を標準化できるようになった。本の製作費も下がった。文字の読めない人でも、この発明の到来によって社会における全体的な情報水準が向上したことで、間接的に恩恵を受けた。しかし、グーテンベルクの印刷機は、表音文字ではなく絵のような記号を使う言語にとっては、出番が限られていた。表象的な絵文字の体系では、一つひとつの文字が単語を表すため、印刷業者が何千もの表意文字を鉛の活字に鋳造する必要がある。ラテン文字のような表音文字の体系では、数少ない同じ文字が使われ、さまざまな単語をつくるために何千通りにも組み替えられるのだ。

読解のポイント Most obviously **は、わかりやすい効果を紹介してから、その後により明確でない効果が続くことを示す。**

1　この文章によれば、印刷機の発明は読み書きのできない人々にどのような恩恵を与えたのか？

a. 読み方を学ぶのに役立った。
b. 社会における情報水準を引き上げた。
c. 本の製作費を下げた。
d. 曖昧な手書き文字を読まなくてすむようになった。

2　なぜグーテンベルクの印刷機は、絵のような記号を使う言語にはあまり実用的ではなかったのか？

a. 文字に基づいた言語は絵文字でできているから。
b. 表音文字のほうがわかりやすいから。
c. 文字の数が多すぎて、それぞれの文字に対応した可動活字をつくることができないから。
d. グーテンベルクはヨーロッパ人だったので、表意文字に基づいた言語を知らなかったから。

Entertainment

Target Words

1. amateurish
2. cast
3. charismatic
4. gala
5. hilarious
6. improvisation
7. incompetent
8. medium
9. skit
10. zeal

Definitions and Samples

1. **amateurish** *adj.* Not good enough to be the work of professionals

Whoever painted this room did an **amateurish** job, with all sorts of uneven edges.

Parts of speech amateur *n*, amateurishly *adv*

2. **cast** *n.* The group of actors in a play, movie, television show, etc.

Some viewers mistakenly start thinking that a TV show's **cast** members are really the characters they play.

Usage tips In U.S. English, *cast* is singular. In some other varieties of English it is plural.

Parts of speech cast *v*

3. **charismatic** *adj.* Extremely attractive and charming

Because of the sparkle in his eye and his confident style, John F. Kennedy was a **charismatic** leader.

Parts of speech charisma *n*, charismatically *adv*

4. **gala** *adj.* Expensive, elaborately arranged, and full of celebration

A college graduation party should be a **gala** affair, not a backyard barbecue.

Usage tips *Gala* is somewhat old-fashioned, far more common in print than in speech.

Parts of speech gala *n*

5. **hilarious** *adj.* Very funny
   In my opinion, the most **hilarious** character on television was Basil Fawlty.
   Parts of speech hilarity *n*

6. **improvisation** *n.* Inventing a solution to an unexpected problem
   Boy Scouts take pride in their **improvisation** when faced with trouble during a camping trip.
   Parts of speech improvise *v*, improvisational *adj*

7. **incompetent** *adj.* Unskilled; lacking the ability to perform a task
   Because we hired an **incompetent** builder to replace our roof, we now have leaks everywhere.
   Usage tips Usually, *incompetent* implies that someone tries to do something but fails.
   Parts of speech incompetence *n*, incompetently *adv*

8. **medium** *n.* A channel or way for a meaning to be expressed
   Watercolor art is often considered childish, but some artists have achieved great things working in that **medium**.
   Usage tips The plural of *medium* is *media*.

9. **skit** *n.* A short, informal play
   Marnie and Chris spent a long time practicing their **skit** for the school show.

10. **zeal** *n.* Enthusiasm; a deep determination to do well
    Unfortunately, Tom's **zeal** to become a rock star distracted him from his studies.
    Usage tips *Zeal* is often followed by *to* plus a verb or by a *for* phrase.
    Parts of speech zealot *n*, zealous *adj*

TOEFL Prep 40-1 **Find the word or phrase that is closest in meaning to each word in the left-hand column. Write the letter in the blank.**

______	1. amateurish	(a) group of people in a movie
______	2. cast	(b) very funny
______	3. hilarious	(c) unable to perform a task
______	4. incompetent	(d) enthusiasm
______	5. zeal	(e) not like professionals

TOEFL Prep 40-2 **Complete each sentence by filling in the blank with the best word from the list. Change the form of the word if necessary. Use each word only once.**

charismatic gala improvisation medium skit

1. The sixth-grade class put on a little ______ about Thanksgiving Day.
2. The year ended with a ______ celebration featuring a professional orchestra.
3. Gena's skills at ______ saved the play when she forgot her real lines.
4. Television is a passive ______ because it demands no input from the viewer.
5. Movie stars that are especially ______ often take advantage of their charm to go into politics.

TOEFL Success 40 **Read the passage to review the vocabulary you have learned. Answer the questions that follow.**

When the artistic *medium* of theater falls into the hands of college students, the results can be unpredictable. At one college, we saw Shakespeare's *Hamlet* done as musical theater. The idea was bad to start out with, and the actual play

---

TOEFL Prep 40-1 1. e 2. a 3. b 4. c 5. d
TOEFL Prep 40-2 1. skit 2. gala 3. improvisation 4. medium 5. charismatic

was *amateurish*, bordering on *incompetent*. The *cast* did not understand the tragic power of the play. Their *improvisation* when they forgot their lines was silly and inappropriate. The costumes and set design looked homemade, like something from an elementary school *skit*. Three months later, **however**, this same group of students did a great job with the comedy *A Midsummer Night's Dream*. Surprisingly enough, the actors were *charismatic*, played their parts with *zeal*, and achieved a *hilarious* result. It was no *gala* event, but we still felt that it was one of the best performances we had seen.

Bonus Structure **However** indicates a change in focus.

1. What word best describes the author's opinion of the student performance of *Hamlet*?
   a. incompetent
   b. charismatic
   c. hilarious
   d. full of zeal

2. What is the author's opinion of student performances in general?
   a. Students should not perform Shakespeare's plays.
   b. Sometimes student productions are good, and other times they are not.
   c. All student shows are amateurish.
   d. Student performances should be gala events.

TOEFL Success 40 1. a 2. b

文化
レッスン 40

エンターテインメント

意味と例文

1 amateurish （形容詞） プロの仕事としては不十分な

例文訳 この部屋のペンキを塗った人が誰であれ、完全に素人仕事で、あらゆる類いの凹凸があった。

関連語 amateur（名詞）素人、アマチュア、amateurishly（副詞）素人くさく

2 cast （名詞） （演劇、映画、テレビ番組などの）出演者の集まり

例文訳 視聴者の中には、テレビ番組の出演者は実際に彼らが演じるキャラクターであると勘違いする人がいる。

ヒント 使い方 アメリカ英語では cast は単数形だが、他の英語圏では複数形の場合もある。

関連語 cast（動詞）投げる、役を割り当てる

3 charismatic （形容詞） 非常に魅力的でチャーミングな（カリスマ的な）

例文訳 その目の輝きと自信に満ちたスタイルから、ジョン・F・ケネディはカリスマ的なリーダーだった。

関連語 charisma（名詞）カリスマ、カリスマ性、charismatically（副詞）カリスマ的に

4 gala （形容詞） 高価で手の込んだアレンジが施され祝福に満ちている

例文訳 大学の卒業パーティーは、裏庭のバーベキューなどではなく、大々的なイベントであるべきだ。

ヒント 使い方 gala はやや古めかしく、口頭よりも文書で使用されることがはるかに多い。

関連語 gala（名詞）祭典、特別な催し物

5 hilarious (形容詞) とても面白い

例文訳 私の考えでは、テレビで最も面白いキャラクターはバジル・フォルティだった。

関連語 hilarity (名詞) 陽気な気持ち、大はしゃぎ

6 improvisation (名詞) (想定外の問題の)解決策を考え出すこと

例文訳 ボーイスカウトは、キャンプ中にトラブルが起こったとき、即興で対応することを誇りとしている。

関連語 improvise (動詞)即席でつくる、improvisational (形容詞)即興の

7 incompetent (形容詞) 熟練していない／(ある業務を実行する)能力に欠けている

例文訳 私たちは屋根の葺き替えに無能な建設業者を雇ったために、現在、あちこちで雨漏りしている。

ヒント 使い方 incompetent は、ある人が何かをしようとするが失敗することをほのめかしている。

関連語 incompetence (名詞) 無能、無資格、incompetently (副詞) 無能にも、無資格で

8 medium (名詞) (伝えたいことを表現するための)手段や方法

例文訳 水彩画は子どもっぽいと思われがちだが、その表現方法を使って偉大な作品を完成させた芸術家もいる。

ヒント 使い方 medium の複数形は media である。

9 skit (名詞) 短く形式ばらない芝居

例文訳 マーニーとクリスは、学校の催しで披露する寸劇を長い時間をかけて練習した。

10 zeal (名詞) 熱意／(うまくやろうとする)深い決意

例文訳 残念なことに、トムはロックスターになりたいという熱意のために、勉強から遠ざかってしまった。

ヒント 使い方 zeal は、後ろに「to ＋動詞」や for 句を伴うことが多い。

関連語 zealot (名詞) 熱狂者、zealous (形容詞) 熱心な

TOEFL プレップ 40－1

左列の各単語に最も近い意味の単語や語句を選び、空欄にそのアルファベットを書きなさい。

＿＿＿＿＿＿	1. amateurish	(a) 映画に出てくる人たちのグループ
＿＿＿＿＿＿	2. cast	(b) とても面白い
＿＿＿＿＿＿	3. hilarious	(c) 業務を実行できない
＿＿＿＿＿＿	4. incompetent	(d) 熱意
＿＿＿＿＿＿	5. zeal	(e) プロらしくない

TOEFL プレップ 40－2

リストの中から空欄に当てはまる適切な単語を選んで、各文を完成させなさい。必要に応じて単語を活用させること。なお、各単語は一度しか使用できません。

charismatic　gala　improvisation　medium　skit

1　6年生のクラスでは、感謝祭についてのちょっとした＿＿＿＿＿＿を行った。

2　その年は、プロのオーケストラを招いての＿＿＿＿＿＿お祝いで幕を閉じた。

3　ジーナの＿＿＿＿＿＿の能力が、彼女が自分の本当の台詞を忘れてしまったときに劇を救った。

4　テレビは視聴者からのインプットを必要としないため、受動的＿＿＿＿＿＿である。

5　特に＿＿＿＿＿＿である映画スターは、その魅力を生かして政治家になることが多い。

TOEFL サクセス 40

文章を読んで学んだ語彙を復習します。後に続く質問に答えなさい。

[例文訳]

演劇という芸術的な表現手段が大学生の手に渡ると、予想もつかない結果になることがある。ある大学で、私たちはシェイクスピアの「ハムレット」をミュージカルとして上演しているのを見た。そもそもアイデアが悪いし、実際の芝居も素人同然で無能と言ってもいいくらいだった。出演者たちは、その作品が持つ悲劇的な力を理解していなかった。台詞を忘れたときの即興芝居も愚かで、その場にふさわしいものではなかった。衣装も大道具も手作りっぽく見えて、まるで小学生の寸劇のようだった。しかしその3カ月後、同じ学生たちが、喜劇「真夏の夜の夢」を見事に演じた。驚いたことに、役者たちはカリスマ性があり、熱意を持って自分の役を演じ、大笑いを誘う結果となった。決して華やかな催しではなかったが、それでも私たちがこれまで見てきたなかで最高のパフォーマンスの1つだと感じた。

読解のポイント　However **は話題の焦点を変更することを示している。**

1　学生が演じたハムレットに対する筆者の感想を最もよく表している言葉は次のうちどれか。

a. 無能な
b. カリスマ的な
c. こっけいな
d. 熱意に満ちた

2　一般的に学生のパフォーマンスについて、筆者はどのように考えているか？

a. 学生はシェイクスピアの劇を上演すべきではない。
b. 学生が上演すると良いときもあれば、そうでないときもある。
c. 学生の公演はすべて素人っぽい。
d. 学生の公演は華やかな催しであるべきだ。

Risky Fashions

Target Words

1. bulk
2. capricious
3. cumbersome
4. exotic
5. inhibit
6. minimum
7. striking
8. trend
9. vanity
10. vulnerable

Definitions and Samples

1. bulk *n.* Largeness and a heavy appearance

The **bulk** of Kevin's athletic body was too great for one small chair, so he sat on a bench.

Parts of speech: bulky *adj*

2. capricious *adj.* Moving unpredictably from one thing to another

Your college studies will go on too long if you make **capricious** jumps from one major to another.

Usage tips: *Capricious* comes from a Latin word meaning "goat" and implies a motion like the jumping of a goat.

Parts of speech: capriciousness *n*, capriciously *adv*

3. cumbersome *adj.* Difficult to wear or carry because of weight or shape

To make it to the top of the mountain before dark, the hikers dumped their **cumbersome** tent.

4. exotic *adj.* Interesting or unusual because of coming from a faraway place

I walked into the restaurant and smelled the **exotic** aromas of Malaysian spices.

Parts of speech: exoticism *n*, exotically *adv*

5. **inhibit** *v.* To discourage or to slow down
This lotion will **inhibit** the itching caused by mosquito bites.
Parts of speech inhibition *n*

6. **minimum** *n.* The smallest possible amount or level
The **minimum** for being accepted to Cavill University is a score of 60 on the test.
Parts of speech minimize *v*, minimum *adj*, minimal *adj*, minimally *adv*

7. **striking** *adj.* Very noticeable; easily attracting attention
Gordon had a **striking** new attitude after he learned self-discipline at the army academy.
Usage tips *Striking* comes from a verb that means "to hit."
Parts of speech strike *v*, strikingly *adv*

8. **trend** *n.* A movement in one direction or a widespread change in fashion
The **trend** among some young men is to wear their caps with the bill off to one side.
Parts of speech trend *v*, trendy *adj*

9. **vanity** *n.* An excessive concern for one's appearance
Mark's **vanity** led him to spend far too much money on haircuts and new clothes.
Parts of speech vain *adj*

10. **vulnerable** *adj.* Exposed to possible harm
Babies and very old people are especially **vulnerable** to the new disease.
Usage tips *Vulnerable* is often followed by a *to* phrase.
Parts of speech vulnerability *n*, vulnerably *adv*

TOEFL Prep 41-1 **Find the word or phrase that is closest in meaning to the opposite of each word in the left-hand column. Write the letter in the blank.**

______	1. capricious	(a) encourage
______	2. exotic	(b) maximum
______	3. inhibit	(c) ordinary
______	4. minimum	(d) predictable
______	5. vulnerable	(e) well protected

TOEFL Prep 41-2 **Circle the word that best completes the sentence.**

1. The (trend / bulk) of his sweater made him look fatter than he really was.
2. Some analysts see a relationship between fashion (trends / vanity) and the ups and downs of the economy.
3. The outfits worn by firefighters are (vulnerable / cumbersome) and heavy.
4. Her necklace was especially (cumbersome / striking) because of the diamonds it contained.
5. (Vanity / Bulk) led my grandfather to dye his hair and to dress like someone 40 years younger.

TOEFL Success 41 **Read the passage to review the vocabulary you have learned. Answer the questions that follow.**

The fashion industry encourages people to spend far too much time and money on clothes. **It's natural for** humans to use clothing as a mark of belonging to a group and to try to keep up with style *trends*. The fashion industry exploits this natural desire and turns it into a *capricious*, impractical, and expensive rush from one style to another. For example, in one recent year, fashion did an abrupt about-face. Early

---

TOEFL Prep 41-1 1. d 2. c 3. a 4. b 5. e
TOEFL Prep 41-2 1. bulk 2. trends 3. cumbersome 4. striking 5. Vanity

in the year, fashionable outfits showed a *minimum* amount of fabric and a maximum amount of skin. By late summer, famous fashion designers were drowning people in *bulky*, *cumbersome* outfits that looked five sizes too big. *Vanity inhibits* people from looking realistically at *exotic* clothing fads. A *striking* new style catches their eye, they look at the clothes they're wearing, and they are suddenly *vulnerable* to the manipulation of the fashion industry.

Bonus Structure **It's natural for** introduces an aspect of fashion that's not bad, but it implies that an "unnatural" aspect will come next.

1. Which word best describes the fashion industry, according to the author?
   a. striking
   b. minimum
   c. capricious
   d. vulnerable

2. What is one reason people buy the latest fashions, according to the author?
   a. Because they want to feel like they are part of the group.
   b. Because they enjoy spending money.
   c. Because the fashion world is bizarre.
   d. Because their clothes from last year don't fit.

TOEFL Success 41 1. c 2. a

文化
レッスン41

危険なファッション

意味と例文

1 bulk（名詞） 大きく重々しい外観

例文訳 そのたくましい巨体は小さな椅子1つで支えるには大きすぎるので、ケビンはベンチに座った。

関連語 bulky（形容詞）かさばった

---

2 capricious（形容詞） （あることから別のことへ）予測不能な動きをする

例文訳 専攻科目を気まぐれにあれこれ変えたら、大学での勉強が長くなりすぎるでしょう。

ヒント 使い方 capriciousは「ヤギ」を意味するラテン語に由来しており、ヤギが飛び跳ねるような動きを意味している。

関連語 capriciousness（名詞）気まぐれ、capriciously（副詞）気まぐれに

---

3 cumbersome（形容詞） （重さや形状のために）着用や持ち運びが困難な

例文訳 暗くなる前に山頂に到着するために、ハイカーたちはかさばって邪魔なテントを捨てた。

---

4 exotic（形容詞） （遠く離れた場所から来ているために）興味深い、または珍しい

例文訳 そのレストランに足を踏み入れると、マレーシアのスパイスのエキゾチックな香りがした。

関連語 exoticism（名詞）異国趣味、exotically（副詞）異国風に

---

5 inhibit（動詞） 妨げる、または遅らせる

例文訳 このローションは、蚊に刺されたときのかゆみを抑えてくれるだろう。

関連語 inhibition（名詞）抑制

6 minimum（名詞） 最小限の量や度合い

例文訳 キャビル大学に合格するためには、最低でも、テストで60点を取ることだ。

関連語 minimize（動詞）最小限にする、minimum（形容詞）最小（限）の、minimal（形容詞）最小（限）の、極小の、minimally（副詞）最小限に、非常に小さく

7 striking（形容詞） 非常に目立つ／注目を集めやすい

例文訳 ゴードンは陸軍学校で自分を律することを学んだ後、目に見えて新しい態度を身につけた。

ヒント 使い方 strikingは、「殴る」という意味の動詞に由来する。

関連語 strike（動詞）打ち当てる、strikingly（副詞）目立って、著しく

8 trend（名詞） （ある方向への動きまたは流行における）広範にわたる動き

例文訳 一部の若い男性の間では、帽子のつばを横に向けて被ることが流行している。

関連語 trend（動詞）傾向を示す、傾く、trendy（形容詞）流行りの

9 vanity（名詞） 自分の外見を過度に気にすること

例文訳 マークは虚栄心のために、ヘアカットや新しい服にお金をかけすぎていた。

関連語 vain（形容詞）虚栄心の強い

10 vulnerable（形容詞） （起こりうる）危険にさらされている

例文訳 赤ちゃんや非常に高齢の人は特に新しい病気にかかりやすい。

ヒント 使い方 vulnerableは後ろにto句を伴うことが多い。

関連語 vulnerability（名詞）傷つきやすさ、vulnerably（副詞）傷つきやすく

TOEFL プレップ 41－1

左列の各単語の反対語に最も近い意味の単語や語句を選び、空欄にそのアルファベットを書きこみなさい。

＿＿＿＿＿＿	1. capricious	(a) 奨励する
＿＿＿＿＿＿	2. exotic	(b) 最大限の
＿＿＿＿＿＿	3. inhibit	(c) 普通の
＿＿＿＿＿＿	4. minimum	(d) 予測可能な
＿＿＿＿＿＿	5. vulnerable	(e) よく保護されている

TOEFL プレップ 41－2

各文を完成させるのに最も適した単語を丸で囲みなさい。

1 そのセーターの（流行／大きさ）のせいで、彼は実際より太って見えた。

2 アナリストの中には、ファッションの（流行／虚栄心）と経済の浮き沈みには関係があると見る者もいる。

3 消防士が着ている服は（傷つきやすく／かさばって扱いづらく）、重い。

4 彼女のネックレスは、ダイヤモンドがあしらわれていたので、特に（扱いづらかった／目立っていた）。

5 祖父は（虚栄心／大きさ）から、髪を染めたり、40 歳も若い人のような服を着たりした。

TOEFL サクセス 41

文章を読んで学んだ語彙を復習します。後に続く質問に答えなさい。

［例文訳］

ファッション業界は、人々が服に時間とお金を過剰に費やすよう促す。人間にとって、衣服を集団への帰属の印として用いたり、流行についていこうとしたりするのは自然なことだ。ファッション業界はこの自然な欲求を利用し、気まぐれで非実用的で、しかもお金がかかるにもかかわらず、人々が次々と別のスタイルに殺到するよう仕向けている。例えば最近のある年には、流行が急激に様変わりした。年の初めは、流行の服は最小限の布地で最大限の肌を見せるものだった。ところが、夏の終わり頃には、有名なファッションデザイナーたちは、本来のサイズよりも５サイズも大きいような、扱いにくくかさばって邪魔な服に人々を埋もれさせていたのだ。人は虚栄心から、風変わりなつかの間の流行の服を現実的な目で見ることができなくなってしまう。魅力的な新しいスタイルに目を奪われてから、自分が着ている服を見ると、とたんにファッション業界の巧みな操作に付け入れられやすくなってしまうのだ。

読解のポイント It's natural for は、ファッションの悪くない一面を紹介しているが、次に「不自然な」一面が来ることを暗示している。

1　筆者によれば、ファッション業界を最もよく表す言葉はどれか？

a. 目立つ
b. 最小限の
c. 気まぐれな
d. 傷つきやすい

2　筆者によると、人々が最新のファッションを購入する理由の１つは何か？

a. 自分がグループの一員であるように感じたいから。
b. お金を使うのを楽しんでいるから。
c. ファッションの世界は奇抜だから。
d. 去年の服が合わないから。

【著者紹介】

ローレンス・J・ツヴァイヤー (Lawrence J. Zwier)

◉——ミシガン州イーストランジング市、ミシガン州立大学英語教育センター副所長。読解、語彙力強化、テスト対策などのためのESL（英語以外を母語とする人のための英語）教科書のほか、一般向けの本も多数執筆している。

リン・スタッフォード-ユルマズ (Lynn Stafford-Yilmaz)

◉——ワシントン州ベルビュー・コミュニティー・カレッジなどで15年以上ESL教師として教鞭をとる。ESLの教科書や試験対策用教材を多数執筆。

【訳者紹介】

島崎　由里子（しまざき・ゆりこ）

◉——早稲田大学商学部、東京外国語大学欧米第一課程卒。訳書に『約束の地 大統領回顧録Ⅰ』（共訳、集英社）、『ジョン・ボルトン回顧録』（共訳、朝日新聞出版）、『365日毎日アナと雪の女王』（共訳、学研プラス）がある。

野津　麻紗子（のづ・まさこ）

◉——早稲田大学大学院教育学研究科修士課程修了。パリ政治学院留学。在フィリピン日本国大使館勤務などを経て、現在フリーランス翻訳者。

TOEFL®テスト対策 必須語彙力トレーニング

2022年6月6日　　第1刷発行

著　者——ローレンス・J・ツヴァイヤー、リン・スタッフォード-ユルマズ

訳　者——島崎　由里子、野津　麻紗子

発行者——齊藤　龍男

発行所——株式会社かんき出版

東京都千代田区麴町4-1-4 西脇ビル　〒102-0083

電話　営業部：03(3262)8011㈹　編集部：03(3262)8012㈹

FAX　03(3234)4421　　振替　00100-2-62304

https://kanki-pub.co.jp/

印刷所——新津印刷株式会社

ISBN978-4-7612-7607-2 C0082